Making Democracy Fun

Making Democracy Fun

How Game Design Can Empower Citizens and Transform Politics

Josh Lerner

The MIT Press
Cambridge, Massachusetts
London, England

© 2014 Massachusetts Institute of Technology

All rights reserved. No part of this book may be reproduced in any form by any electronic or mechanical means (including photocopying, recording, or information storage and retrieval) without permission in writing from the publisher.

Figure 3.15: All Rights Reserved. No part of this work may be reproduced in any form or by any means—graphic, electronic, or mechanical, including photocopying, recording, online distribution, or information storage and retrieval systems—without the written permission of the publisher or the designated rights holder, as applicable.

This book was set in Stone Sans and Stone Serif by The MIT Press.

Library of Congress Cataloging-in-Publication Data

Lerner, Josh, 1978–
  Making democracy fun : how game design can empower citizens and transform politics / by Josh Lerner.
       pages cm.
  Includes bibliographical references and index.
  ISBN 978-0-262-02687-1 (hardcover : alk. paper), 978-0-262-55114-4 (pb)
  1. Video games—Political aspects. 2. Video games—Design. 3. Democracy—Computer games. I. Title.
  GV1469.3.L47 2014
  794.8--dc23

                                                                  2013027451

Contents

Acknowledgments   vii

1   Should Democracy Be Fun?   1
2   Games, Play, and Democracy   27
3   What Game Design Can Teach Us about Democracy   49
4   Not Just Child's Play: Games in Democratic Processes   87
5   Rosario Hábitat: Designing Participation Like a Game   119
6   Toronto Community Housing: Game Design in Less Fertile Soils   149
7   My Game Design Experiment   173
8   Conclusion: A Toolbox for Fixing Democracy   189

Notes   211
Bibliography   243
Index   267

Acknowledgments

This book was a true multi-player endeavor. I especially wish to thank the following good people:

The protagonists of the programs that I studied, for sharing their wisdom and doubts, supporting and challenging my ideas, and inviting me into their workshops, offices, and homes. In Rosario, I am particularly indebted to Carla at the City of the Children; Andrea and Paola of the Area de la Niñez (Department of Children); Pepe, Tucu, Javi, and Julia of the Grupo del Teatro del Oprimido (Rosario Theater of the Oppressed Group); and Guillermo, Duilio, Ximena, Paula, Lucha, Jesica, Alejandra, Mariana, Vicky and Adriana of Rosario Hábitat. In Toronto, my research would have gone nowhere without the support of Evelyn, Alina, Abigail, Julio, Rajesh, Beatriz, Gail, Heather, Jacqueline, Jin, and others.

The institutions that provided financial and in-kind support for my field research: The New School's Janey Program and The Boren Fellowship for research in Argentina, the Universidad Nacional de Rosario (especially Alberto, Cintia, and Claudia) for hosting me in Rosario, and Toronto Community Housing (especially Evelyn, Alina, and Steve) for funding our participatory evaluation.

The colleagues who reviewed my writing or fueled it with ideas. At The New School, this included the PhD Seminar, Janey Seminar, and Politics in Progress Seminar, as well as Victoria, Natascha, Emily, Alex, Maya, and Kalaya. Feedback from presentations at AAG, USAID, the Learning Democracy by Doing conference, and other gatherings smoothed the rough edges of early ideas.

The friends who inspired my research and helped me inch it forward: Catherine, Jason, and Greg for introducing me to the world of game design. Jori, Cora, Sol, Vale, and Emi for helping me navigate Rosario and making me feel at home there. Daniel and Alicia, whose immense resourcefulness and encouragement brought me to Rosario in the first place. Helen, Lindsay,

Chris, and Siue for keeping me grounded (and housed) in Toronto, and for nourishing me with exotic foods, clowns, pedagogy, and chocolates. Rasmus, Ben, Dad, Joanna, and others for giving feedback on my writing.

My co-researchers, who accompanied me in Rosario and Toronto. In Rosario, I was fortunate to work with Paula Ballasteros on our respective research into the City of the Children. I was even more fortunate to count on a research assistant as perceptive, thorough, and patient as Mariana Berdondini, who joined me for most of the workshop observations.

In Toronto, I only hope that our team of tenant researchers learned as much from me as I learned from them. Thank you to Dionne Bailey, Angela Brackett, Tracy Izzard, Kathy Kunsmann, Pamela Mahatoo, Patricia Matthews, Bryan McCarey, Augustre Munro, Rita Oliver, Felipe Palma, Magdalena Palma, MJ Rosenthall, Avril Sandra Salmoon, Simone Samuel, Lorraine Solomon, Sybil Sooknanan, Alecia Spence, Leisin Spence, Bernadette Thomas, Katharine Wallace, and Ivy Wilson. Joanna Duarte Laudon's passion for democracy and participation was the glue that held together this participatory research, as she progressed from research assistant to co-facilitator.

My academic advisors, who shared the tools and insight that made this worth writing and (hopefully) reading. Thank you to Tim Pachirat for methodological guidance, to Katie Salen for masterfully guiding me through the world of games, to Carlos Forment for encouraging me to stir up tensions that made the book more compelling, and to Steve Duncombe for grounding my work in practical concerns and sharpening my ideas into activist tools. I am especially grateful to David Plotke for his dedication and for not only challenging me to produce more rigorous work, but also teaching me how to rise to this challenge.

Most of all, I thank Renate, who kept our home afloat and tolerated my lengthy absences from it, who read every awkward word and discussed every loopy idea, and who walked with me stride by stride in an uncertain quest to make the road by playing.

1 Should Democracy Be Fun?

Everyone loves democracy—except for most of the time, when they hate it. Despite its wide appeal, democracy has a remarkable ability to be fantastically boring, bitterly painful, and utterly pointless. This ability is so incredible that, in mere hours, democracy can transform a thousand passionate activists into a room full of lifeless faces and empty chairs.

Case in point: A public hearing on the largest development project in New York City history—Brooklyn's Atlantic Yards.[1] On a late August afternoon in 2006, hundreds of opponents and supporters crammed into a university auditorium, with latecomers lined up outside. Officially, the hearing's goal was to collect input on the project's Draft Environmental Impact Study. In other words, to help determine if the developer could plant a new basketball stadium and 16 soaring apartment towers in the middle of Brooklyn's brownstone neighborhoods. And if so, how?

The hearing was a nasty battle. Opponents protested that they only had 66 days to review 4,000 pages of technical documents. They warned about endless traffic jams and sketchy guarantees of affordable housing, claiming that the new apartments would just be "rich folks' housing." Unions and other supporters praised the new jobs, housing, and basketball team that the project vowed to deliver. Amid the chaos, the hearing organizers called in the police to remove an outspoken critic. Speakers faced constant heckling and threats. "The bulldozers are coming," boasted an ironworker, "and if you don't get out of the way, they're going to bulldoze right over you."

The Atlantic Yards hearing was about as much fun as, well, your average municipal hearing. After listening to waves of repetitive presentations and canned rhetoric, most of the crowd left early. Those who remained looked dazed. Many walked away frustrated, after signing up to present and not having time to speak. Thousands of other 'concerned citizens' had, no doubt, opted to stay home entirely, to avoid a futile shouting match. In the end, the hearing also failed to deliver a clear sense of how to improve the Environmental Impact Study.

The problems that plagued the Atlantic Yards hearing are typical of democratic participation. Governments and organizations are calling on citizens to engage more actively in political processes, beyond voting in elections. In most cases, though, participation is dominated by the 'usual suspects' and extreme voices, and widely dismissed as pointless. It rarely resolves conflicts or changes decisions. For most people, these opportunities to participate are simply not very attractive, compared with the countless other ways to pass time.

Is this the best that democracy can offer? Is democratic participation destined to be an undesirable civic chore for all but the most passionate citizens?[2] To borrow a phrase from Oscar Wilde, perhaps the problem with democracy is that it takes up "too many evenings."[3] Scholars of democracy offer few alternatives to this view. Even when proposing reforms, they generally accept that, for most people, participating in democracy will be a costly sacrifice. As the political philosopher Iris Marion Young concluded, "Democracy is hard to love."[4] Some champions of participation suggest redesigning the institutions of democracy, to open up new spaces for engagement. Yet too often, these new spaces are no more enticing than the old ones.

After spending too many evenings suffering through public hearings, I glimpsed a different approach in an unlikely place. In July 2006 I was in Venezuela, researching a new national initiative to develop community councils.[5] One Sunday afternoon in Caracas, a local organizer invited me to the parking lot in front of a huge dilapidated apartment block. Tenants had been working for months to prepare for this day, when they hoped to launch a new council for their building. If successful, they would gain control over government money for community projects. But first, the law had presented a series of obstacles. The organizers had to complete a building census, hold elections for two commissions, and draw at least 20 percent of the tenants to the founding assembly, when they would elect dozens of spokespeople for the council. And that was just to *start* the council.

I thought the council was a tough sell, considering these demanding requirements and the general mistrust of government promises in Venezuela. I was wrong. Over 400 people turned out for the assembly, well over the 20 percent threshold. But what really struck me was that people seemed to be enjoying themselves. They were laughing, hugging, chatting, dancing, and—most impressively—lingering. The assembly did not feel like a sacrifice or chore, but rather like something that people actually wanted to attend. Democracy felt *fun*.

Still skeptical, I wondered if the assembly was fun only because it was in Latin America. Were people in Venezuela and other Latin countries just more likely, as Celia Cruz sang, to embrace life as a *carnaval*? Perhaps, but I later toiled through other community meetings in Venezuela that were deathly boring, so there had to be other reasons.

To better understand what could make an activity fun, I turned to the experts: game designers. I had some game designer friends, and over the years they had preached about the importance of level design, clear rules, and playtesting. As we talked more, I learned about a wider galaxy of concepts and mechanics that game designers use to craft enjoyable experiences, such as magic circles, artificial conflict, quantifiable yet uncertain outcomes, status indicators, feedback loops, hidden information, choice points, vivid visuals, sound effects, and core mechanics.

I also began to realize that, in a sense, the Venezuelan assembly was fun because it was *designed like a good game*. The legal regulations created two compelling artificial conflicts: tenants strived to overcome the requirements for forming a council, and to do so before other neighborhoods. Winners received a big monetary reward, but the results were uncertain and depended on reaching a certain score (number of votes). Organizers felt a sense of progress as they advanced through multiple levels of the council process (census, commissions, founding assembly). At the assembly, the vote count provided a constant status indicator for this progress. The experience was more engaging thanks to vivid sights, sounds, and sensations (posters, music, and food).

Once I looked at public participation through the lens of game design, I began to question what I thought I knew about democracy. I reflected back on my experience as an urban planner and facilitator, designing and leading scores of workshops and meetings for community development programs in North America, Latin America, and Europe. I revisited the lessons learned from years researching participatory democracy in a dozen countries. And I realized, more so than ever before, why some meetings worked better than others. I glimpsed the power of good game design.

In the case of Atlantic Yards, game design concepts explain why the hearing was not fun, and how it was designed to fail. The organizers made conflict more antagonistic, asking presenters to explicitly identify as either for or against the development. They offered no opportunities to tackle problems collaboratively. They did not announce the hearing rules in advance, and the facilitator ignored rules about speaking time limits for many politicians and project supporters. People did not really know what they could accomplish by attending, and they had no way to measure progress toward any particular outcomes. There were almost no engaging visuals or sound effects. Combined, these design choices doomed the hearing.

People may be tuning out public hearings—and politics more broadly—but they are tuning *in* to games. Each week, people around the world log three billion hours playing video games.[6] In the United States, 97 percent of youth play computer and video games.[7] So do 70 percent of top corporate executives—while at work![8] Video game revenues have surpassed those of music and movies. Professional sports—and their fantasy offspring—generate even more money. And these games are not necessarily steering people away from public life. Many of the most popular video games entice millions of players to talk, play, and work *together*. So why are most people more interested in games than in democratic processes that directly impact their lives?

The answer is simple. *Games are designed to be enjoyable, and democracy is not.* Game designers work tirelessly to craft enjoyable experiences, drawing on the rich lessons of game design theory and practice. Designers of democratic processes are in fact largely unaware of these lessons. Most political practitioners and scholars have an entirely different understanding of games. Politicians, activists, and pundits generally think of games as metaphors for electoral politics. For political scientists, games are abstract methodological models for analyzing decisions—"game theory."

In recent years, however, games are beginning to play a different role in politics. Increasingly, institutions as diverse as the United Nations, US Army, and grassroots community groups are using games and gamelike processes to engage people in political issues. Their motivations are varied. In some cases, champions of participatory democracy hope to empower citizens. In other cases, political leaders aim to educate the masses or win them over to a particular cause. And while some programs are inserting digital and nondigital games into campaigns and meetings, others are designing these processes to be more like a game, as in the Venezuelan assembly. In this book, I unravel these experiences and ask: *Can games make democratic participation more appealing? If so, how?*

On my quest for answers, I began by exploring the world of game design. I dove into the research on games, participated in game design conferences and online groups, and interviewed game developers. I even went so far—at the urging of several designers—as to play (and analyze) dozens of real live games. Yes, game research has perks.

Next, I set out in search of existing political programs that used games. I uncovered many hotspots in Latin America, but none more prolific than the Argentine city of Rosario. The first city in the world to pass an ordinance endorsing game-playing as a public policy strategy, Rosario has integrated games and game techniques into dozens of municipal programs for over a decade. I studied three programs that exemplify how the city uses games: Children's Councils (youth participation), Rosario Hábitat (participatory planning), and Theater of the Oppressed workshops (policy implementation).

To see if political games would grow in less fertile soils, I traveled to the other end of the Americas. In Canada, I studied participatory budgeting (PB) at Toronto Community Housing (TCH), where thousands of public housing tenants have decided how to spend $9 million annually via assemblies designed like game shows. At TCH, I also designed a participatory evaluation process, using games and game mechanics to engage tenants and staff in improving PB. The evaluation grew into an adventure of its own, as I learned about the art of game design by designing my own games.

During over a year of research in Rosario and Toronto, I observed 40 meetings that used games or game mechanics, interviewed 81 meeting participants and 38 staff, and surveyed 464 participants. Through this research, I hoped to pose the key questions and issues to consider when using games for democratic participation, and when studying these efforts. Throughout, I tried to engage both the design perspective and the participant perspective. In other words, I explored how designers of democratic processes could apply the lessons of game design *and* how participants experienced these processes.

I found that game design can make democracy fun—and make it work. When governments and organizations used games *and* designed their programs more like a game, they tended to make participation not only more attractive, but also more effective, transparent, and fair. But I also found that this approach can backfire—manipulating citizens or trivializing their efforts—unless facilitators effectively weave together certain games and game mechanics. To maximize the fun and minimize the dangers, I propose that governments and organizations redesign democratic processes to include 5 kinds of games and 26 game mechanics. When appropriate, they should use animation, team-building, capacity-building, analysis, and decision-making games. But, more important, they should design democracy to be more like a game, by drawing on *game mechanics* that engage the senses, establish legitimate rules, generate collaborative competition, link participation to measurable outcomes, and create experiences designed for participants.

In this chapter, I explain why fun and games are essential to the future of democracy. Despite widespread popularity, democracy is suffering from less engagement, less trust, and less power. After reviewing several causes of these problems, I focus on one that has been mostly neglected: democratic participation is relatively unappealing. I then suggest why games might make participation more enticing, and warn about the dangers they could pose. Finally, I give an overview of the book and what I hope it accomplishes.

Our Love–Hate Relationship with Democracy

Democracy is both wildly popular and deeply unpopular. While most people now see it as the ideal form of government in theory, they are increasingly skeptical of it in practice. As I will explain, this leaves us with three big problems: people are engaging in democracy less, trusting it less, and granting it less and less power.

Before delving into these problems, what exactly do I mean by democracy and participation? There are countless definitions, so I will take a broad approach. By *democracy*, I refer to the original Greek meaning of 'rule of the people'. This includes representative democracy, direct democracy, participatory democracy, and any other system that enables a group of people to govern itself. This is not limited to the representative democracy of many Western governments, or even to government itself. Democracy can be just as valuable for governments deciding on policies as for organizations deciding on campaigns or friends deciding where to eat.

Participation in democracy also means different things to different people. Most political scientists focus on voting and other efforts to influence elections—what they usually call political participation. Others stress civic participation (in organizations and institutions), community participation (in local community affairs), or public participation (in government decision-making). When I discuss participation in democracy, I refer to all four concepts. In other words, *I understand democratic participation as any effort to influence or participate in decision-making about how a group of people is governed.*[9] This can include voting, lobbying, campaigning, organizing, protesting, deliberating, and other forms of participation, at various levels of government or in other institutions that govern communities.

While democratic participation encompasses a wide range of activities in a wide range of institutions, this book mainly discusses one type of participation at one level of government. I focus on public participation at the local level, in which city residents help shape local government policies. This focus is not accidental. Advocates of deeper democracy see local participatory programs as a key space for reconnecting citizens with government,

Should Democracy Be Fun? 7

since they link concrete neighborhood issues with broader policies. Many of these initiatives are also experimenting with games and gamelike processes, to make democratic participation more popular. State and national programs have dabbled less in games, though at the end of the book I suggest how they might scale up local experiences.

In a sense, governments should not have to struggle to attract democratic participation. Over the past century both democracy and participation have become quite popular, in theory. Democracy—or at least representative democracy—is the political norm in much of the world, emerging as a new common sense. Parties across the political spectrum sing its praises, as do global institutions such as the United Nations and World Bank, and grassroots movements from the Tea Party to Occupy Wall Street.

Since the 1960s in particular, most parties and institutions have also been calling for more participation—not only in elections, but throughout policy-making. Citizens and officials increasingly expect that they will be able to (or have to) work together, and that this will make government better.[10] While political leaders have championed almost any issue imaginable, none are openly calling for "undemocratic government" or "an end to citizen participation." This is true even in countries that are utterly undemocratic and nonparticipatory, such as North Korea—formally known as The Democratic People's Republic of Korea.

But there is a problem. While democracy and participation are widely accepted ideals, we are having trouble living up to them. Most people love democracy and participation in theory, but seem to hate them in practice. Democracy has become the political version of spinach. Almost everyone says it is good, but few people actually want to eat it. This is bad news for democracy, for three main reasons: disengagement, distrust, and disempowerment.

Disengagement

Few people participate in democratic politics, and arguably, even fewer than in the past. Most observers have focused on declining voter turnout. Since 1970, turnout has decreased by an average of 8 percentage points in OECD countries (the advanced democracies).[11] In some countries the drop has been much greater—around 30 points in Japan and 20 in the United Kingdom. People are dropping out of political parties even quicker. Since 1965, party membership has plummeted on average around 60 percent in OECD countries.[12] While there is less data on other types of formal participation, studies suggest that fewer people are attending political meetings and serving on committees.[13] As Robert Putnam warned in *Bowling Alone*, civic engagement in local organizations, clubs, religious institutions, and unions is also dropping, in the United States at least.[14]

It is not clear, though, if people are participating less across the board. Many scholars, such as Theda Skocpol and Morris Fiorina, see a change in the form of participation, more than an overall decline.[15] They argue that people are still participating, just in different ways. While they are voting less at the ballot box, they are voting more with their wallets, through consumer boycotts, shareholder activism, and donations. While they are going to fewer meetings, they are communicating with politicians and the media more, via the Internet and protests. And while they are opting out of traditional civic groups like bowling leagues, they are participating more in large mass-membership groups like MoveOn and Greenpeace. The picture is even more complicated in less developed countries, where voter turnout has risen since the 1950s.[16] This may reflect the initial growth of new democracies, however, more than long-term trends.

Even if some people are participating more in some ways, citizens seem less engaged overall. Large civic organizations are increasingly managing rather than enabling democracy.[17] Affluent professionals run most of them, with little meaningful member involvement. Meanwhile, rises in donations, petition-signing, and letter-sending—while important acts of participation—generally involve minimal effort. In these cases, people are participating more but engaging less. They are turning what were once social processes into individualized tasks with little human interaction. And none of this changes the fact that people in 'advanced democracies' are participating less in elections and other formal political processes. Even before these declines, turnout in most elections (state, local, and national) was embarrassingly low, with less than 50 percent of registered voters showing up on average.[18] Low participation is not a new problem, even if it may be getting worse.

Then, again, even if participation is low, does this really matter? As long as some people turn up at the polls and give input to decision makers, is this not good enough? In their 2002 book *Stealth Democracy*, John Hibbing and Elizabeth Theiss-Morse argue that we should not expect citizens to participate more in democratic deliberation, since they are neither interested nor prepared. Those who do participate are driven mainly by their disgust with corrupt politicians and incompetent bureaucrats. Even if people want to participate, their involvement is not always appropriate.[19] Imagine if governments had to hold public consultations before deciding on earthquake responses, hospital admissions, military maneuvers, or spaceship designs. When speed, safety, confidentiality, or technical expertise is critical, democratic participation may not be ideal.

Should Democracy Be Fun? 9

For most big decisions, though, low participation comes with high costs. First, it means unequal participation.[20] When turnout is low, more affluent and privileged people are usually overrepresented, as are those with extreme views.[21] Young people, people of color, and people with less income and education are systemically underrepresented.[22] Because these groups often have different beliefs and preferences, the outcomes of elections and other public participation processes do not represent the will of the people. Instead, they disproportionately represent the will of certain people—those who are better off, more educated, and older. Politicians also pay more attention to these people once in office because they know they are more likely to vote. Other populations are thus doubly disempowered—they have less say at the polls *and* in between elections.

Second, low participation means that decision makers get less input, resulting in decisions that are less informed, effective, and legitimate.[23] Ordinary people have priceless first-hand information about their communities' problems and needs. "[T]he man who wears the shoe," said the philosopher John Dewey, "knows best where it pinches."[24] Voting, however, is a blunt tool for communicating this knowledge.[25] It only lets people pick from among a handful of shoes, not say how and where their feet are pinched, or what might alleviate this pinching. Deeper participation, such as writing letters and participating in meetings, better conveys complex views and preferences, giving politicians more information to craft effective policies. When people see that they played a meaningful role in decision-making, they are also more likely to view the outcomes as legitimate.

Finally, low participation matters because, in practice, many people are trying hard to reverse it. If politicians, officials, planners, and activists are expressing frustration with low turnout (which they are), we should seek solutions.[26]

Distrust

Any declines in engagement seem measly when compared with free-falling trust in government. People may like democracy, but they now have little faith in democratic governments. In 1964, almost 80 percent of Americans said that they trusted the government most of the time.[27] By 2010, only 22 percent did. In 1964, only 29 percent said that government mainly serves a few big interests. By 1994, 76 percent did.[28] The biggest drop in trust occurred in the 1960s and 1970s, but rates have fallen further since then. The declines have been similar around the world.[29] In fact, by 2005, trust in politicians was highest in North America—less than 15 percent of people trusted them in every other continent.[30]

Such widespread and massive drops change how we think about politics. People are losing trust not only in their governments but in the very ideas of government and politics. Most people now hate politics, as the philosopher Colin Hay has observed. The practice of politics has never been especially loveable. Yet before the 1960s many citizens felt positively about the *idea* of politics, seeing it as a respectable way to pursue the common good. Now politics is almost always a dirty word. When we call someone's actions "political," says Hay, we invariably "question that actor's honesty, integrity or capacity to deliver an outcome that reflects anything other than his or her material self-interest."[31]

Distrust of government is a problem, but it could also lead to a solution, if it causes more people to monitor and scrutinize government. In a sense, mistrust is healthy. For Pierre Rosanvallon, it indicates that the public is paying critical attention, rather than just accepting blindly.[32] For this mistrust to deepen democracy, however, people need to take action to hold government accountable, beyond and alongside the ballot box.

Citizen distrust is only part of the problem. With the global rise of neoliberal ideology, even politicians distrust government.[33] While conservatives spout the most impassioned antigovernment rhetoric, elected officials across the political spectrum now preach about making government smaller, cutting wasteful public spending, and letting the free market and entrepreneurs lead the way. When polled off the record, most officials say that engaging the public in democratic decision-making is irrational and inefficient—which leaves them less likely to invite people to participate.[34]

This widespread alienation from government makes people less enthusiastic about participating. As an OECD survey found, the top reasons people give for not participating are "low interest in policy and/or politics" (78 percent of respondents) and "low trust in how government uses citizens' input" (48 percent).[35]

Disempowerment

As people are trusting and engaging in government less, they are depriving democracy of power. Citizens are losing their ability to shape—through democratic means—the decisions that affect their lives. The rising popularity of public choice theory in the 1960s and 1970s, and of neoliberalism since then, has led politicians to shift government power toward the market.[36] Politicians have rushed to privatize public agencies and functions, hand over responsibilities to boards and banks, give businesses more say through public-private partnerships, and ask nonprofit organizations to take more responsibility for social services. Private contractors now even manage core government functions such as defense. As governments transfer power to (generally) undemocratic corporations and organizations, fewer issues are decided democratically.

Democracy was weak even before this hollowing out, according to participatory democrats. In 1984, Benjamin Barber condemned the dominant model of representative democracy as thin and weak, since it barely involved citizens in the act of governing.[37] In most 'democracies', political decision-making falls well short of democratic ideals.[38] Community members usually have little say in how decisions are made, and these decisions often do not reflect their preferences. Even most public hearings and consultations are not very democratic, with a few experts or 'usual suspects' dominating discussions. This limited model of democracy widens the chasm between citizens and representatives, and constrains our imagination and aspirations for what democracy can be.

The actual disempowerment of democracy is compounded by *perceived* disempowerment. In an era of globalization, pundits and politicians increasingly cast governments as powerless and ineffective against the whims of global forces.[39] When faced with such towering global problems as climate change, terrorism, and financial meltdowns, what can democratic governments really do? As citizens see politicians bow before global forces and corporations, government starts to seem less powerful, and less deserving of power. Perhaps it should be no surprise that by 2005, only 30 percent of people around the world—and less than 40 percent even in North America and Europe—believed that their country was "governed by the will of the people."[40]

Defenders of thin representative democracy argue that it is sufficient and inevitable, and that thicker or deeper democracy is not necessarily better.[41] They applaud the waves of democratization in recent decades, as clusters of developing countries have switched from oppressive regimes to elected governments.

Once these thin democracies are established, though, they tend to stay thin, and often become even thinner. For supporters of participatory democracy, this low-intensity model is neither unavoidable nor very democratic.[42] They point to successful examples of deeper democratic participation, and to countless cases of elected governments acting against the will of the people. They also argue that when political decisions involve competing interests or power imbalances, democracy is essential for protecting the interests of the less powerful.[43] In any context, democracy can help build active citizens and communities, as scholars since Tocqueville have observed in wonder.[44]

For these reasons, many advocates are fighting back against the disempowerment of democracy, asking how decision-making can be more democratic, not less.[45] Public engagement practitioners have invented a colorful array of participatory processes, such as 21st Century Town Meetings, Slow Democracy, Citizens' Initiative Review, Deliberative Polling, World Café, and Future Search.[46] Social movements around the world are organizing to open up government and build participatory democracy, through groups such as the Right to the City Alliance, MoveOn, Brazil's Landless Workers Movement, and the global Occupy movement.[47] And elected officials are pushing for deeper democracy via institutions such as the National League of Cities, the Columbia Institute, and the Forum of Local Authorities for Social Inclusion and Participatory Democracy.[48] These efforts have engaged thousands more people in democratic discussions, building community capacities and often changing policy decisions. But they have generally struggled to tackle one of the deepest problems with democracy.

Why Is Democracy Broken?

Before prescribing treatments for democracy's ailing health, we should diagnose the causes. There are many! I will briefly mention the usual suspects, and then shift the spotlight to another troubling culprit, one that has mostly avoided attention.

Most scholars blame democracy's problems on changes in civic participation, technology, attitudes, demographics, or laws. First, for political scientist Robert Putnam, democracy is suffering because of *declining civic participation and social capital*. As people participate less in the community, their social ties erode, which leads to lower engagement and interest in politics.[49] There is little evidence, though, of declining civic participation outside the United States. Scholars such as Theda Skocpol and Morris Fiorina, as I explained earlier, also argue that even in the United States, participation is *changing* more than declining.[50]

Second, people may be engaging less because of *technological changes*.[51] Over the past century, leisure and entertainment became more private in many respects. It is now easier to watch movies, listen to music, and play games from the comfort of one's home, or through the device in one's pocket. But new technologies have also enabled people to connect in more ways, from mobile phones to blogs to Facebook.

Third, citizens' *attitudes toward political authority are changing* as they become more informed, according to Pippa Norris and others.[52] The new wave of "critical citizens" is expecting better government, deferring to it less, and scolding politicians when they fail to deliver. While this might explain growing distrust, it seems less likely to account for disengagement

Should Democracy Be Fun?

or disempowerment. Critical citizens should arguably participate *more* and demand *more* from government.

Fourth, the public has not just become more critical—it has also gone through a wave of *demographic changes*.[53] People are marrying later and less, divorcing more, having fewer children, and moving more often. Women have entered the labor force in increasing numbers, and noncitizens make up a greater percentage of the voting-age population in many countries. In the United States, more people are in jail—4.5 million by 2004, up from half a million in 1960.[54] All of these changes depress participation, by weakening people's community ties, occupying more of their time with work, or leaving more of them disenfranchised. But these trends are at least partly canceled out by the rise in education levels, the biggest predictor of voter participation.[55] None of these changes have clear effects on political distrust or disempowerment.

Finally, a key legal change has depressed voter turnout: the *lowering of the voting age* around the world. Not only are youth less likely to vote, but initial voting habits seem to stick with them later in life.[56] If they start their voting eligibility by not voting, they appear less likely to vote as adults.

These changes are all significant, even if their effects may not be as grand as some scholars claim. They only deal, however, with one side of the story—what Hay has called the "demand side."[57] Each factor shapes citizen demand for democracy—how many people are motivated to engage in, trust, and empower democracy, and how many of them can act on these motivations. But none of these changes have much effect on the supply of democracy—how worthy democratic processes are of engagement, trust, and power. Perhaps people are tuning out because they are tired of what the radio is playing.

Hay suggests one supply-side problem: politicians and pundits constantly disparage democratic politics, warning the public that it is corrupt and wasteful. Public choice scholars and their neoliberal followers assume the worst of politicians and bureaucrats, inspiring broad public cynicism. They present politicians and parties as strictly self-interested and often corrupt, aiming only to amass votes and power.[58] They brand bureaucrats as lazy and wasteful, only wanting to maximize their income, benefits, and influence, while doing as little work as possible. As the preachers of neoliberalism spread their gospel far and wide, they paint a rather ugly picture of democracy. It is no wonder that so many people look away in disgust.

In this book, I focus on another big problem with the supply of democracy: *For most people, democratic participation is relatively unappealing. It is boring, painful, and pointless.* It is boring because it offers little of interest. It is painful because it often involves nasty conflicts and bitter defeats. It is pointless because it rarely provides any intrinsic pleasure or concrete outcomes. Most people feel that there are better ways to spend their time. According to the OECD survey mentioned earlier, besides low interest and low trust, the top reason why people do not participate is "lack of time or other priorities."[59]

"Lack of time" can mean many things. People may simply not have much time left to participate, after work, family, and other basic obligations. It would be tough to increase the number of available hours in a day, though shorter work hours and free child care can help. "Lack of time" could also mean that the act of participation takes more time than necessary. Technological innovation and more efficient processes might make participation quicker, though perhaps at the cost of meaningful dialogue. But even if it took an hour less, or if there were an extra hour a day, would many people devote their precious free time to zoning hearings, community meetings, or political rallies?

Usually, saying that you do not have time is code for "I'd rather do something else." Compared with the millions of other ways to spend time, democratic participation ranks low. "Perhaps some people enjoy making speeches, or confronting those with whom they disagree, or standing up to privileged and powerful people with claims and demands," writes the philosopher Iris Marion Young. "Perhaps some people like to go to meetings after a hard day's work and try to focus discussion on the issue, to haggle over the language of a resolution, or gather signatures for a petition, or call long lists of strangers on the telephone. But most people would rather watch television, read poetry, or make love."[60]

Politics has never been the epitome of pleasure. Yet, while this phenomenon is not new, politics has slid further down the fun rankings over the past century. Voting was more festive (and corrupt) in the nineteenth century, when parties routinely offered free drinks and entertainment to draw the masses to the polls.[61] These festivities helped boost turnout to record levels. As stricter voting regulations and political ethics have stamped out this revelry, participation has become less fun. Meanwhile, many other aspects of people's lives have become more fun. Entertainment, media, and other social activities have grown more engaging, while political participation has lagged behind.

How could democratic participation move up in the rankings, to better compete against the other draws on people's time? One option would be to suck the fun out of everything else (see North Korea). Otherwise, governments and organizations would have to offer more attractive opportunities to participate. The good news is that, while community meetings

Should Democracy Be Fun? 15

are unlikely to compete with love-making anytime soon, democracy is not inherently undesirable. Research by Michael Neblo and colleagues found that 83 percent of people expressed interest in participating in a deliberative political meeting.[62] Younger people, racial minorities, and low-income people were even more interested. The demand is there, but attractive democratic processes are in short supply.

If unappealing participation is boring, painful, and pointless, what would an appealing participation look like? In a word, it would be *fun*.

Fun is an exceptionally elusive concept.[63] Game scholars have tried, but largely failed, to pin it down. Part of the problem is that fun is subjective—shoveling snow may be fun for some people, but many would disagree. It also contextual—shoveling snow is more fun after the year's first light snowfall than after the fourth blizzard in a month. Whether an activity is fun depends on the person and the context, but in the end, we know fun when we see it. So what is it?

The short answer, as game designer Raph Koster writes in *A Theory of Fun for Game Design*, is that fun is a source of enjoyment.[64] The word itself comes from either the Middle English term for fool (*fonne*) or the Gaelic term for pleasure (*fonn*). Fun, Koster writes, is "our brains feeling good—the release of endorphins into our system."[65]

The long answer is that fun is a broad proxy for a range of pleasures. Through talks at the annual Game Developers Conference, Marc LeBlanc has developed one of the most common frameworks for fun.[66] He breaks the concept down into eight kinds of experience:

1. Sensation: Game as sense pleasure.
2. Fantasy: Game as make believe
3. Narrative: Game as unfolding story
4. Challenge: Game as obstacle course
5. Fellowship: Game as social framework
6. Discovery: Game as uncharted territory
7. Expression: Game as soapbox
8. Submission: Game as mindless pastime

Something is fun when one of these stimuli generates a sense of pleasure.

Regardless of where it comes from, fun is inherently interesting. It feels good, not bad. And its pleasures are naturally rewarding. The point of having fun is to have fun.

Fun is not, however, the opposite of work. In fact it is often quite serious.[67] For a chess player, staring deeply at the board and weighing the consequences of different moves can be fun. For a surgeon, making a series of precise cuts in just the right places and at just the right times can be fun. For a graphic designer, tinkering with computer code to find the perfect shade of purple can be fun. For a community organizer, mobilizing neighbors to march in a protest can be fun. Nearly anything can be made fun.

When something is fun, people are more likely to do it. On this point, even Bertolt Brecht and Volkswagen agree. In 1926, the radical playwright Brecht wrote an essay to his peers, who were frustrated that the public seemed to prefer soccer over serious theater. Whether they liked it or not, he argued, playwrights needed to find better ways to appeal to the people's interests. "We pin our hopes," he wrote, "to the sporting public." As Stephen Duncombe and Andrew Boyd note, Brecht saw a valuable lesson: "people participate in what they enjoy, and unless theater was made enjoyable the people wouldn't come."[68]

The same is true for social change, according to Volkswagen. Yes, Volkswagen. Its initiative "The Fun Theory" spotlights public projects based on a simple premise: "fun is the easiest way to change people's behaviour for the better."[69] An experiment in Oslo, for example, encouraged people to walk up stairs rather than take the escalator, by making walking fun. Organizers transformed the stairs at a subway station into a giant keyboard, such that each stair played a different musical note when stepped on. During the experiment, subway riders were 66 percent more likely to walk up the stairs.

If Volkswagen and radical playwrights have made activities more alluring by making them fun, could governments and organizations do the same? If so, how? They might start by looking at games.

Game Designers to the Rescue?

Games are the epitome of fun. Of course, there are also other models for fun, such as play and entertainment. But what sets games apart—and makes them particularly useful here—is that they are also models of and for democracy.[70] Games are inherently democratic in some key ways: they always involve participation and decision-making, by design. Unlike democracy, though, games are inspiring engagement, earning trust, and gaining power. Could they have similar effects if used in democratic politics?

First, what are games? In brief, they are systems in which players engage in an *artificial conflict*, defined by *rules*, that results in *measurable outcomes*.[71] In soccer, for example, two teams engage in a conflict that is artificially confined to the game field and time period. Rules, such as 'no hands' and 'kicking the ball through the opposing net yields a goal', dictate how players play. When the game ends, each team has won, lost, or tied, depending on how many goals they and their opponent have scored. I delve into more detail on the meaning of games in the next chapter.

Soccer may not seem to have much in common with a town meeting, but it and other games are similar to democracy in important ways. First, both games and democracy are *inherently participatory*. Games require player participation, and usually very active participation. "Unlike movies or television," writes game guru Tracy Fullerton, "the show does not go on if players cease to play."[72]

Second, *decision-making is the core activity* of both games and democracy. In games, players are constantly deciding when to kick the ball, where to move their game piece, and how to zap the alien. As in democracy, these decisions are highly complex. For each decision, players must consider the positions and interests of diverse friends and foes, the resources and time at hand, and the broader context and goals of the game. Not to mention how sore their thumbs may be from pressing down on the controller, or how much they need to cram for an exam the next morning.

Third, games and democracy are *designed*. They rarely just 'happen', especially at large scales. Elections, consultations, and community meetings are only democratic to the extent that they are planned and facilitated. Both political organizers and game designers lay out rules, arrange spaces, set agendas, and designate roles, building on norms and precedents from the broader community. Ideally, this does not dictate what people do, but instead enables them to engage in better ways. Designers create structures for experience, but then players use these structures to create experiences.

Despite these similarities, games are inspiring engagement, earning trust, and gaining power, while democracy is not. To start, *games are attracting and enabling massive participation*. In the United States, 183 million people report playing computer or video games regularly—on average 13 hours per week.[73] There are over 200 million active gamers in China, 105 million in India, 100 million in Europe, and 23 million in Latin America.[74] These figures do not include the billions of people who play sports, cards, or board games; who gamble or play fantasy sports; or who watch sports or game shows.

Each year, more people are playing games. Since 1999, the number of US children playing digital games has increased over 50 percent, and the amount of time they spend playing has nearly tripled.[75] While participation in democracy is stagnating, participation in games is growing.

Games also attract diverse participants. In the United States, 40 percent of gamers are women,[76] and black and Latino youth play video games even more than white youth.[77] The average video game player is 34 years old, and over a quarter of Americans older than 50 are gamers.[78] Parents' education level (a proxy for class) has little effect on gameplay—kids actually play a bit more in lower education families.[79] In sum, the people who participate

18 Chapter 1

the least in politics (youth, people of color, low-income families) seem to participate the most in games.

Besides enticing participation, games also develop people's capacity to participate. In 1971, the psychoanalyst D.W. Winnicott established that play is essential to personal development, allowing people to test out the world around them, and redefine themselves in relation to it.[80] Play and games teach people to recognize different perspectives, read multimodal texts (words, images, and sounds), and understand social roles and rules.[81] Information and skills learned through play seem to stick longer.[82] A study by Richard Blunt found that games can even increase student grades by as much as one letter, when used in university courses.[83] Through games, players learn practical and contextualized know-how, not just abstract knowledge. This learning enables them to engage more, and more effectively, in the future.

While participants of democratic processes often walk away disillusioned with democracy, *players rarely lose faith in games*. Even when they repeatedly fail, they come back for more, or they seek to change the game. Why do games inspire such commitment? Largely because the rules are clear, transparent, and unbiased. Players know the rules of the game, and know that they will not change. The rules give everyone an equal chance, so players have only themselves to blame for failure. Corporate lobbyists and special interest groups do not rig video games.

Players trust games, but not blindly. Gamers are relentless critics. When they see a rule as unfair, they speak out on blogs and online forums, often forcing changes. Many gamers change the rules themselves, hacking the game and creating 'mods' (modifications). When players violate the rules (for example, by fixing matches or taking performance-enhancing drugs), other players, officials, and fans are quick to crack down and punish violators. Gamers learn to understand the system and have faith in it, but also to criticize and change it when necessary.

Finally, as democracy is losing power, *games are becoming more influential*. Video games now gross more than movies and music, with global sales expected to grow from $67 billion in 2012 to $82 billion in 2017.[84] Global revenues from professional sports were $114 billion in 2009, and are expected to reach $133 billion by 2013.[85] As games become more popular, they are commanding more public attention and occupying more of people's time.

Meanwhile, as I discuss in chapter 3, games are having greater influence over education, business, and other fields. Educational games are sprouting up online and in schools. Scholars of learning are asking what games can teach them. CEOs are recruiting *World of Warcraft* players and asking employees to take more game breaks. The video game *America's Army* has become the military's most efficient recruitment tool. *American Idol* is one of the biggest sources of superstars, and its contests attract more votes (178 million in 2008) than presidential elections.[86] Games are, in the words of Tom Chatfield, "the 21st century's most serious business."[87] But are they also its most perilous?

It's All Fun and Games Until . . .

Even if games could boost democratic engagement, trust, and power, would this come at a high cost? Skeptics often worry that games will lead to violence, though this seems unlikely for democratic processes. Games could, however, trivialize serious political issues or manipulate citizen participation. Or they might lead to unfair outcomes, or simply not be any fun. These dangers lurk for those wishing to use games for democratic participation.

Most concerns about the growing role of games in society focus on a single topic: violence. For years, worried parents and politicians have crusaded against video game violence. They claim that games such as the *Grand Theft Auto* series—in which the protagonist on occasion runs over strangers, slashes their throats, and bashes their heads in with baseball bats—instill violent thoughts and habits in impressionable youth.

They may have a point, according to researchers.[88] Studies have found that kids who play violent video games may be more likely to get into fights and be hostile.[89] In some experiments, kids who play such games become more emotionally aroused and have less activity in brain areas related to self-control and inhibition, compared with those who play nonviolent games.[90] But for other researchers, exposure to video game violence is not correlated to serious acts of aggression or violence.[91]

None of this debate, however, suggests that games, *in general,* lead to violence. While critics have focused on blood-splattering shooter games, most games are not particularly violent.[92] *Grand Theft Auto* does not brand games as violent any more than *The Texas Chainsaw Massacre* brands cinema as violent. Violence—in or out of games—might (or might not) inspire violence. But there is nothing inherently violent about games. Many games, such as chess and *Risk*, actually model peaceful ways to engage in violent conflicts.

Even if they do not lead to violence, games might *trivialize serious issues.* Can governments and organizations trust important decisions about real dollars and policies to a game? Are games serious enough for politics? By nature, games oversimplify information and situations.[93] If citizens play along, games could desensitize them to the human costs of complex political decisions.[94] "You lose an avatar; just reboot the game," said Ken Robinson, producer of the US Army game *Army 360*. "In real life, you lose your guy; you've lost your guy. And then you've got to bury him, and then you've got to call his wife."[95]

If policy makers see games as trivial, they might marginalize game-based participation, keeping it separate from real decision-making. *Budget Hero* and other online public budget games, for example, have attracted much attention and praise, but have had little visible impact on actual budgets.[96] Even potential players could shun political games, rejecting their simplified scenarios and game activities as child's play.

When citizens do decide to play, games might *manipulate participation*. Early in the twentieth century, the Russian psychologist Lev Vygotsky concluded that through play, children learn to regulate themselves and to limit their behavior.[97] Could political games have the same effects on adults?

By nature, game designers impose rules that steer people in certain directions and constrain their possible actions. But for a game to be a game, players must have the power to decide their actions. These in-game decisions, however, such as where to move your avatar, are only one type of power. Political scientists refer to this as the first face of power—the power to make decisions.[98] But designers usually dominate the second and third faces of power—the power to set agendas and to shape preferences.[99] They decide the options on the agenda—which passageways your avatar can and cannot enter. They also make subtler decisions about the vision and aesthetics of the game, which influence what options players might want to consider or even imagine. For example, the visuals, sounds, narrative, and language of first-person shooter games often lead you to instinctively unleash a stream of bullets into any creature that moves, even if you might otherwise unleash a friendly greeting.

Designers are not necessarily benevolent, and they sometimes use their power to promote undemocratic behavior. Some popular games, such as American football or Simon Says, discourage free thinking and democratic decision-making. Recently, and especially since 2010, droves of corporations and marketers have been using games to sell products, through "gamification." This buzzword generally means adding game mechanics to websites, services, applications, and other nongame experiences, to make them more gamelike.[100] Social networking sites (*Foursquare*), consumer goods providers (*Campusfood*), health programs (*HealthMonth*), and many others began using points, progress bars, leader boards, achievement badges, and levels to reward users and attract customers. An iPhone app, *Epic Win*, even promised to "level-up your life," by making your to-do list into a game.[101] All of these efforts try to steer player behavior. Or in other words, to manipulate people (for better or worse). Gamification typically makes nongame interactions more gamelike *so that* people take some predetermined action, such as consuming a certain product.

Even when designers have good intentions, their games can have unintended consequences. A BMW game that challenged drivers to be more fuel-efficient caused some of them to drive less safely, dashing through yellow lights to avoid wasteful stopping and starting.[102] No design choice is neutral.[103]

Game design choices could in fact easily benefit the most powerful. Games designed from above could intentionally distract attention and mask power relations. Since the Roman 'bread and circuses', political leaders have used play and games to deflect attention away from 'real' political issues.[104] Like a safety valve, these games allow frustrated citizens to let their emotions loose in controlled environments, without threatening those in power. Such distractions have been especially popular among clientelistic political parties in Latin America, which regularly hold festivals full of fun and games.[105] Behind the razzle-dazzle, these spectacles often conceal and sustain unequal power relations.[106]

In the end, games could also lead to *unfair outcomes*. Even when their internal rules are fair and transparent, games privilege certain players over others. If budget decisions are delegated to a game, for example, will players with greater skills and resources take home more of the loot? Will less privileged communities leave as losers?

Designers might manage to steer games toward fair results, but players will always find ways to game the system, creatively bending or re-interpreting the rules for personal benefit. Sebastian Deterding highlights the case of economist Joshua Gans, who tried to make child-rearing into a game.[107] To potty-train his daughter, Gans promised to reward her with Skittles each time she used the toilet. One step ahead of her father, the girl regulated herself so that she would go to the bathroom every twenty minutes—and stuff herself with Skittles in between.

If games make participation fun, they could attract the wrong kinds of players, further skewing outcomes. In most games, a select group of hardcore gamers plays *much* more than other people, becoming extraordinary experts and sometimes dominating gameplay. In democratic processes, would games create a new class of hardcore participants, rigging the results in their favor? Or would games attract the "unqualified masses," and lead to unwise decisions? Since the French psychologist Gustave Le Bon warned about "crowd psychology" in 1895, political theorists have fretted about the folly of the masses, and what their unbridled emotions might lead to.[108]

Finally, really serious games might *not be any fun*. Game design could sap the fun out of democracy by commodifying participation, turning it into just something else to consume and accumulate. For example, while gamification techniques may boost engagement, critics warn that they can make participation empty and superficial.[109] Gamification, they say, often entices people to take undesired actions just to accumulate more points, out of compulsion. Participation becomes meaningful only when it increases your score.[110] This may help corporations boost profits in the short term, but if gamified activities do not offer intrinsic rewards (such as fun), people eventually lose interest.

Political processes might also be too real to be fun. Many attempts to apply game design to nongame activities result in what Russell Davies calls "barely games," which lack the make believe necessary for genuine play.[111] People play games largely to escape from the real world, not immerse themselves in it.[112] Even if governments sprinkle game mechanics into public meetings, these meetings will not necessarily be fun. Gaming is not, as game designer Will Wright points out, "a form of 'MSG' that [can] be added to anything to make it more palatable."[113] Rather, games require fresh ingredients and a chef with the skills to use them. "To make something fun," writes Deterding, "you need all the hard work of game design . . . preferably performed by real game designers."[114]

Deterding is right that game design is hard work, and the risks above present serious challenges. But he is wrong that game design should be left to "real game designers." Community organizers and political activists have been designing fun games—with real-world impacts—since before game design was a profession. While gamification aims to manipulate people, these political games and gamelike processes aim to empower people, by expanding their opportunities to shape policies. In the rest of this book, we will see if these experiences live up to their lofty goals. Can governments and organizations mix games into democratic participation, while avoiding the perils above?

Overview of the Book

In the next chapter, "Games, Play, and Democracy," I map the terrain for our discussion of games, and chart a new direction for how they can deepen democracy. I begin by defining games and play, then explaining how the media, politicians, and social movements use sports as political metaphors, and how political scientists use 'game theory' to study decision-making. Next, I present the growing social issue games movement, in which game designers develop (mostly) digital games about issues such as poverty and protests, to educate and activate the public. Finally, I discuss how politicians and activists have used play to engage citizens and indirectly influence political decisions, and how social movements and community organizations have wielded games to directly shape public policy. After laying out the various political roles of games, I propose that governments and organizations use games *in* and *as* political action, by directly integrating them into political campaigns, meetings, actions, and discussions.

Chapter 3, "What Game Design Can Teach Us about Democracy," describes how game designers craft fun games, to begin laying out how these design approaches might be applied to public participation. After introducing game design theory and practice, I present key game design concepts and 26 specific game mechanics that are most relevant for politics. I show how, unlike technocratic design that transfers power from citizens to experts, game design provides players with greater skills and opportunities to participate meaningfully. To illustrate how game design concepts can apply beyond games, I show how they are already contributing to the fields of education, business, and architecture.

The following four chapters test how games and game mechanics play out in five democratic processes. Chapter 4 focuses on games in Latin America, chapter 5 on game mechanics in Latin America, chapter 6 on game mechanics in North America, and chapter 7 on games in North America. In chapter 4, "Not Just Child's Play: Games in Democratic Processes," I tell the stories of two programs in Rosario, to show such games can enhance—or undermine—participation. In the City of the Children program, Children's Councils draft public policy proposals largely by playing games. Youth also participate in urban design workshops, however, in which abstract and isolated games marginalize and trivialize their efforts. As a separate initiative, the Department of Children runs Theater of the Oppressed workshops, in which adult youth workers devise strategies for implementing a new national Children's Law. The workshops' theater games show how bodily movement can inspire productive dialogue, but also how facilitators' power is difficult to wield and easy to abuse.

In chapter 5, "Rosario Hábitat: Designing Participation Like a Game," I explain how governments and organizations can incorporate *game mechanics* into participatory processes. Even when games themselves are not appropriate, designers can use game mechanics to make participation more *like a game.* Through the experience of the development program Rosario Hábitat, I find that when facilitators systematically use particular mechanics that engage the senses, establish legitimate rules, generate 'collaborative competition', and link participation with outcomes, they build more democratic community agreements.

Chapter 6, "Toronto Community Housing: Game Design in Less Fertile Soils," tests whether game mechanics can transform democracy outside of Latin America. Governments in the Global North face additional obstacles to designing participation like a game: less supportive context, less playful citizens, and less precedent for games. Yet, starting in 2001, the Toronto public housing authority used game mechanics to engage tenants in "participatory budgeting" (PB). Each year, tenants decided how to spend $9 million through events that resembled game shows. Like Rosario Hábitat, Toronto Community Housing designed participation like a game. And like in Rosario, this approach made participation more enjoyable and effective. In 2009, however, the housing authority expanded PB more widely across the city, creating new opportunities and challenges.

In chapter 7, "My Game Design Experiment," I recount how I used the lessons of the book to help address these new challenges. Over two years, I led a participatory evaluation program at TCH, in which I worked with a team of tenants to evaluate and improve PB. We studied game design and tried to instill game mechanics in the PB process, to address the problems raised in chapter 6. I also practiced the change we were seeking by designing the evaluation meetings around games and game mechanics. The participatory evaluation showed how games—not just game mechanics—can work in democratic processes in the Global North. It also modeled how to redesign democracy to make it work more like a game—and showed that such a redesign improves the quality of participation.

In the conclusion, "A Toolbox for Fixing Democracy," I draw on the lessons of game design and my research to propose how governments and organizations can and should use games to engage citizens. First, I present the types of games and game mechanics that I found particularly useful, and offer examples from my research. I then review the effects that these games and game mechanics may have on democratic participation, and suggest strategies for fulfilling the potential of games while overcoming the challenges.

I conclude by suggesting that we rethink democracy and games. Governments and organizations should make democratic participation more fun, to increase citizen engagement and trust in democracy, and to empower people to democratically decide more issues that affect their lives. To accomplish this, we should directly—and carefully—embed games and game mechanics in democratic processes.

It may seem odd that, in an age of video games, the programs that I discuss all involve nondigital games. Scores of visionary thinkers are championing video games as a tool to solve the world's problems, so why focus on old-fashioned meetings?[115]

Video games have great potential to change the world. But lower tech games and game mechanics are even more useful. Most political decisions are still made in face-to-face meetings, and these are the processes that need changing the most. Digital games may be sexier than political meetings, but they often have less impact and cost more. In most of the world, governments and organizations lack the resources to create digital games for most major decisions. And they do not necessarily need to. Technology does not make games fun, and it will not make democracy fun either. Good design makes games fun, and it can do the same for democracy. Digital features may complement face-to-face engagement, but they should not replace it.

Nondigital games are especially useful models for learning the art of game design. In fact game design classes often start with board games and card games, to focus students' attention on the underlying mechanics and logic of games. Students are usually over-eager to jump into the details of coding and graphics—a recipe for gorgeous but utterly unplayable games. Most enthusiasts of political games also start with digital tools. I instead focus on the basic mechanics of games, through the lens of face-to-face examples. This design know-how can then be applied to digital *and* nondigital games, and everything in between.

In the rest of this book, I hope to make the craft of good game design more accessible to political activists, organizers, facilitators, planners, and scholars. Redesigning democracy may not be easy, but with the right tools, it could be fun.

2 Games, Play, and Democracy

A game is a purely imaginary idealization of a social interaction.
Andrew Colman, *Game Theory and Its Applications in the Social and Biological Sciences*[1]

Games are unique as a medium in that they're interactive and participatory. . . .
Games can be that bridge to more civic engagement.
Alan Gershenfeld, Chairman of *Games for Change*[2]

At a defining moment like this, we don't have the luxury of relying on the same political games. . . .
Barack Obama, 2008 stump speech[3]

What do games have to do with politics? It depends on whom you ask. For most people, Barack Obama included, games are something that politicians play, a metaphor for electoral politics. For most academics, such as Andrew Colman, games are abstract models used to study political decision-making, in the form of game theory. These two outlooks—games as metaphors and as research method—have dominated discussions about politics and games for decades.

Not anymore. Games—the ones ordinary people actually play—have become one of the most influential forms of social interaction. Games are pervasive on TV and the Internet, and in schools, corporations, community organizations, and government programs. The politics of these games has become a serious matter, whether in congressional debates about video game violence, court rulings on performance-enhancing drugs, campaigns for and against the Olympics, military recruitment through *America's Army*, or voter turnout for *American Idol*.

Games are playing more roles in politics than political scientists and pundits generally acknowledge. But why does this matter? There are many reasons, but in this chapter I focus on one: Our understanding of games can open up—or close off—possibilities for democracy. How we talk about and use games affects who participates in democratic politics, and how they participate.

Using games as political metaphors and research methodologies has done little to deepen democratic participation. Game metaphors spark some people's interest in politics, but they usually cast citizens as spectators with little power. Game theory has offered some ideas for encouraging participation, but these ideas have rarely had much impact outside of academe. Both approaches have been useful for understanding politics, but less so for making it more democratic.

If democracy is to be more than a spectator sport, citizens need new ways to play the game. Video games are modeling new approaches. Game designers have developed innovative techniques for engaging people in democratic decision-making, and the social issue games movement has put these ideas in practice through games on diplomacy, immigration, elections, and other political and social issues. Meanwhile, governments and organizations are increasingly designing their own play and games, for political programs, campaigns, and actions. Can these efforts enable more people to participate in democratic politics, in more meaningful ways? Or are they just marginal experiments that have little effect on "serious" politics?

In this chapter, I review the main ways that people have used games for political purposes, and how they have in the process affected democratic participation. I begin by developing a working definition of games, and distinguishing games from play. I then explore how games have been used as *metaphors* and *methodology*, and how games are now being designed *about* and *as* politics. The chapter focuses on experiences in North and South America, but with an eye to broader trends and lessons. Ultimately, I argue that games can play a greater role in deepening democracy if governments and organization use them *in* and *as* political action.

Games and Play

Before discussing how they have been used, what exactly are games? How are they different from play? These questions have puzzled great minds for ages. Games and play are tricky concepts, and scholars and designers have put forward countless definitions. Linguistic obstacles have complicated their task—many game scholars have written in languages that have only one word for both game and play (e.g., *juego* in Spanish).

Games, Play, and Democracy   29

Is there anything in particular that makes a game a game? Most people would say yes. Table 2.1 lists several of the most influential definitions of games/play.[4] In their book *Rules of Play*, game design scholars Katie Salen and Eric Zimmerman synthesize these and other understandings of games and play.[5] They arrive at distinct definitions, which I use with only slight changes. Following Salen and Zimmerman, I understand games, on the one hand, as systems where players engage in an *artificial conflict*, defined by *rules*, that results in *measurable outcomes*.[6] I define play, on the other hand, as free and enjoyable movement within a more rigid structure.[7]

Both definitions require unpacking. First, in games, players are pitted against each other or a system in an *artificial conflict*. This artificiality means that the conflict is kept largely separate from the "real world," in time and space. Most games include elements of both competition and collaboration, but they must be driven by some kind of conflict. In this conflict, players are constrained by *rules*, which limit what they can and cannot do. The game ends in *measurable outcomes*, meaning that players win, lose, or receive some kind of score or reward.

Play is a more slippery concept. It involves relatively free action or movement within a relatively rigid system or context. For example, bouncing a

Table 2.1

What are games and play?

Johann Huizinga: "[Play is] a free activity standing quite consciously outside 'ordinary' life as being 'not serious,' but at the same time absorbing the player intensely and utterly. . . . It proceeds within its own proper boundaries of time and space according to fixed rules. . . ."
Roger Caillois: "[Play is] an activity which is essentially free . . .; separate . . .; uncertain . . .; unproductive . . .; governed by rules . . .; make-believe . . .."
Clark Abt: "A game is a context with rules among adversaries trying to win objectives."
Bernard Suits: "[P]laying a game is the voluntary effort to overcome unnecessary obstacles."
Chris Crawford: "[A] game is an artifice for providing the psychological experiences of conflict and danger while excluding their physical realizations . . . a safe way to experience reality."
Greg Costikyan: "A game is a form of art in which participants, termed players, make decisions in order to manage resources through game tokens in the pursuit of goals."
Elliot Avendon and Brian Sutton-Smith: "Games are an exercise of voluntary control systems, in which there is a contest between powers, confined by rules in order to produce a disequilibrial outcome."

ball around the confines of a basketball court, inserting wordplay into a prepared speech, and skateboarding in a public square. In each case, players take advantage of a space of possibility by trying out new ways of acting within it. This action must also be pleasurable in some sense. So walking aimlessly in a public square would not usually be considered play, while skateboarding around the same square in trying out tricks would be. Like games, play can be quite serious.

Play and games are not mutually exclusive. As Salen and Zimmerman explain, play takes place within games, such as when a basketball player experiments with new moves during a game.[8] Games, in turn, can be a type of play, such as when a game of tag emerges amid less structured schoolyard play. Nevertheless, play and games are distinct creatures, each with its own characteristics and history.

Games as Metaphors for Politics

Scholars, politicians, pundits, and activists have long used games as metaphors for politics. In these cases, games serve as a symbol or rhetorical frame, to illustrate how politics works. At least since Plato, observers have compared politics to a game.[9] For Plato, once the Gods have imposed an order upon the world, "all that remains to the [mortal] player of the game is that he should shift the pieces, sending the better nature to the better place, and the worse to the worse, and so assigning to them their proper portion."[10] In this game of politics, citizens are the players, and they play by allocating resources.

Most often, politicians and the media use game metaphors to fuel interest in politics.[11] They hype electoral campaigns as dramatic races between competitors, each hoping to cross the finish line first. Candidates duke it out in debates, each striving for a knockout punch, slam dunk, or home run. If the race stays tight, it may end in a "photo finish," as in Australia's 2007 federal election between the Coalition's John Howard and Labor's Kevin Rudd (see figure 2.1). Candidates themselves play up these game metaphors (and their uncertain outcomes) to attract more votes. Studies have shown that since the 1960s, games have grown into *the* dominant media frame for covering and discussing electoral politics.[12]

In social movements, leaders such as Saul Alinsky (widely considered the inventor of community organizing) and Martin Luther King have framed organizing as a series of theatrical games.[13] For Alinsky, community organizing was a long-term game between the haves and have-nots.[14] "It is tedious, but that's the way the game is played—if you want to play and not just yell

Games, Play, and Democracy

Figure 2.1
Cartoon of the 2007 Australian Federal Election Race. Image courtesy of Mark Knight.

'Kill the umpire.'" King used game metaphors to highlight the greater purpose of social struggles and their rules.[15] "Football games are not played to get a ball across a goal, but to get it there under certain conditions, in a certain way, with certain results in the lives of those concerned. Power to get the ball across the goal is to be interpreted in terms of purposes and only makes sense in the light of those purposes. Action, then, which defeats purpose is weakness." This game rhetoric helped communicate movement ideas and differentiate between opposing sides, mobilizing more people for action.

In other cases, game metaphors are vehicles for critiquing the status quo. Citizens, the media, and politicians themselves charge elected representatives with the partisan crime of "playing" politics. They lash out at officials for playing with numbers, budgets, words, or—worst of all—people's lives. When governments invite the public to participate beyond elections, games usually become anti-democratic metaphors. In public consultations, community members use game metaphors to complain about tokenism and decisions made behind closed doors. The urban planner Sherry Arnstein referred to this false participation as "the Mickey Mouse game."[16] Activists regularly decry the rigged rules, uneven playing fields, and foul play that limit and undermine participation. At its worst, democratic politics is "just" a game, a ritualized performance with little actual importance.

How have games as metaphors affected democratic participation? Perhaps most important, they shape public opinion, making democratic politics more exiting—or more irrelevant. For many, sports imagery injects energy and drama into politics. By drawing on the language and frames of games, politicians and the media can turn elections into more compelling stories, making citizens feel more engaged in government. For most people, though, excessive focus on the "game of politics," rather than real political issues, eventually leads to a "spiral of cynicism" and disengagement.[17] Game metaphors trivialize politics as "just" a game, or highlight its unjust and rigged nature. Since game rhetoric often refers to male-dominated professional sports, it also tends to resonate more with men than women.[18]

Game metaphors can change how governments govern, heightening party competition and inspiring more dramatic political rhetoric. They may also reinforce one of the basic premises of democratic politics—that even losing parties will stay in the game and play by its rules. As the political scientist Adam Przeworski put it, "Democracy is a system in which parties lose elections."[19] In nondemocratic states, the losers may instead break the rules, via a revolution, coup, or vote manipulation. Even if the losers stay in the game, though, game metaphors often leave them marginalized and disillusioned.[20]

In the end, game rhetoric does not seem to make decision-making more democratic or participation more appealing. Game metaphors present a deceptive image of widespread participation, while in practice most citizens stay on the sidelines, hoping that their cheers and hollers will eventually reach the open ears of a decision maker. As the political commentator Walter Lippmann lamented, electoral politics is largely a spectator sport, one in which politicians do most of the playing.[21] Political fans can rally around their team, giving it money, publicity, a supportive environment, and occasionally even a vote. But when it comes time to govern, citizens remain marginalized from policy-making. Popular game metaphors may increase some people's interest in politics and expose democratic shortcomings, but they do little to engage citizens in democratic decision-making.

Games as Research Method (Game Theory)

In contemporary political science, especially in North America, games are all about decision-making, in the form of "game theory." For game theorists, games are abstract models used to represent and analyze interactions and decisions. Under the broader umbrella of rational choice theory, game theory has become one of the dominant methodologies in political science. Perhaps the most famous example is the "prisoner's dilemma," whereby two prisoners must each decide whether to testify against the other or remain silent, based on the expected results of their decisions. Each prisoner will get the least possible jail time if he testifies and the other does not, but if they both testify, they both get high sentences. Other games model everything from auctions to evolutionary biology to voting behavior.

Game theorists Martin Osborne and Ariel Rubinstein explain that each of these 'games' is "a description of strategic interaction that includes the constraints on the actions that the players *can* take and the players' interests, but does not specify the actions that the players *do* take."[22] By developing models that mirror real-world political conflicts, game theorists hope to identify the possible and rational decisions of actors in the given situation.[23] Since Anthony Downs illustrated in the 1950s how game theory models shape voter decisions, game theorists have studied why and how people participate in politics.[24]

Despite its name, game theory does not necessarily involve games, or at least not what most of us would understand as games. In game theory, players do not make a voluntary effort to play a game. In fact they are not even aware that they are playing a game. As far as they are concerned, they are just living their lives. Is something a game if the people involved do not recognize it as such? Likewise, the conflicts in game theory are not artificial, as in games. They are not separated from the real world in time or space, but rather are fully immersed in the real world. "Game theory," the critic William Poundstone concludes, "is inspired by, but not necessarily *about*, games."[25]

Even if game theory is not about games, it has provided useful ideas about how democratic participation could be more attractive. It suggests how rules, rewards, punishments, and personal characteristics might influence decisions to participate. Game theorists, and rational choice scholars more broadly, have extensively studied how electoral rules, such as registration requirements and election scheduling, affect voter turnout.[26] They have speculated on how participation is motivated by expected rewards and punishments, such as policy outcomes, social relationships, sanctions, psychic gratification, and a sense of satisfaction from acting altruistically.[27] And since these factors rarely explain why certain people participate more than others, game theorists have also investigated personal factors that might motivate people, such as their resources, their "taste" for acting altruistically, and whether they surround themselves with altruists.[28]

But game theory's effects on democratic participation have been modest, for three main reasons. *First*, the assumptions of game theory lead to questionable conclusions. Game theory's models generally assume that people act rationally, but critics argue that we are also motivated by nonrational and even irrational urges.[29] Defenders of rational choice have tried to include these motivations within a broader "procedural view" of rationality, suggesting that actors behave rationally within the limits of available information.[30] Such definitions, however, may stretch rational choice so far as to be of little practical use. Most game theory models also assume that politics boils down to individual decisions based on distinct, rather than overlapping, interests. Many interactions, however, are not based on such zero-sum competition. Finally, game theory assumes that universal, absolute, and knowable principles govern human actions, and that we just need to discover these principles.[31] "Interpretivist" critics have challenged this view, asserting that our behavior is inherently particular and subjective, often driven by hidden forces and desires.[32]

Second, game theory has neglected some of the factors most responsible for participation. For many critics, game theorists either ignore or oversimplify social and emotional motivations.[33] Groups often reach decisions collectively, through social interaction and dialogue. People commonly participate because they are emotionally attached to a group or cause. These social interactions and emotional attachments are highly subjective and complex, and they lose much of their meaning when reduced to static variables in game theory equations. Most important for this study, game theory is incompatible with fun.[34] Fun and enjoyment are main motivations for action, but they are highly complicated and imprecise concepts, ill-suited for the formal models of game theory.[35] Game theorists have tried to include notions of "psychic gratification" or "warm glow" as variables in the decision-making equation, but to understand why and when people enjoy participation, we need to delve deeper.[36]

Finally, game theory has had limited reach because its language is so inaccessible. Game theory's complex models are dry and unintelligible for most politicians, activists, and citizens. These are the people responsible for fostering democratic participation, and they are largely oblivious to the lessons game theory might offer. Rational choice and game theory research has had relatively little effect on political practice.[37] Ironically, while political science research on games has receded into academe, a different species of political games has blossomed outside the academy.

Games about Politics

For game designers, games are radically different creatures. They are sports, board and card games, street games, and increasingly, digital or video games. Though designers disagree on the precise definition of games, most agree with the basic elements presented at the beginning of the chapter: artificial conflict, rules, and measurable outcomes.[38] 'Political game,' for game designers, means a game about politics, designed to educate, raise awareness, or motivate.[39]

Political games date back at least to the Prussian board game *Kriegspiel*, which was used for military training in the 19th century.[40] Civically minded games got a boost in the 1960s, when North American designers and advocates founded the New Games Movement.[41] Through cooperative physical games, these activists promoted play as a tool for social change.

The New Games Movement did not last, but digital game designers now pursue similar aims through a broad movement of social issue games, which includes the industry's Serious Games Initiative and the group Games for Change. As this organization's website proclaims, a game for change is "a digital game which engages a contemporary social issue to foster a more equitable, just and/or tolerant society."[42] Examples include video games on poverty (*Ayiti*), international negotiation (*Peacemaker*), party politics (*Koalition*), nonviolent direct action (*A Force More Powerful*), and elections (*Obama: Race for the White House*). These games are usually played online, by single players or groups. In the role playing game *Ayiti*, for example, you control a Haitian family struggling to make a living, get an education, and stay healthy, while confronting endless challenges (figure 2.2).[43]

The serious games industry is most active in North America and Europe, but designers have also created social issue games in Latin America and elsewhere. Besides digital games such as Uruguay's *Cambiemos* (about building a political campaign), Latin American activists have used nondigital

Figure 2.2
Ayiti: The Cost of Life Game. Screenshot by author.

games such as "street football" to practice and teach democracy on the sports field.[44]

These political games can have deep impacts on individuals and communities, which may indirectly influence political practices. Joseph Kahne, Ellen Middaugh, and Chris Evans found that youth who play civically minded video games are more likely than their peers to say they are interested in politics, to seek out information about politics and current events, and to raise money for charity.[45] While the causal relationship is not yet clear, other scholars have also found that when people play a game, they become more interested in the game's issues.[46] Through the experimentation of play, players' values and social relationships outside the game may also be transformed.[47] Many social issue games encourage players to learn more after they play, offering lesson plans for teachers and links for more information. In theory, as players learn and become more aware, they participate more actively in politics and the community. This relationship, however, has yet to be proved empirically.

Games, Play, and Democracy

The tenuous connection to politics and community groups is perhaps the greatest limitation of social issues games. The games are generally designed by independent developers or design companies with little political experience, only sometimes in partnership with politically or socially engaged organizations. Most of the games are isolated projects, not embedded in longer term campaigns or political processes. When they are connected to a campaign, they tend to have hazy goals, such as raising awareness. They rarely help translate this awareness into action: for example, by actively connecting players with community organizations, political parties, government agencies, or other vehicles for action. Nor have many social issue games tried to intervene in political decision-making processes, such as by helping players write letters to elected officials or attend protests.

These games *could* engage more closely with political practice, however, and there are some exceptions to the generalizations above. Chris Swain's online *Redistricting Game*, for example, lets players map out new electoral districts, and in the process learn how redistricting can corrupt democratic elections (see figure 2.3).[48] While making and promoting the game, Swain and his team engaged advocacy groups and elected officials, and as

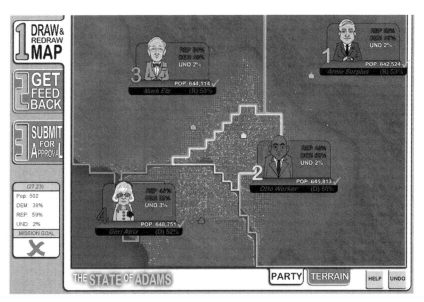

Figure 2.3
ReDistricting Game. Image courtesy of Jonathan Aronson.

a result the game has been used by organizations lobbying for redistricting reform.[49] The game website also includes a "take action" page, where players can arrange a meeting or send a letter to their congressional representative. *The ReDistricting Game* combines the educational power of social issue games with direct political action. If other games could better connect with governments and community organizations, they might have more political impact. In fact political activists outside the game design industry have already bridged this gap, designing games within social and political movements.

Play as Political Action

Politicians and social movements have been using play and games for social change since before video games were born. For them, play and games are practices or actions aimed at directly shaping political campaigns or policies. Unlike the predominantly digital social issue games, these actions typically take place in the streets and in face-to-face meetings. While I draw on the experiences of game metaphors, game theory, and game design throughout the book, I will focus mainly on games and play as political action.

Three main types of political play pave the way for experiments with political games: *populist play* directed by politicians, *dissident play* staged by oppressed people, and *activist play* orchestrated by social movements. These tactics begin to show how game design principles can be inserted into political practice, and they present some challenges that games are well-suited to address.

For many people, the concept of political play brings up images of festive political rallies. Since the Roman circuses, politicians have used this *populist play* to attract and/or distract the masses. In Latin America, political parties routinely organize festivals to win over (or buy off) voters, featuring theater, music, dance, and other spectacular entertainment.[50] In the United States, such playful politics were most common from the mid-19th to early 20th centuries, when political parties were strongest.[51] Festive polling stations were at least partly responsible for driving up voter turnout to record levels—as much as 80 percent at the end of the 19th century.[52] Recent research confirmed that polling station parties still boost turnout.[53]

Electoral festivities, however, only allow for a very constrained form of play. While citizens are welcome to come out and play, these festivals are usually stage-managed by a tiny elite of political insiders.[54] Playful rallies can increase turnout and make participation more representative, but they can also enable politicians to bribe or manipulate voters. In the end, populist play may appeal to the masses, but it is directed by elites.

Politicians have not held a monopoly on play. Poor people have long used playful tactics as "weapons of the weak," to express disapproval with political elites.[55] This *dissident play* dates back at least to the carnivals of the Middle Ages. As the philosopher Mikhail Bakhtin noted, peasants gathered in these carnivals to mock and parody the "official" culture, publicly contesting authority and practicing their own culture.[56] Later, in the Americas, slaves played with subversive and mocking songs and dances, for similar reasons.[57] In many Latin American countries, citizens have challenged authority through playful traditions of dance, music, and theater, such as *fandango* parties in Mexico, *capoeira* in Brazil, and theatrical *murga* groups in Uruguay and Argentina.[58] In Ecuador, for example, *Año Viejo* celebrations have served as annual platforms for political critique.[59] At the end of each year, neighborhood organizations display mocking effigies of unpopular politicians and public figures in the streets (see figure 2.4), then burn the figures to ashes on New Year's Eve.

Figure 2.4
Año Viejo celebrations in Cuenca, Ecuador: An unflattering public model of the mayor. Photo by author.

Dissident play has opened up safe spaces for bottom-up community participation. This participation is often one of the first acts of resistance by oppressed people, a critical step toward more active organizing.[60] But dissident play is usually limited to individuals or small groups, and it rarely has direct political goals or impacts. While it expresses dissatisfaction, it does not necessarily lead to further action. It may even discourage action, serving as a safety valve that lets people voice dissent without disrupting the system. If individuals can let off steam through play, public pressure may not build up enough to burst into collective action.

In North America, in particular, social movements have also used playful theater, music, and performance more purposefully, to win campaigns, change social relations, and intervene directly in political decision-making. This *activist play* began to emerge by the end of the 19th century, when labor groups and Jane Addams' Settlement House Movement experimented with public theater to raise public support.[61] In the 1930s and 1940s, artists connected to the leftist Popular Front used popular theater and agitprop political art to transform people's worldviews.[62] This inspired local guerrilla theater groups such as The Living Theater, the San Francisco Mime Troupe, and Bread and Puppet.[63]

In the 1950s and 1960s, playful tactics moved further into the spotlight. The civil rights movement used Freedom songs, rousing adaptations of older slave spirituals, as a main mobilizing tool.[64] Singing in the streets provided an organized and fun opportunity for people to assert their voice in public, which often led to further action. These playful moments inspired the antiwar movement and the New Left. The 1960s counterculture group the Yippies brought radical play to new heights, trying to levitate the Pentagon and nominating a live pig ("Pigasus the Immortal") as presidential candidate. As ringleader Abbie Hoffman explained, "One of the worst mistakes any revolution can make is to become boring. It leads to rituals as opposed to games, cults as opposed to communities and the denial of human rights as opposed to freedom."[65] Not to be outdone by the Yippies, radical feminists protested the objectification of the Miss America pageant by crowning a sheep as the next Miss America.[66] The gay liberation movement also kicked off with play. During the raid of New York's Stonewall Inn, protesters brushed back the police with outlandish Rockettes-style kicks and chants: "We are the Stonewall Girls / We wear our hair in curls / We wear no underwear / We show our pubic hairs."[67]

Since the 1960s, queer and anti-capitalist activists have made play even more common. The AIDS activist group ACT UP has been especially influential, fusing pleasure with movement politics.[68] In the late 1980s and 1990s,

ACT UP chapters in various cities organized around the right to safe sexual pleasure and play. They announced their demands through graphic posters, provocative costumes, and rambunctious "zaps" (theatrical interventions in public events). ACT UP shaped play into a polished and media-savvy organizing tactic, and the global justice movement has followed suit. Since the 1990s, protests and rallies have routinely featured marching bands, radical cheerleaders, clowns, puppets, choirs, and costumed superheroes. Stylized acts such as Super Barrio Man, the Raging Grannies, Billionaires For Bush, Reverend Billy and the Church of Stop Shopping, and the Clandestine Insurgent Rebel Clown Army often take center stage at actions.[69]

These experiences of activist play have had four main impacts on democratic participation. *First*, they have encouraged more people to participate. They offer positive and easy entry points for political engagement, and energizing ways to stay involved.[70] Billionaires For Bush, for example, invites people to have fun protesting by just dressing up in classy clothes (figure 2.5). In only a couple years, the group grew from a handful of activists to 100 chapters across the United States.[71]

Figure 2.5
Billionaires For Bush. Photo courtesy of Fred Askew.

Second, playful actions have amplified the impact of participation. They have helped movements communicate ideas more clearly and win more media attention, often fueling policy victories. This has rarely been clearer than in 2000 in New York, when activists prevented the bulldozing of several community gardens by staging a protest wearing giant vegetable costumes. When asked why he issued a restraining order against the bulldozing, Attorney General Elliot Spitzer responded, "because a giant tomato asked me to do it."[72]

Third, play has often made participation more democratic. In organizations such as ACT UP, play and games have stimulated more fluid exchange of ideas, strategies, and tactics.[73] Play teaches many of the skills and attitudes necessary for democratic participation, helping people recognize different perspectives and develop a heightened sense of community.[74] Because of its democratic nature, activists have used play as a "prefigurative" tactic, aimed at modeling and creating a more democratic world.[75] Reclaim the Streets events, for example, occupy entire city blocks for a day of dancing, partying, clowning, and art, to model how people might use public space in a more democratic society.[76]

Finally, while it attracts some new players, activist play can also deter participation. Groups like Billionaires For Bush have adopted such a distinct style that involvement can be too time-consuming or expensive for many.[77] Some groups, such as the Yippies, become so immersed in their own play that they are inaccessible to most people. When play turns insular, its messages are more likely to be misunderstood or to only preach to the choir.[78] The public stunts of activist play are also riskier for people of color, who are often targeted by police, than for whites.[79] Partly as a result, playful activist groups are disproportionately led by relatively privileged whites, and so they are sometimes dismissed as elitist.[80]

So how has political play affected democratic participation? Populist play increases participation, but it remains directed by elites and susceptible to manipulation. Dissident play is a vital stepping stone for more active participation, but it often has little direct political effect. Activist play can make participation more attractive, impactful, and democratic, but it is inaccessible for many. If political play is often limited by manipulation, marginalization, and inaccessibility, can games do better?

Games as Political Action

Alongside these experiences of play, some social movements have used games to achieve political change. These movements create games not just about politics, but *as* politics.[81] They integrate games directly into political campaigns, meetings, actions, and discussions. Since the 1960s, Latin American activists, especially in Brazil, have developed and popularized an array of political games. More recently, urban planners and activists elsewhere have adapted these games and invented new ones. Unlike political play, these games are structured around specific rules, conflicts, and outcomes. They not only affect political decision-making but often become decision-making processes in their own right.

Social movements have used games for democratic participation in two main ways. First, they have explicitly *inserted games into participatory processes*, as in "popular education" and "Theater of the Oppressed" movements. *Popular education* wields pedagogy as a practice of liberation. As pioneered by Paulo Freire in 1960s Brazil, popular education groups help oppressed people understand their world and in the process change it.[82] Popular educators regularly use game activities, especially puzzles, role-playing games, and physical and mental challenges.[83] By playing and discussing games such as assassin, charades, and model jury, participants explore complex issues (exploitation, democracy, justice, etc.) *and* devise strategies for addressing them. Social movements often use popular education games to establish goals, determine tactics, and plan collective action.[84] These games have spread throughout the world, and North American popular education organizations, such as Tennessee's Highlander Center, Atlanta's Project South, and Toronto's Catalyst Centre, have been central to social movement achievements, from the Montgomery bus boycott to the US Social Forum.[85]

Since the 1970s, Augusto Boal's Theater of the Oppressed has developed an even more ambitious set of political games.[86] In *forum theater*, actors first present a short play in which a character succumbs to oppression, such as police harassment.[87] They then repeat the play, but this time they invite spectators to become "spect-actors," by jumping into the play, taking a character's place, and acting out new ideas to resolve the conflict (figure 2.6). Multiple spect-actors try their hand, until one "wins" by coming up with a strategy that works. As Boal says, "The game is spect-actors—trying to find a new solution, trying to change the world—against actors—trying to hold them back, to force them to accept the world as it is."[88] The game is not easy, and the spect-actors do not always win.

In the 1990s, Boal linked forum theater with politics through *legislative theater*.[89] After being elected city councilor in Rio de Janeiro, he opted to let citizens make their own laws. He held forum theater sessions around the city, and invited participants to suggest new laws based on their spect-acting

Figure 2.6
Theater of the Oppressed performance. Photo by author.

experience. Boal then proposed these laws to city council and got 13 of them passed, resulting in more hospital beds, public daycare facilities, and an expanded witness protection program. Popular theater has always been a form of play and art, but Boal added game elements. Scores of organizations around the world, such as the Theater of the Oppressed Lab in New York and Headlines Theater in Vancouver, have since incorporated Theater of the Oppressed games into their work. Governments in the United States, Germany, Scotland, and elsewhere have experimented with legislative theater.[90]

Since the 1990s, planning programs and nonprofit organizations throughout the Americas have increasingly mixed games into community participation processes. Many of these games are inspired by popular education, while others mimic mainstream games. For participatory planners, games have become a key tool for community engagement, usually in the form of physical icebreaker and team-building games, mapping simulations, and contests.[91] Local governments are increasingly hosting "informal engagement events," which entice residents with games, arts and crafts, music, and other entertaining activities, while also engaging them on more substantive issues.[92] A prime example is Proyecto ENLACE in Puerto Rico, the 2009 winner of the American Planning Association's Social Change and Diversity Award.[93] In addition to including popular education games in workshops, the program has organized a *reggeatón* competition in which youth write lyrics through participatory research, and a basketball tournament in which teams go through violence-prevention training.

Nonprofit organizations have also become enamored with contests. Larger groups such as MoveOn and the Center for Community Change routinely hold online competitions, in which people can submit policy proposals, campaign ideas, videos, or advertisements, and then vote on their favorites. In many cases, the sponsoring organization then carries out the winning entries. Grassroots groups—especially those focused on LGBT issues—are organizing smaller offline games. In New York, for example, FIERCE (a base-building group for queer youth of color) and Queers for Economic Justice have organized a *ReBowlution* bowl-a-thon and an annual *Amazingly Queer Race*, respectively. Following a broader trend among community-based organizations, these events combine fundraising, member recruitment, publicity, and organizing.[94]

Besides using games *in* participatory processes, Latin American movements have also demonstrated how to *make participatory processes more like a game*. In these cases, they are adopting the principles and techniques of games, without including games themselves. A widespread example is *participatory budgeting*. In 1990, inspired in large part by popular education, the Brazilian Workers Party (PT) launched a participatory budgeting process in the city of Porto Alegre. Through a series of neighborhood assemblies and meetings, residents decide how part of the city budget is spent.[95] Each year, this process has attracted thousands of mostly poor participants, while shifting spending to communities with the greatest needs. Since 1990, over 1,500 cities around the world have adopted and adapted Porto Alegre's model.[96]

Although participatory budgeting is not a game, it essentially works by taking an existing participatory process (budget consultations) and making it more like a game. The city adds transparent rules (which structure deliberation, decision-making, and allocation), artificial conflicts (new competition between neighborhoods and districts), and measurable outcomes (specific amounts of budget money and concrete public works). In the end, a typically inaccessible and technocratic process becomes more participatory and democratic. Other experiences, such as the community councils in Venezuela and decentralized planning in the Indian state of Kerala, have adopted similar game-like designs.[97]

Like play, these games and game-like processes seem to have encouraged people to participate, increased the impact of participation, and made participation more democratic. They are not immune to the problems that limit play (manipulation, marginalization, and inaccessibility), but they are better suited to deal with them. Unlike play, games require clear rules and player-driven outcomes, which make it harder (though not impossible, as we will see in chapter 4) for politicians or leaders to manipulate participants. While play tends to be marginalized from decision-making, games are at their core an activity in which players make decisions toward a goal.[98] In legislative theater and participatory budgeting, for example, people directly decide on new laws and spending.

These processes have also accommodated wider and more diverse participation than most activist play. Popular education, theater of the oppressed, and participatory budgeting have attracted unusually high participation from poor people and people of color.[99] This is partly because the organizers explicitly seek out these groups, and partly because the game formats are designed to be accessible and welcoming to people with little education or resources. In North America, games are especially popular among queer organizations and grassroots community groups.

New Frontiers for Games and Democracy

There is no single relationship between games and democracy. Political pundits, politicians, political scientists, designers, and activists each have their own visions of what games are and how they can encourage participation in democratic politics. For most politicians and the media, games are metaphors for describing the spectator sport of politics, and they may help raise some interest in politics. Game theorists understand games as methods for researching and analyzing political decision-making. Their game-like models offer some insight into why people participate in democracy. For game designers, games are real-world activities, mostly in digital form. Their social issue games serve mainly as political education, hoping to indirectly influence politics. Politicians and activists have used play extensively as a form of political action, to directly impact campaigns or policies. Starting in Latin America, social movements have also developed games as political action, enabling citizens to make democratic decisions themselves.

When viewed in this broader scope, the shortcomings of each use of games and play become more obvious. Spectator sport metaphors may attract political fans, but they also lead to cynicism and rarely encourage active democratic participation. Game theory's lessons are limited because of its questionable assumptions, glossing over of social and emotional motivations, and inaccessible language. Educational as they may be, social issue games usually have little connection with community organizations or political decision-making. Political play is more connected to campaigns and policy-making, but it is also susceptible to manipulation, marginalization, and inaccessibility. Finally, to use games for political decision-making, movements first need to convince leaders to give up some power—a daunting task.

These approaches also open up new possibilities for games and democracy. Pundits could encourage citizens to engage in politics as players, not just spectators. Game theorists could study *game design* to understand how people actually play games. Designers could link their games more directly with movements, campaigns, and other opportunities for participation.

Most of all, social movements and governments could deepen their use of games in democratic processes. Among the varieties of political games and play, games as political action have the most potential to encourage democratic participation, by engaging people directly in political decision-making. Since these games are still relatively uncommon, especially outside of Latin America, their potential remains largely untapped.

Not only are these political games relatively unknown, but their designers also know relatively little about game design. Augusto Boal's *Games for Actors and Non-Actors*, perhaps the most influential book on social movement games, only defines games as "physical dialogues" or "a form of contest."[100]

Despite using games more regularly, social movements have only recently begun to reflect on them deeply.[101] Fortunately, they need not start from scratch. In recent decades, game design scholars have built rich theories of how games work. Game design theory explores how rules, conflict, outcomes, play, information, culture, narrative, learning, and other factors interact in the complex systems called games.[102] In the next chapter, I explore what game design theory can teach us about democratic participation.

3   What Game Design Can Teach Us about Democracy

When you first land in Norrath, you hear footsteps all around you.[1] People are running back and forth, talking in cryptic words. Since you are weak and hungry, you start by attacking rats, selling their fur to buy food and water. After killing enough rats, you suddenly gain a level of experience. Congratulations—you are quite the rat killer! Alas, as a passing stranger mentions, you will need a sword to beat other foes. Venturing outside the town, toward the weapon shop in Rivervale, you call out for other brave adventurers to join you. None do, and you are promptly eaten by a bear.

You return to Norrath as a healer, determined to do better. Even with your basic skills, people pay you to heal them. You gradually become more proficient, until one day a group of fighters asks you to join them. As you explore the world together, you heal them after battles, earning a good reputation. Finally, you are making progress at *EverQuest*, one of the most popular "massively multiplayer online role-playing games" (MMORPGs) in history.

As Edward Castronova has masterfully documented, games such as *EverQuest* are home to virtual worlds as complex as many real-world countries.[2] To make these games fun for players, designers have to carefully craft ways to negotiate conflict, establish legitimate rules, make participation meaningful and rewarding, and engage diverse people. In this chapter, I argue that the techniques game designers use to deal with these challenges can also address similar problems in real-world democratic processes.

Of course, most political issues are not played out on virtual worlds, let alone with swords and magical healing powers. In recent years, however, game designers and developers have identified a universe of underlying rules, structures, elements, and processes that make games work. In *EverQuest*, these *game mechanics* include a mix of *conflict types*; *just-in-time information* about weapons and enemies; *measurable yet uncertain outcomes*, dependent partly on *chance*; *status indicators* measuring player health and skills; *resources* such as money and experience levels; *characters* such as healers and fighters; *hidden information* in the form of unexplored map terrain; an endless stream of decision-making *choice points*; and *vibrant visuals* and *sound effects* that help immerse the player in the game, within its *magic circle*. If such game mechanics can make players more interested in joining teams and undertaking quests, could they also make citizens more interested in joining community meetings and undertaking electoral campaigns?

This chapter explores what game design, and in particular, game mechanics such as those outlined above, can teach us about democratic politics.[3] First, I offer a brief introduction to game design and game design theory. In the bulk of the chapter, I present key game design concepts and mechanics, focusing on those that are most relevant for politics. I show how, unlike technocratic design approaches that transfer power from citizens to experts, game design provides people with greater skills and opportunities to participate meaningfully. Finally, to illustrate how game design concepts might apply beyond games, I review how they are already contributing to the fields of education, business, and architecture, where they are modeling new ways to process information, develop skills, build confidence and efficacy, collaborate in groups, think creatively, and motivate participation.

Game Design and Game Design Theory

Before delving into the theory behind it, what exactly is game design? In general, it is the process of crafting the structures and rules of a game. As discussed in chapter 2, while there is no single definition of games, most scholars roughly agree that they are systems in which players engage in an artificial conflict, defined by rules, that results in measurable outcomes.[4] This includes video and computer games, board games, card games, social games, and sports, to name a few categories. To create these game systems, designers establish a game premise, goals, rules, procedures, and other features that I will review below.

Game design may sound like a technocratic process, but it is not. Technocratic design transfers power from citizens to experts, prioritizing technical solutions over human experiences. Game designers instead strive to create meaningful human experiences. As Katie Salen and Eric Zimmerman describe, play becomes meaningful when a player's actions clearly lead to outcomes that have meaning within the game.[5] In *Pac-Man* for example, if ghosts suddenly run away and become vulnerable when Pac-Man eats cherries, seeking out cherries becomes meaningful. To sustain meaningful play, designers need to provide players with ever greater skills and opportunities to participate. While technocratic design renders people passive, game design activates them.

Game designers design games, but they do not directly design *gameplay*. They build the structures that shape players' experiences, but then players create their own game experiences by interacting with these structures.[6] In the end, designer intentions, player goals, and the broader social context combine to shape gameplay.[7] Designers set up interesting situations and provide opportunities for play—what Salen and Zimmerman call "spaces of possibility"—but they do not dictate the outcomes of the game.[8] If they do, it ceases to be a game worth playing.[9]

Game design is a young profession with an old history. People have been designing nondigital games for centuries, without necessarily calling themselves game designers. In recent decades, however, video game design and development has become a booming industry, encompassing corporations such as Electronic Arts and Nintendo, hundreds of smaller studios, and countless independent designers. By 2009, global video game sales had reached $46.5 billion, compared with $30 billion in box office film revenue.[10]

As game development has grown as an industry, game design has emerged as an academic field of study. As opposed to *game theory*, which studies game-like abstract models, *game design theory* studies digital and nondigital games that people intentionally and consciously play in the real world. In university departments, journals, blogs, and conferences, game design scholars debate the importance of narrative, the culture and ecology of games, relations between games and other media, player learning and experiences, the game design process, game aesthetics, and other topics.[11]

While games are played around the world, both the practice and study of game design are more geographically concentrated. Most major game design companies and academic programs are based in North America, Europe, Japan, and South Korea. While there are (some) game developers and scholars in less developed countries, they usually depend on their Northern counterparts. In Argentina, for example, the small lot of game companies serves mainly as cheap labor for foreign corporations, taking on such illustrious tasks as designing the digital grass of sports fields in US video games.[12] Argentine game designers and academics have only recently begun to organize their own conferences and forums for debate. As one local designer told me, "If I wanted to make an Argentine game right now with Argentine culture, I would have no idea how to do it."[13] Meanwhile, developers in the Global North are making most of the games played in developing countries, based on Northern cultures, perspectives, and biases.

Indeed all games are designed with particular kinds of players and playing styles in mind. The great diversity of real-world players is one of the main reasons why designers cannot predict exactly how a game will be played. In an influential essay, Richard Bartle described four main player types, which he called diamonds, spades, hearts, and clubs.[14] Diamonds are achievers who aim mainly to win. Spades are explorers, always trying to dig up new information and secrets. Hearts are socializers who play games to talk and interact with other players. Clubs are killers who go around clubbing as many other players as they can. Fullerton has added even more variations: collector, joker, artist, director, storyteller, performer, and craftsman.[15] Often players will combine elements of multiple play styles. Each player might also be a casual, experienced, or hardcore gamer. Because the sense of engagement comes from different things for different players, successful games appeal to and plan for various types of players and the interactions between them—just as successful democratic processes plan for various types of participants and forms of participation.

To ensure that their games accommodate diverse player styles and interests, designers rely on *iterative design*.[16] Through this process, designers and *playtesters* play successive iterations of a game, to test it out. After each round of playtesting, designers evaluate players' experiences and alter the game as necessary. Playtesting is hard work. For the video game *Halo 3*, for example, Microsoft Games User Research conducted over 3,000 hours of playtesting with more than 600 players, in a room fully wired with video cameras to track player movements and expressions.[17] In general, the design process constantly alternates between prototyping, playtesting, evaluation, and redesign, gradually honing in on a final product. Because designers cannot fully anticipate player actions, this process is essential for making games that people will actually play and enjoy.

Tricks of the Trade: Game Mechanics

How do game designers make fun and engaging games? Not by magic. Behind each successful game is a system of interweaving structures, rules, features, and elements—what I refer to as "game mechanics." In the following pages, I review key game mechanics, drawing on examples from popular games.

This may seem like a straightforward task, but it is not. Game design is a relatively new discipline, and designers are still struggling to build a common vocabulary and theoretical framework. As Doug Church has observed, "game designers can discuss 'fun' or 'not fun,' but often the analysis stops there."[18] When the analysis does not stop there, it frequently wanders off in quite different directions. There are still many disagreements on what it takes to make an engaging game.

Game designers and scholars in fact do not even agree on what game mechanics means. Reading through various definitions is enough to make one's head spin:

- "rule based systems/simulations that facilitate and encourage a user to explore and learn the properties of their possibility space through the use of feedback mechanisms"[19]
- "any part of the rule system of a game that covers one, and only one, possible kind of interaction that takes place during the game, be it general or specific"[20]
- "means to guide the player into particular behaviour by constraining the space of possible plans to attain goals"[21]
- "methods invoked by agents, designed for interaction with the game state."[22]

Other designers avoid the term game mechanics. Tracy Fullerton breaks games down into categories such as *formal elements* ("elements that make up the essence of games"[23]) and *game procedures* ("the actions or methods of play allowed by the rules"[24]). Staffan Björk and Jussi Holopainen analyze configurations of *game elements*: "the physical and logical attributes that help maintain and inform players about the current game state."[25] Church discusses *formal abstract design tools*.[26] Others write about game *components* or *features*.

While these terms have somewhat different meanings, there is relative agreement on many of the basic concepts that they represent. Richard Rouse and Marc LeBlanc offer perhaps the most straightforward descriptions of this universe of game concepts. For Rouse, game mechanics are the guts of a game, describing "what the players are able to do in the game-world, how they do it, and how that leads to a compelling game experience."[27] For LeBlanc, mechanics are "all the necessary pieces that we need to play the game . . . the rules . . ., the equipment, the venue, or anything else necessary for playing."[28] He considers mechanics to be the complete description of a game system, determining how the game will behave.

Following Rouse and LeBlanc, I understand game mechanics to include *the rules, structures, elements, and processes that designers use to shape gameplay*. Game mechanics are the internal gears that make games work, their basic design ingredients. They pave the way for (and do not include) what LeBlanc has called "game dynamics"—the actual events and phenomena that occur as the game is played.[29] In baseball, for example, mechanics such as rules, points (runs), and the shape of the playing field enable and encourage different gameplay dynamics, such as fly balls, ground balls, foul balls, and stolen bases.

Like a good recipe, a good game is the sum of its parts. Games are systems of mechanics—"groups of interrelated elements that work together to form a complex whole."[30] Most game mechanics can play a variety of roles (or no role at all), depending on how they are mixed and matched. Mechanics can also have distinct roles and effects in different games, or for different players. All of this variation is what makes iterative design and playtesting so essential, to see how particular combinations of game mechanics play out in practice.

Admittedly, my definition of game mechanics is very broad—for a reason. As Salen and Zimerman point out, definitions are useful for designers to the extent that they serve as tools for understanding and solving design problems.[31] While the definitions cited above may be helpful for game designers, this book is not written primarily for game designers. Rather, it is written for scholars and designers of political processes, including planners, officials, facilitators, organizers, and activists. After discussing games with such people for several years, I have found that "game mechanics" resonates more than other terms, and that a broad definition suffices. That said, if you prefer to substitute "elements," "procedures," or other terms for "game mechanics," feel free.

In the following four sections, I review 26 game mechanics that are particularly relevant for democratic politics. I group the mechanics according to four main design issues that they might address in democratic processes: conflict and collaboration, rules, outcomes, and engagement (see table 3.1). Any attempt to cluster game mechanics into categories is at least somewhat arbitrary, since many mechanics serve various purposes and take various forms. Hopefully, though, the four categories will make the stream of mechanics more navigable for designers of democratic processes.

Conflict and Collaboration

All games involve some kind of conflict. Players may be pitted against other players, teams, or even the game system. Conflict creates dramatic tension and challenges, which fuel a player's emotional investment in a game.[32] This conflict is often framed as competition, but it usually includes some collaboration as well. Each conflict ultimately ends in victory, defeat, a tie, or some kind of score for each side. While conflict outside of games can

Table 3.1
Key game mechanics

Conflict and collaboration

1. Conflict type

2. Magic circle

3. Balancing feedback loop

4. Reinforcing feedback loop

Rules

1. Multimodal presentation

2. Just-in-time information

3. Modeling

4. Player-generated rules

5. Sanctions

6. Rulings

Outcomes

1. Clear goals and objectives

2. Measurable outcomes

3. Uncertain outcomes

4. Chance

5. Points

6. Status indicators

7. Levels

Engagement

1. Vibrant visuals

2. Sound effects

3. Enjoyable core mechanics

4. Choice points

5. Resources

6. Hidden information

7. Characters

8. Narrative

9. Metagaming

be destructive, games make conflict safer by making it more artificial. As I explain below, they at least partly separate conflict from the real world, so that it takes place between players in the gamespace, rather than between people outside of the game. To create and manage this artificial conflict, designers rely, in particular, on the following game mechanics: different conflict types, magic circles, and balancing and reinforcing feedback loops.

1. Conflict Type

The type of conflict shapes the basic relationships that players have with each other and the game.[33] Conflict takes place among individual players, groups or teams, and game systems. Game systems include, for example, a computer program, which presents challenges for players, or a deck of cards, which limits the possibilities of game play. In politics, individuals could refer to citizens; groups to parties, organizations, and institutions; and systems to electoral systems or other legal or budgetary constraints. There are at least five different conflict relationships, and many games combine two or more types of conflict.

Individual vs. Individual Two or more individuals compete against each other. This competition may be direct, as in boxing or *Monopoly*, with one player's gain being another's pain. Or it can be indirect, as in a footrace, with each player's performance having little or no effect on other players.

Individual vs. Group One individual competes against a group of players. This conflict often creates a social tension, unless there are easy ways to bring the individual player back into the group. In the game of tag, for example, the player who is "it" competes against everyone else in the game, but she can also swap out of this role and integrate with the other players by tagging one of them.[34]

Individual vs. System One or more individuals compete individually against the computer or game system. This may involve one player, as in *Tetris* or Solitaire, or multiple players competing side by side, as in BINGO. In these cases the computer code, deck of cards, or random selection of numbers determines the system that opposes the player. These games can be socially isolating but also quite engaging. They generally do not encourage interactions between players, but solitary gameplay also gives the individual more control over and stake in game outcomes.

Group vs. Group Two or more groups or teams compete against each other. Competition may be direct, as in football or hockey, or indirect, as in a relay race. This conflict offers perhaps the greatest unpredictability and variation, since it depends on complex interactions within each team, between players with different skills and playing styles.[35] In team sports such as football, for example, a single missed pass may change the competitive balance in any number of ways, depending on how players on each team are positioned, their individual skills, and which opposing players are covering them.

Group vs. System A group of players competes together against a game system. This is perhaps the least common type of conflict, though it may encourage the most cooperative play. In the board game *Lord of the Rings*, for example, players struggle together as a fellowship against pressures imposed by the game system, represented by the villain Sauron.[36] On the top part of the playing board, the players' colored hobbit figures and the black Sauron figure move closer or farther apart, depending on the players' performance (see figure 3.1). When Sauron overtakes a hobbit figure, that player is out of the game. The team's quest continues, though, as long as it keeps the player with the ring away from Sauron. While each player obviously wants to stay alive, the only way to beat the game is by playing together as a team.

2. Magic Circle

A magic circle is a play space that is temporarily separated from the ordinary world, within which special rules apply.[37] Johann Huizinga first coined the term in the 1950s. Magic circles are a basic element of games, often established through several more specific game structures. Designers try to separate magic circles by both space (sports fields, stages, boards of board games) and time (agreed-upon game times). They usually accentuate the circle's physical boundaries, to create the feeling of safety necessary for play.[38] To further mark boundaries, players often must perform rituals to enter the magic circle: for example, reading the game rules aloud, shaking hands before a match, or singing the national anthem. By clearly defining the boundaries of magic circles, designers and players create a safer space for dealing with conflict.

Magic circles enable what Bernard Suits called a *lusory attitude*: a state of mind in which players willingly choose to employ less efficient means for obtaining a goal.[39] This inefficiency is essential to games—it provides the challenge that makes them fun.

For example, the rules of soccer only apply in a space designated as a soccer field, within a time period designated as a soccer game. Within this magic circle, players adopt a lusory attitude. If the goal is to get the ball in the net, the most efficient way to do this would be to pick up the ball and run full speed toward the net. Once players walk onto a soccer field and start the game clock, though they refuse to pick up the ball. Instead, they

Figure 3.1
Group versus system conflict—*Lord of the Rings* board game. Photo by author.

kick it—a relatively inefficient approach—because the rule of "no hands" applies within the magic circle.

The division between magic circle and real world is always a bit blurry, and a source of tension for games.[40] Winning a game inside a magic circle may lead to prizes and social rewards in the real world. Likewise conflicts and relations in the real world can affect how players interact in the game world. Nevertheless, the more that designers can envelop play within a defined magic circle, the more artificial (and compelling) the game conflict seems to players. Similarly sharper boundaries around spaces of political

What Game Design Can Teach Us about Democracy

deliberation and negotiation might make real-world conflicts seem less threatening and easier to address.

3. Balancing Feedback Loop

Feedback refers to the game system's response to player actions.[41] In balancing feedback loops, the game response counteracts player actions, leveling out performance. If a player is having success, the game gets harder, by adding additional challenges. If a player is having difficulties, the game gets easier, by reducing the challenges. Balancing feedback helps maintain competition between strong and weak players, or between players and the game system. It can slow the advance of successful players and give weak players the extra support they need to compete.

In the video game *Space Invaders*, for example, players try to shoot all the descending alien invaders before they bomb or run into the player's avatar at the bottom of the screen, as shown in figure 3.2. After completing each

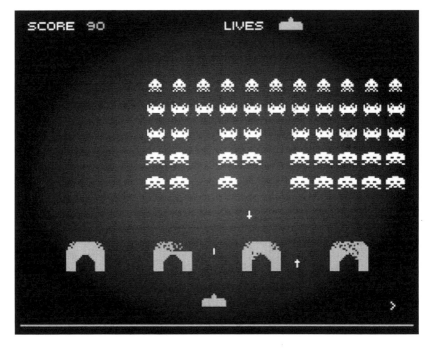

Figure 3.2
Balancing feedback loop—*Space Invaders*. Screenshot by author.

level, the next level presents a more difficult set of enemies—invaders that are faster, more numerous, or better able to shoot the player. As players advance in level (and skill), the game becomes harder and harder. In a town hall meeting, such a feedback loop might mean that once someone (successfully) speaks multiple times, he is automatically placed at the bottom of the speaker list, or faces other obstacles to speaking again.

Balancing feedback loops are essential for creating what Mihaly Csikszentmihalyi calls "flow."[42] A flow state is when a player's skills equally meet the challenges of the activity. In this state of mind the player achieves the highest focus and enjoyment. She feels in control of her actions and master of her fate. The task for game designers is to keep raising the difficulty and competition level enough to challenge players, but without overwhelming them or taking away too much control over gameplay.[43] If a game becomes too difficult too quickly, it generates anxiety, but if it stays easy for too long, it leads to boredom.[44] To create flow, good games manage to adapt to the level of the player, adding difficulty at just the right speed to stay at the outer edge of the player's "regime of competence."[45] This allows a game to feel challenging but not impossible—a tough competition, but one that players can win.

4. Reinforcing Feedback Loop

In reinforcing feedback loops, the game response mirrors and multiplies player performance. The game becomes easier in response to player success, or harder in response to player difficulties.[46] This feedback makes successful players breeze through the game quicker, and drags down unsuccessful players in a spiral of defeat. Reinforcing feedback thus widens the gap between more and less successful players. Generally, designers avoid too much reinforcing feedback, since it disrupts the game's competitive balance. It can be useful, though, for ensuring quick resolutions to conflicts, creating a sense of finality, increasing the stakes of activities, or illustrating systemic inequalities (e.g., the rich get richer).[47]

For example, in the TV game show *Jeopardy*, when a player provides a correct response, she stays in control and gets to pick the next challenge. This generally favors the successful player, since it allows her to pick the categories and dollar amounts that are most advantageous to her. In a town hall meeting, a reinforcing feedback loop might mean that after (successfully) speaking, a participant is given automatic access to the mic, making it easier for her to speak again.

Rules

Rules are the internal formal structures of games that limit or dictate what a player can do.[48] They are explicit and unambiguous, shared by all players, fixed, binding, and repeatable. While the concept of rules suggests some higher authority, in games there is generally no specific person or body associated with that authority.[49] Instead, the authority lies in the agreement between the players to abide by the rules. As the psychologist Erik Erikson observed, what distinguishes play from work is that the rules of play (and games) are self-imposed.[50] The same can be said of democracy, as opposed to other forms of government.

The official rules of a game only represent a small portion of the total rules. Beneath these guidelines lies a web of unwritten rules.[51] Some of these are constituative, meaning that they are based on the underlying game structure and mathematical logic—for example, the limited number of possible moves in tic-tac-toe.[52] Others are implicit—they go without saying, even if sometimes they might be better off said. These include many rules of etiquette or procedure, such as when and where a player can take a game break, how long she can take for her turn, and what players can say or do while playing and not playing. There are so many unwritten rules that it is virtually impossible to document them all.[53]

Nevertheless, designers should not ignore unwritten rules. When important rules remain unwritten, veteran players tend to understand them better than newcomers, giving them an unfair advantage. Jo Freeman observed similar dynamics in social movements, in her article "The Tyranny of Structurelessness."[54] For Freeman, the often romanticized "structureless" movements and meetings of the 1960s may have rejected traditional hierarchies, but they also imposed "informal" hierarchies. Because men were more familiar with the informal (and unwritten) rules of the game, they could dominate meetings. By refusing to write down rules, movements were keeping women in the dark.

Oddly, rules are both limiting *and* enabling. Although they constrain player actions, players accept them largely because they make creative gameplay possible. Bernard Suits demonstrates this unusual relationship with the case of high jumping contestants: "Their goal is not *simply* to get to the other side, but to do so only by using means permitted by rules, namely, by running from a certain distance and then jumping. And their *reason* for accepting such rules is just because they want to act within the limitations that rules impose."[55] Rules can thus allow players to adopt a lusory attitude, finding enjoyment in constrained tasks that they might otherwise have no reason to pursue.

Whether or not rules actually make a game enjoyable depends on how they are created, communicated, changed, and enforced. To start, designers need to avoid creating too many or too few rules. Too many rules can constrict play and overwhelm players with complexity. For Linda Hughes and other game scholars, "Games aren't much 'fun' when rules, rather than relationships, dominate the activity."[56] Then again, too few rules can leave players unclear on what to do.

Once rules are created, games need to clearly communicate them to players. As Fullerton warns, "The less well that players understand your rules, whether rationally or intuitively, the less likely they will be able to make meaningful choices within the system and the less sense they will have of being in control of the gameplay."[57] Many games also need to accommodate rule changes, either by the players themselves or by game authorities. Finally, games need mechanisms for enforcing agreed-upon rules, such that gameplay seems fair. To accomplish these tasks, designers use multimodal presentation, just-in-time information, modeling, player-generated rules, sanctions, and rulings.

1. Multimodal Presentation

Multimodal presentation involves communicating rules (and other information) in multiple formats—through spoken and written words, symbols, images, interactions, sounds, and other modalities.[58] Good games do not assume that players instantly understand the rules, but rather that rules need to be constantly presented, explained, and reinforced. They often write rules in rulebooks or instructions, embed them in game content, read them aloud, and display them prominently throughout gameplay.

The board game *Monopoly*, for example, communicates rules (such as "collect \$200 on passing *Go"*) by presenting them in the instructions *and* writing them on the game board, as in figure 3.3. In many digital games, players also discover rules through interactions, as they test out what they can and cannot do. In political processes, different modes of presentation include websites, videos, PowerPoint presentations, signs, symbols, handouts, and oral announcements. Most processes use relatively few modes, however.

2. Just-in-Time Information

Just-in-time information is information presented at the moment when it is actually useful for a player. As James Gee points out, humans are not very

What Game Design Can Teach Us about Democracy

Figure 3.3
Multimodal presentation—*Monopoly*. Photo by author.

good at learning from lots of overt information given to them outside the sorts of contexts in which this information can be used.[59] So while games may provide a full stock of rules and information in their instructions, they also present specific rules and information during the game, when they are in context and players can act on them. These timely cues help players better understand and follow rules.

In the computer game *SimCity*, for example, all buildings must be connected to the electricity network to be used. The game quickly teaches the player this by displaying a flashing lightning bolt on any unconnected lots (see figure 3.4). Unless electricity is reconnected, buildings on these lots will soon disappear. Similarly democratic processes can provide information about voting rules, speaking times, or agenda items close to the moment when this information is most necessary.

3. Modeling

Modeling is when a game demonstrates or walks the player through actions she will soon need to undertake, or rules she will need to follow. Games often start with training modules, or their early levels function as training

Figure 3.4
Just-in-time information—*Sim City*. Screenshot courtesy of Conor Lauzon.

modules, enabling players to observe and act out common rule-bound tasks before their actions really count.[60] One way to achieve this is through what Gee calls "concentrated samples," when the player starts by seeing many more instances of key game features than would be the case in a less controlled sample.

For instance, in the classic arcade game *Teenage Mutant Ninja Turtles*, and many other arcade games, the machine displays a looped segment of gameplay before players insert coins. Before play starts, players can watch the game model basic actions they will need to undertake and respond to. This demo loop demonstrates how the turtles walk, jump, and fight, and how enemies move and attack. It shows off the pizza power-ups that the turtles can consume to refresh their energy, and how this energy is depleted by enemy attacks. Armed with this information, players are more prepared to launch into the game. Once they start playing, the initial stages provide relatively easy opportunities to practice basic moves and actions, with little risk of being killed right away. In a public hearing or meeting, modeling might mean a facilitator giving a mock presentation, demonstrating how to speak into the microphone, before asking community members to speak.

4. Player-Generated Rules

Player-generated rules are game rules that players write or help decide, before or while playing. While most games start with fixed rules, some allow players to make, change, or erase the rules. These player changes only become rules if everyone in the game agrees that they are the rules. Linda Hughes, in her study of the playground game *four square*, found that not only did kids constantly invent new rules but also that they were more interested in the rules that they generated and controlled.[61] Dekoven, Salen, and Zimmerman have argued that games *should* empower players to be more like designers by including rules that are meant to be broken or modified.[62] Regardless of the intentions of designers, people often opt to set their own rules when playing popular games such as Poker, basketball, and tag. "The search for the well-played game is what holds the community together," DeKoven explains. "But the freedom to change the game is what gives the community its power."[63]

The card game *Democrazy* offers one of the best examples of player-generated rules (see figure 3.5). Players attempt to pass new laws (rules) that benefit themselves, increasing the relative value of their playing chips. Each

Figure 3.5
Player-generated rules—*Democrazy*. Photo courtesy of Catherine Herdlick.

player, on her turn, puts forward a card that proposes a change to the rules. All players then vote on the change, and if the rule passes, it becomes law. Players can add new rules such as "red chips are worth two points," "all players with beards get five points," or "each time a law is adopted, the player who proposed it takes an extra turn"—but only if they win a majority vote. Some participatory budgeting initiatives—including ones that I have helped design in the United States—use a similar approach, letting local stakeholders write the rules and then revise them periodically.[64]

5. Sanctions

Sanctions are automatic penalties or other kinds of enforcement that a game imposes for rule violations. They are most commonly used in sports, to provide incentives for players to follow the rules, while still allowing the game to continue.[65] Too much rule enforcement can take the fun out of a game, but regular and predictable sanctions can help players learn the rules through trial and error.

In US football, for example, if an offensive or defensive player moves over the line of scrimmage before the ball is in play, the referee punishes his team with an automatic five-yard penalty. The play is then repeated, with the line of scrimmage moved five yards to the disadvantage of the violating team. Sanctions are obviously also popular in international politics, for regulating issues such as global warming emissions and nuclear weapons. Unlike in professional sports, however, these sanctions are usually decided on an ad hoc basis, sparking substantial controversy.

6. Rulings

Rulings occur when a designer or authority is called on to act as a judge, to say whether and how a rule applies. No matter how thorough a game's rules, there will always be ambiguities.[66] In nondigital sports in particular, such as tennis or football, an umpire or referee is typically designated to make rulings. Too many rulings can make the decisions of judges seem more important than the actions of players. If the conditions and process for rulings is clear, however, there may be less criticism.

In baseball, for example, umpires often make rulings when applying the rules of the base paths. According to the rules, if a player arrives at a base before the ball arrives, he is safe. Whether a player beats the throw in any specific instance, however, is determined by a judgment of the umpire. If the umpire rules that the player is safe, he spreads his arms wide. Hearings or disciplinary committees can serve a similar role in democratic politics—if they have clear mandates and support.

Outcomes

People play games for many reason, but usually at least one motivation is to win. After investing energy and time to overcome a game's challenges, the moment of victory delivers the intrinsic pleasure of a job well done. For some games, real-life rewards such as prizes or trophies make winning yet more gratifying. Even a loss or tie can be rewarding, if players feel that they have performed well.

When we know that a game will end in a concrete outcome, conflict becomes more thrilling and rules more acceptable. Good games therefore closely link participation with outcomes throughout gameplay, so players feel that they are making progress and keep sight of the light at the end of the tunnel. Designers create this link mainly by using clear goals and objectives, measurable outcomes, uncertain outcomes, chance, points, status indicators, and levels.

1. Clear Goals and Objectives

Clear goals and objectives let players know what they are supposed to be doing and accomplishing. If games do not communicate this, players feel lost and often abandon the game. Game goals therefore tend to be straightforward, so that they are more easily grasped—for example, to find the treasure, chase the enemy, build the city, or solve the riddle.[67] Clear goals are essential for motivating players, but to maintain players' attention, they should be both challenging and achievable. "[T]he goal is never easily attained," explain Salen and Zimmerman. "[R]ather, it is the obscure object of desire, the carrot held just out of reach, pulling players forward through the varied pleasures of gameplay."[68] If a goal seems impossible, in contrast, players are likely to give up.

In the card game Blackjack, for example, the main goal is to collect cards that add up to as close to 21 points as possible, without going over that total. This clear goal makes it easy for new players to quickly pick up the game.

Beneath the overarching goal, designers provide short-term and intermediate objectives.[69] These objectives may range, for example, from jumping over a hole to collecting all the coins on a level. Some games also have different objectives for different players, and others allow players to choose from among various goals and objectives. By enabling more variation and complexity, these approaches can extend the life of a game. Unfortunately, town hall meetings and public hearings rarely make distinct and achievable goals so clear for participants.

2. Measurable Outcomes

All games end in measurable outcomes, meaning that a player wins, loses, ties, or receives some score.[70] These outcomes distinguish games from play. The clearer the potential outcomes are, the greater is the motivation to play the game. When a player knows how she will be able to measure the precise outcome of the game, she can more easily sense how the game is advancing toward its end.[71]

In the board game *Trivial Pursuit*, for instance, players try to answer six categories of trivia questions. When they successfully answer a question, they receive a colored pie slice representing that question's category, to insert into their circular game piece on the playing board (see figure 3.6). The number of slices in each player's game piece provides a clear measurement of the outcomes so far. When a player collects all six slices and returns to the center of the board, she wins. In US presidential elections, the electoral college provides distinctly measurable outcomes. Each candidate (and his supporters) knows how many electoral college votes he needs to win (270), how many votes each state offers, and how many votes he has collected so far.

Figure 3.6
Measurable outcomes—*Trivial Pursuit*. Photo by author.

3. Uncertain Outcomes

Designers try to keep outcomes uncertain so that players cannot predict or know in advance who will win. Uncertain outcomes are key for sustaining people's attention. As long as the outcome is unknown, any player could still win or lose. Otherwise, as Fullerton observes, "If players can anticipate the outcome of a game, they will stop playing."[72] Once the outcome becomes certain, players become spectators, and they detach from the game emotionally.[73] The same is true of democratic processes. Once citizens know the results, and know that their participation will not change the results, they are more likely to disengage. In most participatory processes, unfortunately, the outcomes are rather predictable.

The game show *Who Wants to Be a Millionaire* illustrates the power of uncertain outcomes. Players try to answer a series of trivia questions, to win sums of money up to one million dollars, pounds, or other currency. With each correct answer, the contestant moves higher up the list of questions, and has the potential to win even more money. But if the player answers any question incorrectly, she is instantly kicked off the game. As a result at every point in the game the outcomes are entirely uncertain. Both full victory and full defeat are possible.

4. Chance

Games often leave some results to chance, whether through dice, spinners, coin flips, or randomized computer feedback. Chance can help equalize player outcomes and add uncertainty. It gives less successful players hope that the outcome might still somehow veer in their favor, motivating them to keep playing.[74] If players lose, they can deflect some of the blame to chance, and hope that next time the results might be different.[75] Leaving outcomes to chance may seem unfair, though, if it happens too often or for key moments of the game. In these cases, players begin to feel that their skills and efforts are pointless, and that game outcomes are arbitrary. To prevent resentment, games can warn players in advance about the possibility of chance events, and offer ways to minimize potential damage.[76]

The TV show *Wheel of Fortune* is one of the most iconic examples of a game driven by chance. Contestants try to solve a word puzzle by guessing letters to fill in the puzzle blanks. On a player's turn, she first spins a giant wheel. The wheel usually stops on a dollar amount, which indicates how much the player's guess is worth. When the player then guesses a letter, she gets that dollar amount for each instance of the letter in the puzzle. The wheel may also stop on special spaces, which can change the order of turns or lead to prizes. The game's dramatic tension depends largely on the *chance* of the wheel. Neither players nor spectators can know or determine exactly where it will stop, or how this will affect the game balance. In community meetings, chance can be used (or misused) to resolve some decisions, such as by picking names out of a hat to determine responsibilities or positions.

5. Points

Points measure progress toward goals, through a numerical score. They quantify the results of gameplay. Points may take the form of tokens, dollars, or other currency, goals, runs, baskets, or simply "points." In democratic processes they might also be counted as votes, signatures, or endorsements.

The board game *Scrabble* shows how points can drive gameplay (see figure 3.7). Each letter tile is assigned a point value, based on how common the letter is. Players try to lay out words with the highest sums of letter points. These points can be multiplied by double and triple score spaces on the game board. As a game progresses, players track their score, trying to accumulate the most points by the time the letter tiles are exhausted.

Figure 3.7
Points—*Scrabble*. Photo by author.

What Game Design Can Teach Us about Democracy

6. Status Indicators

Status indicators signal to players what stage the game is at, how much progress the player has made, or how much time is remaining. Clocks tick down, hourglasses fill up with sand, milestones are achieved, time warnings pop up, and energy or health bars rise and fall. If games warn of impending dangers and the time remaining, players are less surprised if they fail, and less likely to blame the game.[77]

For example, in the popular fighting game series *Mortal Kombat*, the top of the game screen displays a horizontal health bar (see figure 3.8). Each side of the bar tracks the damage that one player has sustained. When the health bar depletes to zero, the player dies. The bar thus functions as a constant indicator of player success. Fundraising bars or counters can have similar effects for grassroots campaigns.

7. Levels

Levels create intermediate goals for players, requiring them to complete a set of tasks and achieve an objective before moving on to the next part of the game. In video games, levels are usually called such, but they may also take the form of rounds, quests, or stages. As players move through levels, they build a sense of progress, a feeling that they are advancing toward the end of the game. Games usually start easy with immediate rewards, to allow players to build up competence and commitment to the game.[78] Early

Figure 3.8
Status indicator—*Mortal Kombat*. Screenshot by author.

levels rarely include time pressures, tough enemies, or harsh punishments for mistakes.

Celebrity, for example, is a party game usually based on three rounds (or levels) of charades-like play. Players each write the names of celebrities on pieces of paper, and then put the papers in a hat and divide into teams. In the first round, players try to get their teammates to guess celebrity names picked out of the hat by describing them orally. In the second round, players can only say one word for each celebrity name, but can use gestures to act out the celebrity. In the third round, players can only use gestures and cannot speak. Each level of the game adds a new type of challenge, building on the skills and knowledge from previous rounds. The Venezuelan community council meeting described in chapter 1 also used levels to drive participation. First, organizers had to complete a building census, then form provisional commissions, and finally hold a founding assembly.

Engagement

In addition to the basic mechanics described above, designers use other techniques to further engage players. These engagement mechanics make games even more attractive and rewarding, by making them more aesthetically pleasing, emotionally gripping, or intellectually stimulating.

1. Vibrant Visuals

Designers deeply integrate rich images, graphics, and other visual effects throughout games. They try to make games inherently enjoyable to look at, so that play is more enticing. These visuals envelop players in the game's narrative, world, and aesthetics, to transport them away from their real-world surroundings and make them emotionally invest in the game. As Henry Jenkins reasons, to achieve a "holding power" that lets players transcend their immediate environments, "game spaces require concreteness and vividness."[79] While many digital games, such as *Halo* and *Assassin's Creed*, are famous for vivid graphics, other games also highlight visual elements.

For instance, slot machines would be a rather uninteresting game without engrossing visuals, if the machine simply displayed a number in each of its three columns each game. Rather, it shows each column's roll spinning wildly, eventually settling on a colorful and highly stylized number, word, or image. Likewise, the rest of the machine is usually covered with bright colors, impact fonts, arrows, and pictures, drawing players in and keeping them visually engaged (see figure 3.9). Democratic processes rarely integrate visuals so thoroughly. At most public consultations, people are lucky to see a PowerPoint presentation or cheesy clip art.

What Game Design Can Teach Us about Democracy 73

Figure 3.9
Vibrant visuals—Slots. Photo courtesy of Jeff Kubina.

2. Sound Effects

Designers often use music or sounds to establish the gamespace and further immerse players in the game experience. While at any given moment a player can only engage with a small fraction of the visual gamespace, the game's soundscape can flow throughout gameplay, connecting players with the broader game world and stimulating emotions.[80] Music and sounds may be pervasive, occasional, or even noticeably absent at times. For many scholars the tight linkage between engaging visuals, sounds, and actions generates the deep and meaningful experience of immersion that is common to games.[81]

Few games have put sound effects to better use than the 1993 computer game *Myst*. In the game the player is transported to the apparently deserted island of Myst, which gradually reveals its secrets as the player explores it. Ambient synthesizer music envelops the player in a mood of mystery and exploration, while incidental sounds such as bells and seagulls draw attention to the island and its surroundings. Player actions often result in squeaks, clicks, and clunks. The music proved so popular that it was released separately as a soundtrack. While electoral campaigns may blast theme songs and some community meetings feature music, few democratic processes include sound effects more deeply, to call attention to particular information, actions, or rules.

3. Enjoyable Core Mechanics

Core mechanics are the basic actions that players perform again and again in a game.[82] Good games are based on inherently enjoyable and accessible core mechanics, such as running, jumping, throwing, catching, hitting, kicking, shooting, clicking, and trading. Successful core mechanics generally require players to move physically and/or virtually (via their game avatar), engaging players more viscerally. Some people are more drawn to or skilled at certain core mechanics. Highly social players, for instance, often engage more in gifting and trading mechanics that are common in *Facebook* games such as *Farmville*.

Bowling is a prime example of an otherwise boring sport blessed with a fun core mechanic. For most of a game, players wait for a ball to roll down a lane. Yet bowling is an incredibly popular sport, largely because it relies on a single enjoyable core mechanic—rolling (or throwing, for less polished players) a really big ball, as in figure 3.10. The simple act of rolling the ball toward a set of pins is fun enough to keep players eagerly awaiting their turn. Meanwhile, the core mechanics of most democratic processes

Figure 3.10
Enjoyable core mechanics—Bowling. Photo courtesy of Xiaphias.

What Game Design Can Teach Us about Democracy

(listening, presenting, and arguing) are as much fun as your average Monday morning staff meeting.

4. Choice Points

Choice points are moments when players can make a decision that will affect the course of the game. In the words of Sid Meier, author of the *Civilization* computer games, "a game is a series of interesting choices."[83] Even in shooter games, players need to choose whether to shoot left or right. Under time constraints, this becomes a quite meaningful choice. To enable these choices, designers must lay out multiple possible ways for a player to make progress or move ahead.[84] The choices must also have real consequences, pushing the player closer to victory or defeat.[85] Designers try to strike a delicate balance between offering too many and too few choices. Too many choices can make a game overwhelming or tedious, but if players are not asked to make new choices regularly, a game can feel stagnant.[86]

The video game *Tetris* thrives on choice points. As each block drops from the top of the screen, the player needs to decide how to rotate it and where to position it, before it falls to the bottom (see figure 3.11). If the player decides wrong, blocks soon accumulate up to the top of the screen, ending the game. If the player manages to position blocks right, she can erase rows and stay alive. This stream of decisions keeps most players glued to the screen. In contrast, a typical community meeting offers each participant only a handful of opportunities—if any—to make decisions.

5. Resources

Resources are things that are valuable because they can help players achieve goals, but that are also scarce by design.[87] They can be lives, units, cards, health, currency, moves or turns, power-ups, inventory, special terrain, or time, for example. Because resources are scarce, players must manage them efficiently to achieve goals. If players can accrue things, and later use them, they have more incentive to keep coming back to the game.[88] If there are multiple kinds of resources to collect and manage, player decisions become more complex. "These are not just complex decisions"; Greg Costikyan adds, "these are interesting ones. Interesting decisions make for interesting games."[89]

In the *Super Mario* video game series, for example, players can collect mushrooms, stars, leafs, and other resources, often by jumping up into "?" blocks (see figure 3.12). The resources give the player extra powers, such as the ability to fly, live longer, or shoot fireballs. Democratic processes often provide votes as a basic resource, though some also use tokens, passes,

Figure 3.11
Choice points—*Tetris*. Photo by author.

turns, currencies, and arts and crafts supplies to inspire more creative participation.

6. Hidden Information
Some games hide basic information about a situation from players at first, so that they can gradually discover it during the game. The technique is sometimes known as the "fog of war," referring to hidden areas on war game maps, which players uncover by exploring the map.[90] For complex

What Game Design Can Teach Us about Democracy

Figure 3.12
Resources—*Super Mario Brothers*. Photo by author.

games in particular, providing too much information at first can paralyze or overwhelm players. If they need only become familiar with a limited set of information first, it is easier to get hooked on the game. Leaving parts of the game unknown also creates interesting situations for strategizing—it forces players to more carefully consider what they do and do not know when mapping out a game plan. The promise of being able to uncover new information keeps players coming back for more.

Sid Meier's turn-based computer game *Civilization* shows how hidden information can keep players engaged. In the game, the player attempts to build an empire in competition with other civilizations. She starts with one unit of "settlers" and knowledge only of the settlers' immediate geographic surroundings, with the rest of the world map clouded in black. Gradually, she builds cities and explores the world, coming into contact with new regions, civilizations, and challenges, and revealing more terrain on the map (see figure 3.13). In elections, the gradual unveiling of vote results on maps, district by district, can create a similar draw.

7. Characters
Role-playing games in particular often create compelling characters that let players experience and interact with different identities and points of view. Strong and vivid characters help players empathize with the game situation and live vicariously through it.[91] They build emotional attachment to the game and raise the stakes and complexity of decisions.[92] No other medium lets people play with identity so actively as games. Every game has some kind of role playing, as people first become players, and then usually characters inside the game as well.

For example, the computer game *Grand Theft Auto IV* allows players to assume the identity of Niko Bellic, depicted in figure 3.14. A Serbian

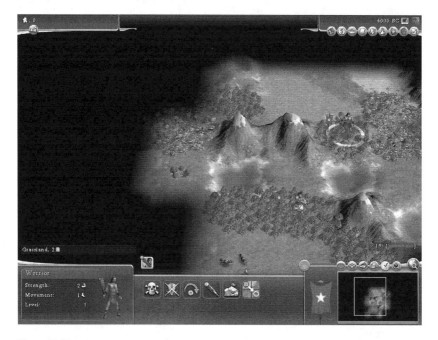

Figure 3.13
Hidden information—*Civilization*. Photo courtesy of Jason Haas.

Figure 3.14
Characters—*Niko Bellic, Grand Theft Auto IV*. Grand Theft Auto IV Screenshot Courtesy of Rockstar Games and Take-Two Interactive Software, Inc.

immigrant and veteran of the war in Bosnia, Niko came to America in the hope of starting a new life. Despite these ambitions, he is drawn into criminal activity to save his cousin. As the game unfolds, the player is forced to make difficult choices that will decide the fate of Niko and his loved ones. The game has become widely popular in part because it offers players the opportunity to experience a fully detailed virtual world in an alternate persona.

8. Narrative

Many designers build narrative elements into games, to place game actions in the context of a broader story. Narrative threads bind events together and drive players forward toward completing the game.[93] Games usually start with exposition, establishing their setting, characters, and premise.[94] Often this provides explanation and justification for the rules. The game conflict then drives the story forward, with intermittent signs that the player is approaching the climax. After the climax, many games include a recap or formalities as a denouement, easing down the dramatic tension and giving players a sense of closure.[95]

In the board game *Life*, for example, players move game pieces along a winding path, trying to progress through the milestones of life (going to college, buying a car, getting married, having kids, etc.) while avoiding life's challenges (buying furniture, paying taxes, getting in car accidents, etc.). Along the way, players forge a story of their character's life. The well-known (if caricatured) narrative of life helps put the game activities in a broader and more meaningful context (see figure 3.15).

The role of narrative has inspired a contentious debate in the game design community. On one side, "ludologists" argue that the linear flow of stories is in direct conflict with the freedom of action allowed by games.[96] If players can change the story, how can designers hope to craft narratives? As Markku Eskelinen puts it, "If I throw a ball at you I don't expect you to drop it and wait until it starts telling stories."[97] "Narratologists," in contrast, argue that compelling storylines help immerse players in the game world, creating greater dramatic tension.[98]

Henry Jenkins and others have tried to bridge these two sides, illustrating how designers can work as "narrative architects" by building game spaces with narrative elements and possibilities.[99] For example, they can include elements from popular narratives such as *Star Wars* (evoked narratives) or let players perform or witness narrative events (enacted narratives). Or they can include narrative events that players discover at key game moments (embedded narratives) or provide players with plentiful raw material to craft their own narratives, as in *The Sims* (emergent narratives).

Figure 3.15
Narrative—*The Game of Life*. THE GAME OF LIFE® & ©2013 Hasbro, Inc. Used with permission.

These techniques might also help weave meaningful yet flexible narrative into democratic participation. As Rogers Smith has argued, stories are vital for building communities.[100] Democracies have struggled, though, to shape them in a participatory fashion, allowing for contesting views while still bringing people together around a shared narrative.

9. Metagaming

Metagaming consists of game-related activities that happen around and during a game, outside of the game itself.[101] It includes the broader culture of parallel chat sessions, web forums and magazines, conventions, media coverage, merchandising, and countless other extensions of games. These additional venues give people more ways to engage with the game world. Players often engage in metagaming to harness information and resources outside of the game, in order to improve their performance inside it. Enhancing the metagame can increase a game's lifespan, attract new players, and be deeply satisfying on its own.[102]

For example, *America's Army* is a series of video games and accompanying media projects produced by the US Army. The game allows players to simulate combat through an unusually realistic first-person shooter game. But the reach of *America's Army* extends far beyond the game itself. Its online network includes active community forums, newsletters, blogs, news updates, *YouTube* and *Facebook* links, and interactive information about the army, as depicted in figure 3.16. The game has also been extended into a graphic novel, student education seminars, and mobile gaming experiences at sporting events. Likewise democratic processes could (and sometimes do) develop online forums, *Facebook* groups, blogs, and listservs, and organize offline newsletters, parties, and happy hours.

The Influence of Game Design

The concepts discussed above are not just for game designers. In recent years educators, businesses, and architects, along with their respective academic branches, have begun to learn lessons directly from game design. By applying game mechanics, they have modeled new ways to help people understand information, develop skills, and build confidence and efficacy. They have boosted group collaboration, creative thinking, and motivations to participate. In the process they have shown how game design can transform diverse social and political settings, such as schools, workplaces, and cities.

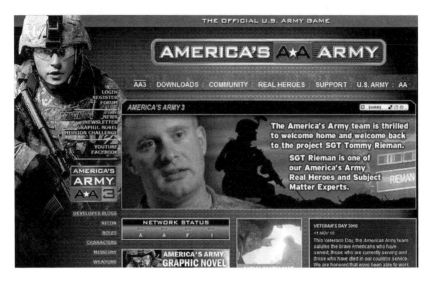

Figure 3.16
Metagaming—*America's Army*. Image courtesy of the US Army. AMERICA'S ARMY and the AA logo are registered trademarks of the Department of the Army.

Games are increasingly shaping *educational institutions and practices*. James Gee's classic 2003 book *What Video Games Have to Teach Us about Learning and Literacy* made perhaps the strongest argument for linking games and learning: "better theories of learning are embedded in the video games many children in elementary and high school play than in the schools they attend."[103] Gee demonstrated how, contrary to skeptical media reports, people are learning deeply, actively, and critically when they play games. Even better, games make learning fun—something that people intrinsically want to do.[104] Game-based learning may also translate into civic learning and change. Scholars are beginning to find that certain kinds of games and gameplaying are correlated with higher civic and political participation.[105]

Gee and others have shown how many of the game mechanics outlined above also function as good learning principles:[106]

• Just-in-time learning allows people to apply new learning immediately and limit data overloads at the beginning of activities.
• Modeling situates learning within the domain where people will later act.
• Multimodal presentation makes information accessible to different learning styles and prepares people for the multimodal texts and images they encounter in the real world.

What Game Design Can Teach Us about Democracy

- Balancing feedback loops and levels enable people to develop new skills and knowledge at their own pace, gradually stretching out their capabilities.
- Status indicators provide learners with instant feedback, which helps them hone skills.
- Dividing assignments into levels, and requiring a certain number of points before completion, provides additional incentives for students to make progress.

Educators and game enthusiasts have applied these game-based learning principles in two main ways.[107] First, they have supported and amplified the learning that occurs through commercial games outside of educational institutions. This involves promoting, developing, and researching games that teach valuable life skills for communicating, problem-solving, collaborating, and innovating. The other approach has tried to incorporate games and game mechanics into educational institutions, to change their curriculum, design, and structure. In New York City and Chicago entire *Quest* schools have even been designed to facilitate "game-like learning," with games and game mechanics embedded throughout the school environment.[108] Most organizations focused on games and learning, such as The Education Arcade, The Games for Learning Institute, and the Institute of Play, are swinging from both sides of the plate, working inside and outside of schools to promote game-based learning.[109]

The logic of games is also leaving its mark on *businesses*. As John Beck and Mitchell Wade argue in *The Kids Are Alright: How the Gamer Generation Is Changing the Workplace,* the new generation of workers learned big lessons from their years spent playing video games, and their bosses need to catch up.[110] Beck and Wade find that games teach workers to focus on the individual, assume that everyone can eventually succeed, expect there to always be an answer, experiment through trial and error, and learn from the team, not bosses. The learning that takes place through games translates into good management skills, according to John Seely Brown and Douglas Thomas.[111] Many corporations agree. McDonalds, Hilton Hotels, and others have launched employee training games on platforms such as Nintendo DS and Sony Playstation Portable.[112] MBA programs such as MIT's ask students to shoot baskets and hop around the room, as they square off in team challenges.[113]

Some business leaders suggest that companies should facilitate and harness this "gamer disposition," by structuring themselves more like games.[114] They argue that, faced with increasing uncertainty and change, companies need employees that seek out challenges and welcome unexpected events as opportunities to innovate.[115] A game approach could help employees develop these traits and transform the workplace, so that it "supports constant experimentation and allows problem solvers to define and redefine the issues."[116]

How exactly might game mechanics help companies change the way they work? John Hagel and Brown offer several ideas, many of which are already surfacing in the business world: [117]

• Make initial levels of the corporate structure easy, so that workers can easily gain a sense of accomplishment and learn to innovate as they move up in level.
• Keep the next level always in sight, with a clear yet challenging path to get there.
• Encourage employees to take on systemic challenges by forming groups, helping them enhance social relations and learn to collaborate.
• Provide people with clear and rich metrics for assessing their performance outcomes, to give them intrinsic motivations to improve and innovate—for example, by integrating point measurements and status indicators into personal "dashboards" for employees.
• Link workers with a rich set of metagame online forums, where they can reach out for guidance about how to find and use resources and where bosses can identify star players.

While businesses are using game design principles to boost innovation and performance, *architects* are increasingly wielding them to improve usability.[118] Just as game developers design virtual structures for players to experience, architects design real-world structures for people to experience. Beyond using games in community workshops and charettes, as discussed in the last chapter, some architects are trying to rethink the entire design process based on the lessons of games.[119]

They start with the assumption that games generally model how people engage with space.[120] Once this logic is understood, they argue, architects can use game mechanics to design better spatial flows that:

• Provide clear goals for use that channel flows of people.
• Include feedback loops that allow buildings to adapt to their users' experiences.
• Insert emergent narrative themes that lend spaces more meaning.
• Build incentive structures into spaces to encourage certain behavior.
• Bring play into the design process to open up new prospects for participation.
• Use game design software and tools to visualize how people might interact with architectural projects.

If game design is already offering valuable lessons for education, business, and architecture, what about politics? How might the insights of game design improve the design of democratic political processes? In the following four chapters, we find out.

4 Not Just Child's Play: Games in Democratic Processes

1989 was a banner year for democratic insurgency. In China, university students occupied Tiananmen Square, demanding democratic reforms. The Solidarity movement toppled Poland's Communist regime, sparking a chain of democratic revolutions in Hungary, Romania, the Czech Republic, and other Eastern Bloc countries. The Berlin Wall was the star of the show, bowing down as the iron curtain fell around it. These revolutions were monumental. But the biggest *innovations* in democracy were happening elsewhere.

In Latin America's Southern Cone, a radically different form of democracy was growing. In the 1980s, dictatorships collapsed or eroded in Argentina, Brazil, Uruguay, Chile, and Paraguay. As in Eastern Europe, these transitions led to liberal representative democracy at the national level. They also, however, inspired ambitious local experiments in participatory democracy. An upsurge of new mayors set out not to copy the standard Western model of democracy, but rather to forge new ways for people to democratically govern themselves. Three cities stood out in this movement to reinvent democracy: Porto Alegre (Brazil), Montevideo (Uruguay), and Rosario (Argentina).

In 1989, progressive new administrations took power in each city, and they quickly opened up government to new forms of democratic participation. Porto Alegre launched participatory budgeting. Montevideo set sail on a wave of decentralization. These stories have been told elsewhere, as I explain below, but Rosario's experiences are less known. The city not only adopted participatory budgeting and decentralization but also other strategies for participation: youth participation, participatory redevelopment, and playful democracy (*democracia lúdica*[1]).

In the next two chapters, I discuss these strategies through the lens of three of Rosario's most innovative programs: The City of the Children,

Theater of the Oppressed workshops, and Rosario Hábitat. The first two programs, which I examine in this chapter, form the core of the city's *youth participation* agenda. In the next chapter, I tell the story of Rosario Hábitat, the city's platform for *participatory redevelopment* in its *villas miserias* (shantytowns). Each program engages people through *playful democracy*, but in different ways. The two youth-oriented programs insert discrete games and game-like activities into workshops and meetings. Rosario Hábitat does as well, but it also uses *game mechanics* to design the entire participatory process *like a game*.

The youth programs discussed in this chapter offer three main lessons. First, they prove that games are not just for kids, and that they can be equally engaging for adults. Second, they illustrate how games and game-like activities, when included in democratic processes, can make participation more active and meaningful. Finally, some of the experiences suggest that too much or too little gameplay can trivialize or manipulate participation, or suck out the fun, especially when play is separated from measurable outcomes.

In the next section, I describe how Rosario emerged as a hub of participatory and playful democracy. I then introduce the City of the Children program, explaining how its Children's Councils use games and play to develop public policy proposals. To show that games are not just for kids, I review how the Department of Children gets adults to play, through Theater of the Oppressed workshops. I conclude with two cautionary tales, of games and game-like activities that trivialize and manipulate participation, sometimes making it less fun and diminishing participation. Taken together, these experiences show how games can be a powerful tool for democracy—if wielded with care.

Participatory Democracy in Rosario

In recent decades, local governments in Latin America have become famous for their experiments in participatory democracy.[2] In Porto Alegre, the *Partido dos Trabalhadores* (Workers' Party), which later took the presidency under Luiz Inácio "Lula" da Silva, began by letting residents decide how to spend city budget funds. Since 1989, its experiment in "participatory budgeting" has spread to over 1,500 cities around the world, earning Porto Alegre a reputation as the world capital of participatory democracy.[3] Meanwhile, starting in 2001, thousands of democratic dreamers from across the globe began to converge in the city for the World Social Forum, an annual gathering of grassroots movements opposed to neoliberalism.

A few hours to the south, Montevideo's *Frente Amplio* (Broad Front), led by future President Tabaré Vázquez, decentralized the city government.[4] It divided the city into eighteen zones, in each zone creating a community center to administer basic city functions and engage residents in democratic assemblies.

These and other experiments were possible because of their countries' strong social movements, dynamic political party systems, and federal governance structures. After dictatorships fell across Latin America in the 1980s and 1990s, repressed social movements began organizing more openly. At the same time, democratically elected presidents such as Carlos Menem in Argentina, Henrique Cardoso in Brazil, and Luis Alberto Lacalle in Uruguay imposed controversial neoliberal economic policies. As they privatized state agencies, opened up markets to free trade, and scaled back social programs, grassroots movements fought back *and* started organizing their own political parties and coalitions, such as Brazil's Workers' Party and Uruguay's Broad Front.

South American countries have historically had unstable political systems, creating space for new parties to gain power.[5] One or two political parties have often dominated, but the array of parties has tended to change every few decades—partly because of frequent dictatorships. This instability allowed the Workers' Party, Broad Front, and other new parties and coalitions to rise from obscurity to the presidency in a few short decades.

Before contending in national elections, these parties won office and built power bases at the local level. After winning mayoral races, the new parties were eager to launch ambitious new policies, to distinguish themselves from their predecessors. Because of their countries' federal political systems, they had the power to do so.[6] The provinces and municipalities have substantial autonomy over local policies and spending, so new administrations have been able to experiment with new channels for participation, without needing approval from central government authorities. Porto Alegre's participatory budgeting and Montevideo's decentralization would likely have been impossible without this local autonomy.

Rosario followed the lead of its sister cities, but also launched its own democratic innovations. With over a million residents, Rosario is Argentina's third largest city.[7] It lies four hours northwest of Buenos Aires along the banks of the Paraná River, the second longest river in South America (see figure 4.1). Founded in the late 17th century, the city's large port and rail terminal helped it grow into an industrial hub.[8] Sprawling agricultural fields also envelop the city, making the surrounding province of Santa Fe one of the breadbaskets of Argentina and one of the world's top sources of soy.

Figure 4.1
Map of Argentina. Courtesy of Google and Inav/Geosistemas SRL, 2013.

Rosario has long been one of the most progressive cities in Argentina. As an export shipping hub, it attracted masses of European working class immigrants toward the end of the 19th century, leading to strong labor and anarchist movements. Another wave of immigrants arrived from Europe during and after World War II. As a result the vast majority of *Rosarinos* are of European descent—mainly from Italy and Spain.

The roots of participatory democracy in Rosario can be traced back to at least 1983, when parliamentary democracy was restored in Argentina after seven years of a brutal military dictatorship. During the military *junta's* "Dirty War," the state and paramilitary groups "disappeared" 30,000 citizens - secretly abducting and usually killing them. Thousands more were tortured in clandestine detention centers. In the early years of democratic rule, Guillermo Estevez Boero, the leader of the *Partido Socialista* (Socialist Party) of the province of Santa Fe gave a series of lectures on participatory democracy.[9] He called for civic engagement in local community organizations and trust in the creative capacity of ordinary citizens. Boero anticipated that exercises in local democracy would nurture the capacities necessary to manage an inclusive, transparent, and participatory city government.

In 1989, a progressive coalition led by the Socialist Party won Rosario's municipal elections, on a platform calling for greater democratic participation. The coalition has remained in power since, winning repeated re-election. Building on its success in Rosario, it later won control of the province of Santa Fe as well.

The new administration quickly got to work. It decentralized key municipal functions into six districts, and drastically upgraded and expanded the municipal health system. Later it launched a solidarity economy program, promoting urban agriculture and worker-owned cooperatives. During the terms of Mayor Hermes Binner (1995–2003), the city introduced participatory budgeting, and the City of the Children and Rosario Hábitat programs.[10]

The national economic crisis of 2001 struck the city hard, leaving over half the population below the poverty line.[11] Since then, however, the city's social policies, the province's agricultural boom, and the nation's economic growth have helped Rosario recover economically, dropping the poverty rate below 15percent.

In 2003, the UNDP (United Nations Development Programme) recognized the achievements of Rosario's participatory model, awarding the city first prize in Latin America for good governance and local development.[12] To celebrate and show off its programs, the municipality hosted a giant international fair. After days of policy discussions, the mood shifted for the final grand plenary. On the stage, the international dignitaries handed the microphone to a shuffling Italian pedagogue, his face nearly obscured by a puff of scraggly white hair. As the crowd fell silent, Francesco Tonucci began to preach about play.

The City of the Children

Tonucci is the founder of the international City of the Children project.[13] In 1991, he launched the project in his hometown of Fano, Italy, as a "laboratory" of urban transformation. His theory was radically simple: Cities are broken, and they can only be fixed by and with children.

For Tonucci, children are "environmental indicators" for our ability to live together.[14] "If a city," he writes, "is safe, navigable, and livable for children, who are its weakest residents, it will be so for all citizens."[15] To identify and fix urban problems, adults should bring children together to discuss the challenges they face, and to propose solutions. Since children typically repeat what they hear from adults, they needed to first be liberated from prejudices and inspired to invent their own ideas. Then, adults needed to help translate these ideas into reality. These were the tasks of Tonucci's urban laboratories.

In 1996, Mayor Binner invited Tonucci to Rosario. Inspired by the visit, Binner created the *Comisión Intergubernamental Proyecto "La Ciudad de las Niñas y los Niños"* (Intergovernmental Commission of the City of the Children Project), to establish Rosario as the first City of the Children in Argentina.[16] In the Commission's first letter to city bureaucrats, its Chair began with two questions: "Can we conceive a city for all, from the perspective of children? Can we do it together, one afternoon, in a magical place, with a cup of coffee or hot chocolate, and a piece of cake from grandma?"[17]

This was no ordinary Commission Chair. María de los Ángeles "Chiqui" González quickly emerged as the creative force behind Rosario's City of the Children. González brought to the project fierce dedication and an ambitious vision, sprinkled with a dose of magical realism. More than anyone else, she also brought games to Rosario.

As an initial step, the commission formed a *Consejo de Niños*—itself a play on words. While *consejo* is pronounced the same as *concejo*—the Spanish word for council, with an "s" the word means advice. Thus the *Consejo* functioned as both a children's council and as children's advice for the city. After the first kids signed up, they began to debate the role of games and play in the city. Then they had an idea. What if the city could encourage people to play more?

In 1998, the Children's Council presented a plan to City Council: institute a *Día Anual del Juego y la Convivencia* (Annual Day of Play and Coexistence).[18] On this day the city would ask its residents, young and old, to set aside work for a bit, and instead play games. The city councilors unanimously approved the proposal, making Rosario the first city in the world to officially devote a day to play and games, the first Wednesday of each October. In the holiday's first year, at least 120 institutions and 30,000 people stopped to play.[19] To encourage more regular play, the city also began organizing mobile *ferias de juegos* (game fairs), full of games and playful activities. Their aim was to "occupy public space for the right to play."[20]

For González, though, one day for play was woefully inadequate. To truly nourish a playful democracy, the City of the Children needed a permanent physical presence in the city.[21] It also needed a more focused pedagogical strategy. Over the next five years, González pursued both goals by launching three high-profile spaces for play and learning: *La Granja de la Infancia* (The Children's Farm), *El Jardín de los Niños* (The Children's Garden), and *La Isla de los Inventos* (The Island of the Inventions). *La Granja* and *El Jardín* are large theme parks, while *La Isla* is an indoor museum.

In these spaces for urban education, children and adults build new instruments in sound laboratories, assemble their own newspapers, and write new urban dictionaries. A workshop dedicated to the "design and construction of ideas and utopias" asks visitors to craft "possible and impossible objects," such as flying hearts and robotic dinosaurs. In an exhibit called *Clandestine Words*, visitors lift up stones to uncover a path of hidden phrases. Some phrases, such as "he looked like him" and "it must have been for something" helped Argentina's last dictatorship to "disappear" citizens with impunity. Others, such as "silences that scream," caused their authors to be persecuted or tortured. Across from the path of stones, professional "animators" guide parents and children through a participatory budgeting game (see figure 4.2).

By 2004, the city had also established six Children's Councils, one in each district. Each council includes 20 to 40 children between 9 and 11 years old. Each school can select one representative from among those who are interested, as can nonprofit organizations and neighborhood groups. Representatives serve for two years, staggering terms so that half the children are new and half can serve as mentors. The councils generally meet once every week or two, from April to December.

Two adult coordinators accompany each Children's Council. Each year, they ask it to propose a public work or policy for the city. The coordinators submit these proposals to the Intergovernmental Commission, which is responsible for making them happen. Ultimately, the purpose of the Councils is "to change the city." This is no easy task. To begin, coordinators have to bring together packs of pre-teens, and somehow translate their ideas into concrete policy proposals. Or, in one case, into a monument.

Figure 4.2
Participatory Budgeting Game: Children and a parent rearranging public works and services in the *Participatory Budgeting Game* at the Island of the Inventions museum. Photo by author.

A Monument to Ideas

One of the Children's Councils' most visible impacts on the city is the *Monumento a las Ideas* (Monument to Ideas). The original idea for the monument surfaced in the Central District's 2004 council. The monument's four-year development process illustrates how the councils use play and games to influence politics.[22]

When the councils begin meeting for the year, coordinators use icebreaker games to create a comfortable and collaborative atmosphere. One example is the *Newspaper Game*, a variation of musical chairs. Each council representative gets a sheet of newspaper and starts by standing on the paper. When the coordinator claps, everyone walks randomly around the room. The next time she claps, the players must find sheets of newspaper to perch on. The coordinator then removes a sheet or two of paper and starts another round with a clap. Each round, more paper disappears, and it becomes harder to find a

Not Just Child's Play

sheet. The players end up sharing sheets, crowding together in precariously balanced formations. To stay alive, they have to stand together.

After introductions and icebreakers, the coordinators of the 2004 Central Council asked the children, "What would the city of our dreams look like?" The council discussed ideas one Saturday, and then played with them the next week. The councilors brought in arts and crafts supplies, and the coordinators laid a giant cardboard sheet on the floor, to form the imagined city's base. Mauro made wire trees for the parks.[23] Laura and Josefina attached a felt river to border the city. Agustina and Juliana set up a glistening carton school. Mauro suggested naming the city Maurolandia. No one seconded his suggestion. Then Eros looked at the growing sea of buildings and made an urgent announcement: "The city is missing a monument!" His idea attracted no more attention than Mauro's, but Eros cobbled together a yogurt container monument anyway.

During the rest of 2004, the council continued discussing what the city could be like, and playing. It was not until the following year that the idea of the monument resurfaced. At the first meeting of 2005, the coordinators asked the second-year councilors to remind the newcomers what they had done the year before. After recounting their experiences, one councilor lamented, "What we're doing now will just be a memory later." The coordinator responded, "*Just* a memory?" "What we're doing now," the kid restated, "will become a good memory in a big city."

Over the following weeks, the council discussed and played with the ideas of memory and difference. The councilors talked about memorials to the people "disappeared" during the dictatorship. They played games questioning the differences between boys and girls, and children and adults. And they drew pictures about these ideas. One picture showed a defiant hand with the slogan "No one can stop us when we think." Another was a locked gate, underneath it the text, "They closed the gate to differences. Let's open it to differences." Then, recalling their imagined city, one councilor suggested turning the pictures into a monument.

After pitching the idea to the Intergovernmental Commission, the Central Council planned the monument. The councilors decided to plant it in a park already dedicated to the memory of the disappeared, across the street from *Alto Rosario* (High Rosario), one of the city's ritziest shopping malls. The Monument to Ideas took the form of a giant locked metal gate, standing alone in the middle of a field and facing the mall. At the top of the gate a banner read, "No one can stop us when we think." Then, after the dedication, the city opened the gate.

Play and games made the monument possible, by encouraging collaboration and sparking creative ideas. The children, most of whom did not know each other beforehand, learned to work together largely by playing icebreaker and team-building games. Then, when confronted with serious ideas (the city of their dreams, memory, difference), they played. By building a model city, the councilors experimented with ideas for how to improve the city, in a concrete and visible way. Group play inspired the ideas for the monument and its slogan.

For staff coordinators, play is an essential practical tool and a deliberate political strategy. It is practical because, as one coordinator told me, "play is how children participate." Play is perhaps the most common form of interaction for children, and thus one of the most comfortable. Besides being practical, the coordinators see play as a conduit for articulating children's genuine ideas and perspectives, with minimal adult influence.

If anything, the councils play too little. Staff boast that Council meetings are grounded in games and play—which is what originally drew me to the program. While the Councils include play in most meetings, coordinators also lead the children in plodding discussions about respect, families, communication, or other general topics. During these less active moments, many councilors stop paying attention, instead fidgeting in their seats or playing covert games with their friends.

The main shortcoming of the Children's Councils, however, is not too little play, but rather too few games. Few of the Councils' activities would qualify as games. While the exercises usually include rules, they rarely engage players in competition or lead to measurable outcomes. Many of the coordinators scorn competition, relying instead on loosely collaborative activities. "We don't work with the logic of competition," Martín announced during a staff meeting, "We work with the logic of the collective." The coordinators often craft artsy and earnest play activities that do not lead to any particular outcomes. Making masks about emotions or inventing movements based on different colors may be playful, but these exercises make little progress toward policy proposals.[24]

The City of the Children staff, like most people I met in Rosario, do not distinguish between play and games. This confusion is largely linguistic—Spanish only has one word (*juego*) for the two concepts. Without a distinct definition of games or an understanding of game design, the Children's Council coordinators tend to design *juegos* that lack basic game features and game mechanics described in chapter 3.

When they avoid the structure of games, staff may be making the Council meetings less fun and less productive. Some children invariably roll their eyes or cringe when the coordinators reject competitive behavior. Or they play their own games. During a break at one council meeting, the boys ran into the yard for a game of soccer. The coordinators struggled to drag them back. Other departmental staff suggested that more structured and competitive games could help the Councils accomplish more. "It's a mess," a staffer told me, "that there's no competition . . . competition makes you want to do better next time."

Yet even with limited games and game mechanics, the City of the Children program has accomplished a lot. It built three high-profile educational spaces, launched an annual day of play and mobile game fairs, and established Children's Councils in each city district. Besides a new monument, the councils have led to a monthly event agenda for kids, a radio show, and public service ads for TV. Councilors designed trash monsters and exhibited them in public, to draw attention to rampant littering. They got the city to install new benches and green spaces, so that parents could more easily watch over kids playing in public. Most important, for González, they changed how the city is run. "The Children's Councils have proposed and implemented many campaigns . . . but none left more of a political and poetic mark on municipal administration in Rosario than the opening to play that they unleashed."[25]

Some leaders of the City of the Children, however, are skeptical about how wide this opening has grown. Ana, a member of the Intergovernmental Council, confessed to me that most city staff are still allergic to play. "It takes two or three days of work to make adults play . . . it's difficult, especially to get them to play spontaneously. Only a psychologist could dismantle all these inhibitions. . . ." Elsewhere in the Department of Children, however, a team of jokers has been proving Ana wrong.

Enacting the Law

While the City of the Children tries to inspire political participation, other city employees focus on protecting children's basic rights. At the end of 2007, this task became harder. A new national law forced organizations and institutions to develop new policies for interacting with children. To help craft and implement these policies, the city turned to the Theater of the Oppressed. In the process, it showed how games can engage adults in democracy.

At the end of 2007, the Argentine federal government passed National Law N° 26.061 *Protección Integral de las niñas, niños y adolescentes* (Full Protection of Children and Adolescents) to comply with the International

Convention on the Rights of the Child. Whereas the previous law understood children as objects to protect, the new law treated them as subjects with rights. Like most national laws, however, people were not sure how to implement it. Rosario's Department of Children saw a challenge. How could it bring the broad-reaching law to life so that it would actually change youth policies?

A manager at the Department of Children happened to be friends with one of the founders of the *Grupo de Teatro del Oprimido (GTO) Rosario*—the Rosario Theater of the Oppressed Group. As explained in chapter 2, the Brazilian activist Augusto Boal launched Theater of the Oppressed in the 1970s.[26] Gradually he developed it into a set of theater games and techniques, designed to empower oppressed people to understand and change the conditions of their lives.[27] Facilitators, known as "jokers," encourage spectators to become "spect-actors," by acting out solutions to conflicts that they face. The Rosario GTO formed in 2006. At first, its six members organized workshops mainly with community groups, mental health centers, and a hospital.

In 2008, Andrea and Paola—staff at the Department of Children—invited the GTO to help them more actively engage youth workers in carrying out the new law. They developed a plan to hold workshops in each district of the city for institutions that worked closely with youth: health centers, youth centers, community centers, schools, child care providers, *ludotecas* (play spaces), and other agencies and nonprofit organizations. To multiply the workshops' impact, the department asked each institution to send only a couple representatives, and then have those representatives relay the experience to their coworkers.

I participated in my first workshop on a Tuesday morning at the city's West District Center. I met Andrea and Paola at the center's auditorium, a dimly lit sloping hall the size of a small movie theater. By 10:00, around 25 people had nestled into the plush seats in the first few rows. Andrea welcomed the participants and directed their attention to a table in front of the stage. Two lawyers, Noelia and Jorgelina, sat at the table, ready to explain the new law. "The lawyers are going to tell us about the text of the law," explained Andrea, "and then, in the second part of the workshop, we're going to work on the concrete practice of the law, as it applies to each of us."

Noelia began by highlighting the differences between the old and new children's laws. The old law, *La Ley del Patronato* (The Patronage Law), understood children as passive objects, subject to the courts. They had basic rights—to school, medical care, a stable family, and so forth—and if

Not Just Child's Play

these rights were violated, juvenile courts were responsible for intervening. Judges in these courts responded to rights violations mainly by putting the children in institutions. Among other things, the old law criminalized poverty. When children's families were unable to care for them, the courts decided their fate.

The new law understood children as active subjects, supported by the government. All institutions and organizations that interacted with youth now had the power and responsibility to work *with* children (and their families) to protect their rights. School officials, child care providers, health workers, and other frontline staff were now obliged to intervene when they saw a child's rights violated. Fundamentally, local governments became responsible for addressing children's issues that were previously relegated to the courts. "The judge," Noelia concluded, "is not going to resolve problems anymore with his magic wand."

Over the next half hour, Noelia delved into the details. She explained the new roles of family courts, the ways that multiple levels of government were to collaboratively implement the law, and the differences between the national and provincial laws. In response, the workshop participants stared blankly, rolled their necks, and scratched their noses. Heads nodded, cell phones beeped, and bodies shifted in seats.

After 40 minutes of law talk, Noelia paused. "I'm not sure if anyone wants to ask something about the theory of the law. . . ." Silence. A couple people laughed awkwardly. "So you understood everything, right?" More laughs. "Coffee," someone called out, "please?" Eventually, a few questions surfaced. Eyes soon wandered, though, to the table with coffee and cakes. Tucu, one of the GTO members, announced a coffee break. In the second part of the workshop, he explained, they would deal with everyday problems of the law—through theater. Noelia scanned the audience's faces and hastily added, "Don't be afraid."

After the break, Tucu, Julia, and Javi—the GTO jokers—led us all up onto the stage. Overhead spotlights cast circles of light on the wood floor. Tucu spread people into an oval and introduced the GTO and its part of the workshop, which would run till 1:00. "The idea is to deal with the theory of the law through practice, by putting the body in play. Through games, we'll devise strategies for acting." These games would inspire new questions and answers by letting people practice new ways of acting. "We're all actors in our lives," Julia added. "We're always presenting a certain character. When we go to a party, we put on a certain attitude; for work, we put on costumes. . . ."

To warm up (literally), Tucu rubbed his hands together, and asked everyone to do the same. Then he led the group in shaking their shoulders, shaking their hips, and stomping their feet. To expel stressful thoughts, he asked everyone to brush off their pants, then the backs of their neighbors. As people began to laugh and play, even the lawyers joined in.

The next exercise activated people's voices and faces. First, Tucu led everyone in reciting their vowels with exaggerated sighs: "Ahhh Ohhh Ehhh Eeee Uuuu." After a few rounds, he began changing the order and intonation of the vowels. Some became laughs, others questions, others shouts. Then each sound was paired with an action, such as throwing back a shoulder, kicking up feet, or whirling an elbow. As I later discovered, the activity was inspired by the Augusto Boal game *How many "A's" in a single "A"?*[28]

Julia now launched entire bodies into movement, with a game of *Stop* (pronounced "estop" in Spanish). "Can we walk a bit?" People started to walk around at random. "A little lower." People crouched down while walking. "Up!" Everyone stood up and walked straight again. Suddenly Julia clapped and yelled "Stop!" People froze. She proceeded through several more variations—walk like you're a 16-year-old strutting your stuff, like you're in a hospital waiting room, like it's the best day of your life. Each time, she interjected "Stop!" and asked everyone to look around at people's poses.

Javier introduced the next game: *Complete the Image*. In the middle of the room he positioned two volunteers, Clara and Julian, facing each other and shaking hands. Javier asked people what they saw. "Friends meeting." "Sealing a deal." Javier removed Julian and asked what people saw now. "Filling up gas." Javier explained, "We have an image, but we can change the image." He inserted Tucu into the original scene, squatting with his back to Clara. Now Tucu was getting a massage. Small changes in the image lead to vastly different understandings.

Javier asked people to form groups of three, to play the game themselves. Each group modeled an image with two members. After a couple seconds the third group member replaced one actor, to change the image's meaning. Then repeat. For 10 minutes, the groups invented a flood of creative images. Some made letters with their bodies, while others ate, played, or argued. Everyone focused intently, mutating their images rapid-fire.

After an hour of movement, Tucu called the group together, to start dealing more directly with the topic of the day. In the next game—*Image of the Word*—the goal was to translate words into images, like in the party game Charades. Tucu divided people into two groups, explaining that one would make an image and the other would describe what it saw. The first word was "childhood." Group A's members posed. Some adopted whimsical looks. Others squatted down low, and a couple joined together in a play position. What did group B see? "Innocence." "Play." "Powerless."

The groups rotated back and forth, presenting their bodily understandings of "street," "school," and "family." The topics then became more specific. Group A formed an image of the old children's law. Some pointed, others covered their eyes, and others squatted down in fear. Group B made an image of the new law (see figure 4.3). Some reached out to comfort each other, others looked around hesitantly, and others held their hands to their ears as if straining to hear. Finally, to open up the game, Tucu invited each side to challenge the other team to represent a particular word. Group A proposed "The Department Chair" (aka their boss). The images were not entirely favorable.

Julia announced that they would move on to the final game—*Forum Theater*. She began with an overview of Theater of the Oppressed, "a technique to understand and transform our reality." As Javier added, participants would now "season the gathering with their own work stories." Julia divided people into two groups and asked each to pick a real story of oppression related to the law. "Think of a scene in which you, in a situation of some power, wanted to apply the law but could not." Then each group would present the scene.

Figure 4.3
Image of the Law: An image of Argentina's new children's law, during the Theater of the Oppressed game *Image of the Word*. Photo by author.

I sat with one group. After exchanging a few stories, my group picked an incident when Maria, a social worker, tried to help a girl who was allegedly being abused by her father. The parents refused to talk, and Maria was frustrated. How could she break through?

Tucu encouraged people to focus on their roles as workers. "What is the problem that we can't resolve?" He suggested thinking of a specific image to represent the situation. The group chose two scenes: one of the social worker and a teacher attending to the girl, and another of the youth center workers meeting to decide what to do.

Then I got dragged in. Several people pulled me into the scene, asking me to play a worker in the meeting. Tucu edged me on—"Now you'll do action research." Soon I was sitting alongside three city employees trying to act out how youth workers would react. I played the apathy card—a guy who just wanted to escape the meeting and go home. After months researching municipal bureaucrats, I had plenty of source material. I took my phone out and held it as if texting, and cast a "when will it end?" look over my face.

As we honed our images, Tucu suggested we look at our fellow actors and adjust our poses. He urged us to act out a repetitive motion, to bring our characters to life. I checked my watch persistently. My neighbor shrugged her shoulders. Another guy clasped his hands, pleading. Then Tucu asked us to add a few words. "Enough already," I repeated. "I'm tired of this," my neighbor moaned. "We have to do something," the pleader pleaded.

It was time to "improvise with a game," Tucu announced. Our group presented first. My cluster acted out our office meeting; then the rest of the group presented its scene. The social worker and teacher walked alongside the girl, her mother following them, mouth sealed shut.

Tucu asked the other group what they saw, and if they identified with anyone. "Those two are trying to help the girl." "Office workers looking for a solution." "But some of them don't want to be there." They saw that some workers wanted to intervene while others did not, and they sympathized with both sides.

We presented again, and this time Julia invited the spectators from the other group to become "spect-actors"—to enter the scenes and try to solve the problem. For the next 15 minutes, several of them intervened. Mario stepped forward and assumed the role of the teacher. He tried arguing with us workers more forcefully, saying it was our duty to file a complaint. We brushed him off, and nothing changed.

Claudia joined the scene as the girl's lawyer, and she persuaded the mother and teacher to talk with the workers. Julia clapped and asked what changed. People said that Claudia added some order, and that now the teacher and social worker had help from an expert in the law. Next, Lucia intervened as the social worker, going to a health center to consult with a doctor. Afterward, people suggested instead visiting the girl's house and talking with both parents directly. Mariela gave it a try. Julia asked if the situation had improved, overall. People nodded, and Lucia admitted that the interventions were easier than she had feared.

The other group then presented its image, about the (now illegal) suppression of sexual education at a Catholic School. Laura stood in the middle, looking down shyly, one hand reaching down next to her crotch and the other up above her chest (an initial version had the hands in slightly different positions, inspiring mock catcalls). Victoria, playing a teacher, was trying to pry Laura's curious hands from her body. Sebastian, a school authority, stood on the side with one hand pointing up to the stage light (aka God) and the other pointing down disapprovingly at Laura. John Travolta would have been proud of the pose. Other actors stood in the background.

Victoria, intent on subverting the law, wanted to train the teachers to lead fake sexual education classes. "The child," she announced, "doesn't need to ask questions about its little body. This law leaves a lot of things open, so we're going to take advantage of what's not clear and insert our own ideas." Ana entered the scene, as an insurgent teacher trying to open space for discussion about more meaningful sexual education. But Victoria fended her off.

The observers said that the scene felt very real—they often had to negotiate similar tensions. Julia asked if anyone wanted to intervene. Duilio tried engaging Victoria and Sebastian, saying that kids came to him with questions about their bodies regardless, and that it would be best for their health to discuss these questions with an expert. Victoria asked Duilio if he was Catholic, and he nodded. "Great, so we can leave it in the hands of God, no?"

Maxi suggested that the school director intervene, but admitted this was hardly realistic. Tucu agreed, but drew out a lesson. In every institution someone higher up can be an ally, and one strategy for dealing with oppression is to find this person.

To wrap up, Tucu asked the group to come together to "decontextualize the issues from the scenes, and contextualize them in our own jobs." The lawyers reflected briefly about how the law related to the scenes, suggesting other possible actions. Finally, Javier asked each person to share an impression from the workshop. "Words confuse, but it's clearer with the body." "The scenes let you see how you actually act." "It's easier to say than to do." "It's hard to come up with ideas when you're rushed." Almost everyone spoke. Julia said she hoped that when they returned to work, similar interventions would come more naturally. Tucu thanked the group and received a rowdy applause. The participants carried their smiles off into the city.

In the Theater of the Oppressed session, play did a lot of work. Like in the Children's Councils, it *encouraged collaboration and creativity*. The theater exercises and games linked people together, making them feel like part of a group. They also inspired participants to invent creative new ways to address common problems. These are standard features of play. "What play signals do," writes leading play researcher Stuart Brown, "is invite a safe, emotional connection."[29] Years of scientific research have found that play increases our "capacity to innovate, adapt, and master changing circumstances."[30]

To get people to play theater games, the GTO had to first *ease into active participation and sweep aside inhibitions*. The jokers started with the most simple and unintimidating of acts—rubbing hands together. Once people were comfortable with that, they gradually transitioned to more demanding exercises. Each step of the way, the jokers built trust by modeled an outlandish new action, before asking others to follow. "First I do something ridiculous myself," Tucu told me, "and then they'll feel good and won't be embarrassed to do it themselves."

The initial exercises primed people to play by getting them to move like children. The jokers asked people to shake their whole bodies, recite exaggerated vowels, and practice silly walks. "One of the best ways to get . . . adults to play," writes the game designer Jesse Schell, "is to make them feel like a child again."[31] In fact any kind of movement can have such an effect. "There are ways to jump-start play," Brown argues. "Physical activity— *movement* of any sort—has a way of getting past our mental defenses."[32]

Once people were activated, they became bolder and challenged power relations. They made mocking images of their boss in Image of the Word, then talked back to school authorities and pressured coworkers in Forum Theater. The theater games led people to reveal what James Scott called "hidden transcripts"—popular critiques of those in power, which are usually uttered only in private.[33]

Researchers have called this newfound openness an "activation phenomenon."[34] In an experiment at Johns Hopkins, for example, nurses who were given a chance to say their names and mention concerns at the beginning of a case were more likely to note problems and offer solutions. "Giving people a chance to say something at the start," wrote Atul Gawande, "seemed to activate their sense of participation and responsibility and their willingness to speak up."[35]

As they acted more honestly, participants learned to better *understand different perspectives and emotions*. "Seeing your colleague acting out a situation that impacts him," Sara told me, "makes you see things differently . . . that really moved me." The games helped Verónica "think about the perspectives of others and what's going on in their heads." As a result, for Argentine popular educator Mariano Algava, games compel people to question common sense.[36]

By moving beyond words, the GTO offered new ways to express and understand emotions. "We try to find other ways of communicating," Tucu explained, "not just with the word, but also with the body." This was the best part of the workshop for Rodrigo, who said the different languages let him "think in different ways." These new ways of thinking were distinctly emotional, forcing people to communicate their inner feelings through exaggerated expressions. Opening up to emotions helped make the law real, according to department staff. "The application of the law is not just rational," Andrea said, "but also emotional, and in the theater exercises you don't have the filter of the rational, just like in everyday life." When confronted with child abuse and stigmas against sexual education, workers' first (and often most important) reaction is usually emotional.

Finally, the theater games *translated the law into practice*. They forced people to consider how the law related to their work, and what they would have to do to fulfill it. "The issue is not the law," Andrea stressed, "but rather institutional practices." The law can only protect children's rights if real people and institutions apply it. In Argentina and elsewhere, passing a law is often the easy part. The real challenge is making it stick in practice, so that it actually changes behaviors.

For the Children's Law to become real, workers had to learn to apply it in real situations, where they faced high pressure and had little time to think. In other words, they had to learn to improvise. "In the workplace you can't just think about the law," argued Tucu. "You have to act"—which is exactly what the workshop participants learned to do. "We acted out real situations," said Verónica, "to figure out how we will tackle them later." But would this really change institutional practices?

Yes and no. The workshop did not directly change practices, but most participants that I spoke with thought it would have this result in the end. "People are going to make decisions based on what happened here," Rodrigo asserted. No one expected changes to take place overnight. They would emerge, for Florencia, "in the short term at the personal level, in the medium term in relations with the public and community organizations, and in the long term in public policies."

In addition to these external outcomes, the workshop was intrinsically fun. All the participants I interviewed said they enjoyed themselves, and nearly all of them said they would like to attend another Theater of the Oppressed workshop in the future.

Only a few people remained lukewarm about games. "This was enough," Julio admitted. "It's not for me so much . . . I don't know . . . if some other opportunity comes up we'll see." Some people are less comfortable playing, and they may participate less in games. "It was really difficult for me at first," said Sara. "You're not used to doing this, to exposing yourself in this way. There's a fear of turning into a clown." But she added, "this is negative at first but positive later, because it helps you express yourself, extend yourself, and talk. Play doesn't have to be off-limits for adults."

It often seems that way, though. It is surprisingly difficult inviting adults to play. Staff did not mention games or play in the invite, afraid that this would scare people. When one community worker heard that the workshop would involve theater, he declined the invitation. "With everything that I have to do in the neighborhood, I can't afford to play." For Rodrigo, though, more people might have attended had they better understood what would be involved. "Why didn't more people come? I think for lack of knowledge, thinking that you're going to have to sit and listen. They told us it would be a training, and that makes you think of something different, more formal."

Games can drive engagement for adults too. People participated more in the Theater of the Oppressed sessions and reported enjoying the workshops more because of the games. While few people spoke during the formal introductory talk with the lawyers, everyone spoke *and* moved—usually a lot—during the theater games. "In Theater of the Oppressed," as Andrea observed, "you can't 'not participate.'" Staff even had to organize extra workshops, after attendees of the early sessions clamored for more opportunities for their coworkers. Adults may be more reluctant to try play, but once they dive in, they want more. Years of scientific research agrees, as Brown has found. "We are designed to be lifelong players, built to benefit from play at any age."[37]

Like in the Children's Councils, the Department of Children's Theater of the Oppressed workshops used play and games to encourage collaboration and creativity. The theater games eased reluctant adults into active participation and swept aside inhibitions. Participants learned to understand different perspectives and emotions, and they translated laws into practice. While a few people found the workshops difficult, everyone enjoyed them and thought they were useful in the end. This was not the case, however, when the Department of Children tried to dream of plazas.

Separating Work from Play

Each year Rosario's Children's Councils churn out dozens of ambitious 11- and 12-year-olds. After serving for two years, these councilors hand over their spots to fresh volunteers. To harness the interest and experience of the ex-councilors, the City of the Children created a new position: *niñas y niños proyectistas* (child project designers). While the Children's Councils and Theater of the Oppressed workshops help shape public policy, the contributions of the *proyectistas* are less clear.

According to the City of the Children, the *proyectistas* are, a "consultative body where children work together with municipal experts to plan, design, and remodel urban spaces and services."[38] Unlike the Children's Councils, which chose what topics to work on, the *proyectistas* respond to city requests. When a department wants youth input on a particular project, they can call the *proyectistas*.

The *proyectistas'* biggest project so far has been *Sueños de Plaza* (Plaza Dreams).[39] Funded through the city's participatory budget in 2006, the project called for remodeling 14 public plazas in Rosario's southwest district. Ana, a city planner interested in youth participation, took note and proposed including youth input in the plaza design. She organized a series of workshops with children living near the plazas.

The first workshop that I observed, for the plaza *Las Rosas*, was on a Monday morning in a rather humble elementary school classroom. Every few minutes, packs of roaming children filled the halls with chatter. In between, a pounding drill sounded off, presumably from a construction site outside. The room was cold, but the electric wall heaters gradually warmed it up.

When I arrived, a team of five facilitators was getting ready—Ana, Alejandro, Sonia, and Barbara from the Planning Department and Mariela from the City of the Children. As they pushed the knee-high tables and chairs to the walls, they explained that the purpose of the workshop was to "capture the soul of the plaza." Apparently, it was "floating in the air."

Shortly after 10:00, a dozen kids arrived, ranging in age from 8 to 11. The facilitators divided them into two groups and sat on the floor, chatting while they waited for the others. A few minutes later, two *proyectistas* arrived, accompanied by three City of the Children staff. Two Rosario Hábitat staff followed shortly.

Ana asked the kids if they brought any objects (which they were supposed to), but they shook their heads confusedly and said no. "We're going to think of an object, since you didn't bring one, that you could have and share somewhere in a plaza." "A rock." "A pigeon." "Popcorn." Mariela prodded the kids on, "What else could you find in a plaza?" "Benches." "A tree." "Ants."

At 10:30, Sonia shouted some familiar words, "We're going to play a game of *Stop!*" Like in the Theater of the Oppressed workshops, she asked the kids to walk around, and then freeze when she said "Stop!" They started playing, with someone always moving after "Stop!" and earning a round of pointed laughs. Sonia, who was quiet before, blossomed into a new person. Words popped out of her mouth as she skipped around the room. A daffodil yellow shirt peeked out from under her black sweater, as if on cue.

To add another layer, Sonia asked the kids to think of an object while walking. After saying "Stop!" she asked a few kids to name their objects. "A ball." "Noodles." "A stick." Then she asked them what they were thinking of doing with the object. "Playing catch." "Eating " "Fighting." The next stage was more challenging. Now, at Stop, the players had to make an image of their action with their bodies, pairing with someone else. One kid froze in an image of throwing a ball, and his partner moved into position to catch it. A girl fetched one of the Rosario Hábitat observers and declared, "You are a fork." She then rotated the human fork to twirl imaginary noodles. A boy impaled his friend on an imaginary stick. Some figures outside started banging against the window grates to get attention, but with little success—the kids in the room were too focused.

Sonia divided the room into two groups, asking each to develop a scene in a plaza. One facilitator worked with each group, prodding on their scenes: "What would that look like?" "Then what would happen?" "How would you move then?" A few kids wandered in and out as the groups crafted their scenes, but most were engaged. A couple older boys leaned against the back wall. With all the tumbling around, everyone had by now acquired a nice layer of dust on their pants.

At 11:15, Sonia signaled that it was time to present. In one group, Barbara stood tall and waved her hands like tree branches. She dropped scraps of paper, which her kids pretended were leaves and tried to catch or scoop up. Some of them leaped to pick imaginary apples. The other group's scene had two girls sitting on benches eating ice-cream cones. Some of their teammates crouched down to become benches, and the girls balanced on top of them.

Barbara announced that the groups would present each scene once more. This time, each group would divide in two after the presentations. Half the group would paint what they saw in the other presentation, and the others would brainstorm words about what they saw, to make poetry.

Both groups presented again, and then divided up to paint and brainstorm words. The painters received a paper canvas, watercolors, and brushes. When someone wanted to paint, they were blindfolded, so that they painted "from the heart." Not surprisingly, the paintings were exceptionally abstract, especially as the strokes of multiple artists were layered onto the same canvas (see figure 4.4). One girl painted the wind, making broad waving strokes with green paint. "Nothing limits you," Barbara urged her on. "I don't want to paint," muttered another girl. So she did not. The second group wrote down words with Sonia. Some kids, however, escaped to play outside. Others busted out marbles and played on the floor.

A bit before noon, Ana announced that there was hot chocolate outside for everyone. Whoosh! The kids flew outside, ending the workshop.

Afterward, I asked Ana what would happen now. "We have to assemble poetry with the words," she said, "and build the new plaza." Right. She mentioned that perhaps the *proyectistas* could help with the poetry. Sonia studied the drawings and wondered at the multitude of circles. Was there a

Figure 4.4
Trivializing planning? A blindfolded student painting images to be used for planning a public plaza, during a workshop of the Plaza Dreams program. Photo by author.

hidden meaning? Confused, I asked how the pictures would influence the plaza. "That's our work now," Ana responded curtly, "with the *proyectistas.*" I nodded politely, still with no idea how the workshop would contribute to the plaza.

A few weeks later I met with Ana to uncover more of the story. I asked again how the workshop activities related to the design of the public plazas. "Only an artist can understand that. The drawings and poetry and movements are like primary materials for the construction of the plaza." Play, for Ana, was magical. "It lets kids work from the heart instinctively and not go through the mind to give an opinion. We believe that they already have information about a place unconsciously. We take that information out of the body and soul, using games." By playing, kids could uncover what they really wanted and needed, blocking out ideas absorbed from adults.

But I could not yet grasp how abstract paintings and spontaneous poetry would become a public plaza. When I kept pressing, I got a more direct answer. "We lay out all the material from the workshop and us staff interpret it. For example, here you have roundness like the movement of the body, and the poetry speaks of the sea and the color blue. So we make associations, and a draft is made, and this is presented to the *proyectistas* to comment on." Still unsure of what the *proyectistas* actually did after the workshops, I asked them.

"I have no idea," Gabi told me, her eyes shifting side to side. Hunched over, she was enveloped in a puffy black coat, her head framed in a checkered scarf. "Last time we drew some plans with other *proyectistas*, in the south or southwest for another project." The workshop, for Gabi, was mainly about getting together with other kids and playing. "They told us that we were going to a school, we were going to play, and it'd all be good."

Participation in the Plaza Dreams workshops did not feel very empowering. "They didn't do anything that we suggested," vented Eva, the other *proyectista*. Eva dressed the part of a nerd, with a crisp white turtleneck and gray school sweater, her chestnut hair back in a tight ponytail. She stood up straight, making me self-conscious about my posture. "I was involved last year but nothing was happening, so I left. We left. There wasn't much project design. . . ."

Plaza Dreams was not having much impact. More than three years after winning funding, only one of the 14 plazas had been constructed, and that one only partly. According to Ana, the rest were suffering from "budget problems." "The problem is with the adults. They don't designate funds for the City of the Children, don't put it on the agenda. There's still a lack

Not Just Child's Play

111

of education among the municipal staff. When it comes time to finalize something, they say that it's a mess and nothing can be done." The City of the Children made Rosario look good, but for Ana, the administration was not really supporting the program.

Others placed the blame elsewhere. "It's how the City of the Children positions itself," suggested another member of the Intergovernmental Commission. While the program was officially housed in the Department of Children, it was physically and ideologically isolated. Staff worked in a refurbished train station far from the department headquarters. Most of them were trained as artists or psychologists. Other departmental staff complained that the council coordinators insisted too firmly on implementing children's "authentic" ideas, without adult contamination. As a result the program often came into conflict with the planners, technicians, and other adults who had the power and expertise to turn ideas into reality.

These conflicts were part of a deeper problem with Plaza Dreams (and with the City of the Children program): the coordinators insisted on *separating children's play from adult work*. During the workshop games, facilitators did not share any information about the plaza, nor did they ask the children to tackle the real decisions that planners would have to make. Afterward, planners designed the spaces mainly on their own, without playing.

This separation between play and work distracted children's attention and trivialized meaningful planning decisions. The workshops focused attention entirely on play and games, concealing the children's ultimate lack of power over design decisions. To design public spaces, planners need to address tricky issues such as accessibility, environmental impacts, and safety. In the workshop these serious topics were reduced to abstract splashes of paint and ambiguous snippets of poetry.

When the children painted and picked words, were they even thinking about the particular plaza under consideration? "I don't know," Ana admitted. "There are things that are magically related. We trust that the kids that live nearby have information about the place that can be transmitted through the games. They have a memory of the place, an understanding of the place." Perhaps, but how could children access that memory and understanding if, as in the workshops I observed, the facilitators never mentioned which plaza they were talking about?

If play is divorced from real decisions, it marginalizes and disempowers players. In the end, planners decided what the children's images and words meant, and thus decided how to design the plazas. For Ana, this was necessary. Children cannot, she argued, "sit down and draw a plaza."

Actually they can. Hundreds of kids have been mapping out playground designs, for example, through the Trust for Public Land's NYC Playgrounds Program.[40] They are making real decisions about what goes where. And they are not alone. In Rosario, children and teens have decided how to spend $75,000 in real cash each year, through the city's youth participatory budget.[41]

Children can express what they want in a plaza, but not through abstract play and games alone. With enough time, information, and support, they can make real decisions. In recent years, however, the City of the Children has pursued play and games as ends in themselves, and less as ways to make policy decisions. The program activities rarely challenge children to accomplish anything through hard work. "The most important thing," an Intergovernmental Commission member concluded, "is to have play." Tonucci would disagree. The point of the City of the Children, for him, was "to change the city."[42]

The excessive focus on play has made it harder to change the city. It has marginalized the City of the Children from many officials. "There are departments like Public Services," an Intergovernmental Commission member told me, "that think this is pure stupidity, that it has no value. For them it's just a bother."

The Plaza Dreams program illustrates some dangers of play. By separating play and games from meaningful decisions, it trivialized and marginalized participation. Like some of the Children's Council meetings, the workshops revolved around too much abstract play and not enough focused games. But more structure and games are not necessarily better, as I discovered in another Theater of the Oppressed workshop.

The Dangers of Playing God

Theater of the Oppressed can be hit or miss. At some sessions people failed to present—let alone resolve—coherent scenes about their workplaces. This was not by chance. Rather, the workshops' success depended on how many rules the game facilitators imposed and how long they had people play. Game designers wield a power that is difficult to master, and easy to abuse.

One of the last workshops I observed was in a sprawling sunroom at a cultural center. When I arrived, Paola was setting up four rows of black plastic chairs facing one side of the room, and a table in front of them as a makeshift speakers' podium. Around 30 people drifted in, and the workshop proceeded as before. Two lawyers gave a presentation about the law and took some questions, before breaking for coffee.

Not Just Child's Play 113

After the break, Tucu, Javier, and Julia asked everyone to stand in a circle at the back of the room. Julia started with a warm-up, to "remind ourselves that we have a body." She began by swaying gently on her ankles, and asking others to follow. She inched up to swing her knees around in circles, then her hips and all the way up to her neck. People slowly let their bodies loose, and in a few minutes everyone was gyrating their hips like Shakira.

Tucu eased into vocal stretching, with some rounds of "Ahhh Ohhh Ehhh Eeee Uuuu," each vowel paired with a dance move. To add a layer of competition, he performed a series of vowel and movement combinations, and challenged people to repeat them. Amid spontaneous giggles, someone shouted, "I want more!" She got her wish. Tucu asked people to form pairs and have a conversation with their partner entirely in the vowel and movement language, this time using facial expressions too. We were soon in a monkey house.

Julia proceeded to a game of *Stop* (see figure 4.5). This time, you had to first make noises when you crossed someone's path. Then look at the person and say their name. Then say their name via gesture, without speaking. Then make a gesture of what you were thinking.

Javier and Tucu moved on to Complete the Image and Image of the Word, and by the time we arrived at Forum Theater, we had been playing for nearly an hour and a half. In 45 minutes, people would have to leave.

In Forum Theater my group settled on an abstract scenario in which a worker was oppressed by government bureaucracy. Tucu urged them to think of something more concrete, but Mariano complained that the GTO was imposing too many constraints. Only half joking, he proposed that the group play by its own rules. "There's oppression here [in the workshop], so we're going to try to break out of it."

Tucu had other ideas. He asked the group members to add a repetitive motion to their poses, then a repetitive sound. The actors hesitated, as they struggled to think of motions or sounds. After some picked a phrase as their sound, Tucu added that the repetitive sound should not be words.

By the time my group presented, it had sharpened its scene. A girl lay on the ground, writhing in pain, and a worker was holding her until the medics arrived. Another worker sat in the office with his feet up, refusing to help. "You'll have to figure this out yourself." Their boss stood on the desk, talking on the phone with her back turned. "There's no money in the budget—we have to start thinking about the campaign!"

At 1:00, the girl died, and a few heads glanced down at watches. The workshop was supposed to be over by now. Julia asked if they could stay an extra few minutes, and most people nodded their heads. But no one

Figure 4.5
Too much joy? An extended game of *Stop*, during a Theater of the Oppressed workshop. Photo by author.

stepped up to intervene in the Forum Theater scene, perhaps wary of the time. Julia tried her own idea, calling the office worker to get more help. No luck. Someone else jumped in and combed the street for a doctor. He succeeded, but then admitted that this was not very realistic.

In the second scene, 10 people sat in a row of chairs, their backs facing us. A woman was hurrying back and forth and gesturing frantically in front of them. Julia asked what we saw. "A waiting room." No one offered more specific ideas, so Julia asked the actors to say what they were thinking. Those in seats complained about how long they were waiting, and the woman on her feet complained that no one was responding to her. We still did not know what to make of the scene.

Tucu asked if anyone wanted to intervene. No one volunteered. Javier apologized that we would need to wrap up, since we were running late.

In this workshop people failed to resolve the scenes of oppression. One group failed to even present a coherent scene. Similar problems afflicted some other workshops as well, to a lesser extent. What went wrong?

First, the GTO jokers *played too many games*. They spent over half the workshop warming up, and after playing *Stop*, Complete the Image, and Image of the Word, there was little time to deal with the more concrete work problems. Good games can be addictive. In this case the joy of play seduced the facilitators into extending the warm-up games and paying a heavy cost later. Even if everyone is having fun, facilitators of democratic processes should keep their eyes on the prize, and nudge people along toward broader goals. They need to be realistic about the time required to learn new games—something the GTO's expert actors probably underestimated. Trained actors are used to improvising scenes, but novices need more practice.

The acting novices needed even more practice because the jokers *presented too few rules at the beginning of games*. In Forum Theater the groups struggled to come up with appropriate scenes. The jokers had a vision of what kinds of scenes would work, but they only revealed this vision in bits and pieces. "It reaches a point where you get lost," Verónica told me. "Where are we going with this? I sense that you [the joker] have an idea of where it should go, and I don't know what that is." When groups had trouble, the jokers clarified the rules of the game: pick a scenario where there is oppression, where you could be in the role of the oppressed, and where there are real possibilities for action. But often by the time the jokers clearly communicated these rules, the groups had to perform their (underdeveloped) scenes. As a result observers did not know how to intervene.

Some games stretched on too long because the jokers *introduced too many rules during the games*. "I felt corrected all the time," Verónica complained. "Guide, guide, guide, guide . . . stop, talk, stop, talk. That wore me out. There's a lot of rigidity." In each game the jokers proceeded through a series of steps or rules, perhaps more than necessary. "The rules were too directional," said Pablo. "I asked if we could move in the scene and he told me, 'No, just an image.' And then later, yes, you had to pick a movement. I didn't like how it was so laid out." Adding new rules in the middle of a game shifts the playing field, often disorienting or frustrating players.

Designing games is hard, and integrating them into workshops is even harder. In this second workshop the GTO jokers made the mistake of playing too long, sharing too few rules at the start of games, and adding too many rules changes once games were in progress. As a result the games were sometimes less fun and less productive. Game design is an art, and the GTO jokers sometimes struggled to piece together game mechanics into smooth and cohesive systems.

This is a common problem for game designers, who need to constantly balance between serving as a central game authority and allowing players to make their own decisions. In other words, they need to nurture what Archon Fung has called "accountable autonomy."[43] Designers should grant players autonomous decision-making power, while using their skills, knowledge, and resources to keep players accountable to the broader aims of the game.

Most of the time, the GTO jokers managed to guide people through enjoyable games that advanced the goals of the workshop series. They certainly did a better job than I could have. Using their theater skills, they coaxed people into unleashing their emotions and ideas. Games indeed depend on experienced designers, though official game designers are not the only ones who can fill this role. "There was a level of professionalism with the techniques," Andrea asserted. "If you buy a book of games you're not going to be able to do them like a guy from the GTO." The GTO members were proficient game designers, but as they would no doubt admit, even the best jokers can learn new tricks.

Games as Political Change

In the city of Rosario, games and play are transforming democratic participation. The government, along with community groups such as the GTO Rosario, is mixing games and playful activities into democratic political processes. In 1996 the City of the Children program planted the seeds of play. Its Children's Councils and other initiatives used games and play to tackle a giant political goal: transform the city for the good of all, especially its most vulnerable citizens. Games have since become, as Secretary General Jose Garibay told me, a "cross-cutting issue for the municipality." For their staunchest advocate, Chiqui González, Rosario's games play an even deeper political role. They serve as "a demonstration of the possible utopia."[44]

To travel toward this utopia, the Department of Children is making the road by walking, albeit with some missteps along the way. The Children's Councils and Theater of the Oppressed workshops are using games and play to engage more people in more meaningful ways, shaping public policies while making participation fun. The council and workshop games encourage collaboration and creativity, ease people into active participation, sweep aside inhibitions, help people understand different perspectives and emotions, and translate laws into practice.

These games are not just for kids. Though the City of the Children works mainly with children and youth, it aims to change the way *all* citizens engage with the city and with each other.[45] The Theater of the Oppressed workshops translate games into an adult setting, showing how they can work even with municipal workers. By playing in meetings, workshops, and public spaces, Rosario's children and adults demonstrate that play and games can make democratic participation more engaging and effective. As Chiqui González argues, "to play and live together are the verb form of democracy."[46]

But Rosario's programs are not always winners. In the City of the Children's Plaza Dreams initiative, facilitators separated play and games from meaningful decisions, distracting players from their lack of real power. By refusing to deal with serious planning issues, the Plaza Dreams workshops trivialized and marginalized participation. Throughout the City of the Children program, staff often shunned competition and failed to link play to real outcomes, making participation less engaging and productive. Even in the Theater of the Oppressed sessions, facilitators sometimes got so hooked on games that they had little time to achieve workshop goals. Or they failed to explain rules clearly at the start of games, and ended up adding too many rule changes once play had begun. As a result some people felt manipulated and had less fun.

While these dangers are real, they may also be avoidable. Could game design and game mechanics link play with meaningful decisions, to tackle serious issues? To make participation more fun, without losing track of the work to be done? To introduce just enough rules at just the right times so that players feel neither lost nor controlled? And could governments and organizations apply these game approaches even when games may not be appropriate? Rosario Hábitat offers some answers.

5 Rosario Hábitat: Designing Participation Like a Game

Something was wrong with the map. Mario peered down at it for a minute, a blank look of disbelief on his face. He had sat quietly through the workshop introductions, learning how he and a dozen neighbors were about to turn part of their *villa miseria* (shantytown) into a regular city block. He had stood with his tattooed arms folded as the workshop facilitators laid out a giant map of the area on a table, with new streets superimposed over existing lots. Suddenly, Mario erupted. "That new street," he blurted out, pointing to the map, "is on top of my house. I've lived there my whole life, since my dad built it with his bare hands. My dad just passed away, and now you're telling me that it'll be destroyed for some stupid road?!?" The facilitators looked at each other, and I waited for an ugly conflict between city plans and resident demands.

To my surprise, the residents of Villa La Cerámica had already learned to negotiate the conflict themselves, through workshops of the Argentine development program Rosario Hábitat. Verónica, Mario's neighbor, reminded him that the new road was necessary for the City of Rosario to finally install water, sewer, gas, and electricity connections for their houses. Julio, another neighbor, added that Mario would still get to pick a nearby location for his new house *and* get title to the land, based on rules the residents had already agreed on. In the end, Mario asked the facilitators to check with the Planning Department about shifting the road's location, but then he backed down calmly. "If this is best for the community, I'll move."

Most community meetings do not end so nicely, especially when they involve difficult decisions about who gets what land. Land conflicts have become common in Latin American cities, as shantytowns swell and local governments seek to replace them with formally planned (and often more profitable) developments. In Argentina, these conflicts routinely result in *piquetes*—raucous road blockades that shut down main highways and avenues. More broadly, such disconnect between government and citizens often contributes to failed development programs, social exclusion, and the declining legitimacy of government itself.[1] Rosario Hábitat learned this lesson the hard way. During its first two interventions, in the *villas* Corrientes and Las Flores, the program's attempts at participatory planning inspired violent backlash.

What changed, to allow residents and staff in La Cerámica to resolve their conflict amicably? *Rosario Hábitat learned to design participation like a game.* The program managed to improve its results by changing its process. Like in the programs discussed in the last chapter, staff began to include games as workshop exercises. Rosario Hábitat also went a step further. In their efforts to make participation more engaging, staff redesigned the whole participatory process, grounding it in many of the "game mechanics" outlined in chapter 3. Inspired by the spirit and practice of games, staff crafted better workshops using the same principles, elements, and techniques that game designers use to craft better games.

While the previous chapter showed how games can be inserted into meetings, I now explore a deeper role for games—how entire political processes can be designed to be more *like* games. Most of the experiences below are *not* games. As the learning scholar James Gee has argued, though, the principles of game design should not be confined to games. "Good video games build into their very designs good learning principles . . . we should use these principles, with or without games, in schools, workplaces, and other learning sites."[2] Following Gee, I argue that games also model good principles of participation, interaction, and decision-making. Rosario Hábitat illustrates how these principles can be used in communities, organizations, and governments, with or without games. While Rosario Hábitat could be analyzed in many ways, after five years of research I found that game design was the most useful lens for understanding when and how the program worked, and for defining new practices that could be used elsewhere.

I also found that Rosario Hábitat's game approach effectively resolved disputes such as Mario's above, along with other problems. But did this conflict resolution come at a cost? Did the process manufacture consent, by manipulating or coercing agreement? Did it trivialize participation?

The answers depended mainly on which game mechanics staff used. When facilitators applied particular mechanics that engage the senses, legitimate rules, generate 'collaborative competition,' and link participation with outcomes, they managed to build more democratic community agreement. When Rosario Hábitat did not take this approach, its efforts collapsed.

After presenting Rosario Hábitat in the next section, I describe the program's initial mishaps in the *villas* Corrientes and Las Flores. In the rest of the chapter I then discuss the main changes made to the program, by revisiting four later workshops in the *villas* Itatí and La Cerámica. For each workshop, I highlight the key game mechanics that made participation work. In the final section, I explain how these game mechanics work together as a systemic approach for facilitating democratic participation.

Rosario Hábitat

As explained in chapter 4, the city of Rosario has been at the crest of a recent Latin American wave of participatory democracy. Yet despite the success of its participatory programs, the administration elected in 1989 initially had little effect on one of the city's most visible and serious problems: horrid living conditions in the *villas*. These informal settlements had begun to grow on the outskirts of Argentine cities in the 1960s, mainly because of internal migration and slum clearance.[3] By the late 1990s there were 91 *villas* in Rosario, occupying 10 percent of the city.[4] The *villas* housed 115,000 people, 13 percent of the city's population, in fragile homes made mainly of scavenged materials. Most residents occupy the land illegally, without legal connections to the city's water, gas, or electricity networks. Most have little formal education, low incomes derived from informal labor, and darker than average skin. Because *villa* streets are usually unpaved and lack sewage systems, rain turns them into muddy quagmires. Even without rain, the streets are often lined with standing pools of sewage and household waste.

In 1998 Mayor Hermes Binner called for a participatory program to improve conditions in the *villas*. Rosario's Public Housing Service (*Servicio Público de Vivienda*, or SPV), a city agency that had already led small interventions in the *villas*, proposed Rosario Hábitat as a comprehensive development approach. SPV obtained a loan from the Inter-American Development Bank to cover 60 percent of Rosario Hábitat's initial $71 million budget, and the City of Rosario provided the rest.[5] SPV launched the program's first phase in 2000, aiming to improve conditions in 11 *villas*— home to 5,200 families, almost a third of the total *villa* population. Figure 5.1 shows the first eight villas.

In each *villa*, Rosario Hábitat works on three fronts. First, it develops *urban infrastructure*. It generates plans for streets and sidewalks; gas, water, sewers, storm drains, and electricity systems; and facilities such as health and child care centers. It then coordinates the efforts of several city agencies, public utilities, and contractors to carry out the plans. To install new

Figure 5.1
Map of Rosario Hábitat *villas:* Map depicting the city of Rosario and the location of Rosario Hábitat villas within the city. Image courtesy of Programa Rosario Hábitat.

infrastructure, some households need to be relocated. Rosario Hábitat either helps these families move to vacant areas in the *villa* or builds new houses for them in a nearby neighborhood. The program also delivers property title to each family.

Second, staff provide *support for children and families,* including workshops in nutrition and gender relations, recreation activities, and placement of children in schools. Third, Rosario Hábitat coordinates a *work and income generation* program, to provide job training, internships, and placement services, and helping residents form micro-enterprises and cooperatives.

As María Isabel Garzia, the former SPV director, summarized, "The idea is that the *villa* stops being a *villa* and becomes a normal city neighborhood. For that reason, Rosario Hábitat is considered a plan that delivers citizenship, not just housing."[6] This was the idea, at least. When staff tried to carry out their plan, however, residents had other ideas.

Not According to Plan

Rosario Hábitat began by intervening in two very different *villas*. Villa Corrientes was downtown and already integrated into the city grid, while Las Flores was small and isolated on the city's periphery. In both cases residents violently rejected Rosario Hábitat, and staff learned vital lessons.

Because of its central location in the city, Villa Corrientes already had roads, sewers, and other basic infrastructure. Its 800 families were close to the opportunities of downtown, and many people had formal jobs. In other *villas*, work often involved scavenging trash from city streets, via horse-drawn carts. In Corrientes, the only horse was a pet pony. It was almost a middle-class neighborhood.

Irregular unlighted alleys still permeated the blocks, though, and crime was rampant. Above all, the *villa*'s downtown location made it a political priority. It lay less than 20 blocks from the city center, an embarrassing eyesore for the municipality.

Since security was the most glaring problem, the Rosario Hábitat team in Corrientes decided to open up safer passageways to cut through the blocks (see figure 5.2). Based on a land use survey and the program's criteria, staff mapped out a new plan for each block, indicating which households would be relocated to accommodate new passageways. They then presented these plans at community meetings in the *villa*, and residents signed in agreement. Garzia was optimistic at the time: "It wasn't simple, but after a while people came to consensus, not just based on their own willpower but also to fulfill a series of technical requirements."[7]

Garzia was wrong. In August 2004 the time came for families to move, and they refused. Relations between Rosario Hábitat and the community deteriorated rapidly. As tensions escalated, a resident tried to stab a staff member, and the project team was literally chased out of the *villa*.

What went wrong? As one coordinator recalled, "people weren't interested in the solution we were offering." The program had not offered residents many concrete benefits, instead explaining that some of them would have to move for "regularization." When faced with the real task of

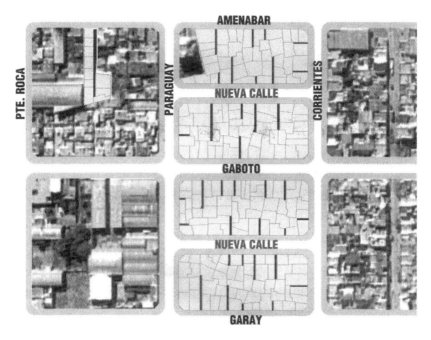

Figure 5.2
Villa Corrientes: An aerial map of part of Villa Corrientes. New mid-block streets are labeled "NUEVA CALLE" and new passageways are marked by dark lines jutting into the block. Image courtesy of Programa Rosario Hábitat.

uprooting their homes, many families decided that the costs outweighed the benefits.

This decision came as a surprise to staff because they had not engaged the community in meaningful ways. People had had little say in the new plans for the *villa* and little opportunity to understand the program's technical relocation criteria. Their participation had been passive, as staff recognized later. "When the residents first signed the agreements," Paula admitted, "they weren't in agreement." As Jesica concluded, "There wasn't anything participatory, and there weren't good relations with the residents."

Rosario Hábitat re-did the planning process, this time with more participation. Staff organized a new round of meetings for each block, in which they tried to get to know families and decide on new block plans from scratch. They never managed to develop a coherent participatory process, but eventually the program reached new agreements with the residents. After several arduous years, the city finally opened four new streets and several new passageways, and relocated 200 families to a new housing development.

At around the same time as the struggles in Villa Corrientes, a different Rosario Hábitat team was intervening in Las Flores, a poorer, smaller, and newer *villa*. Sitting just outside the city's beltway, Las Flores only housed around 360 families. Although it was on the edge of the city, the *villa* was a political hotspot. Several parties had strong bases there, constantly organizing residents to make demands on the government.

Rosario Hábitat started to engage the first two sectors of Las Flores as in Villa Corrientes, presenting new plans and trying to secure agreements. One coordinator reflected, "The program was 'participatory,' but people didn't really participate." The results were similar to those in Corrientes. Because there had been little communication with residents, staff realized late in the game that their land use plans were not very popular. In particular, residents did not understand why the plans left out the 80 new families that had recently moved into the *villa* since the last census.

Community members became furious that not all families fit into the plans, and they blocked nearby roads and highways with *piquete* protests. For the technical coordinator in Las Flores, these conflicts "proved that there had to be another way . . . you can have a perfect land use plan, but without participation, it's not going to work."

This lack of meaningful participation is by no means unique to Rosario Hábitat. Rather, the problems in Corrientes and Las Flores represent some of the most common challenges of participatory programs: translating and communicating technical information, incorporating and negotiating diverse community opinions, agreeing on rules, facilitating democratic decision-making, and keeping the process relevant for the community.[8]

After the initial setbacks in Las Flores, Rosario Hábitat tried to redesign its process, to better address these challenges. The program invited Gustavo Romero, a Mexican expert in participatory planning, to lead several trainings, where staff learned about participatory facilitation, decision-making, and design techniques. Rosario Hábitat also recruited more experienced facilitators.

The training workshops and new facilitators inspired staff to design a new participatory process and implement it in the remaining sectors of Las Flores. The experiment paid off. The work in the other sectors went smoothly, without protests. Mariana, a veteran facilitator, explained, "with the same people, after having gone through a participatory design process, we didn't have any more problems . . . the treatment was completely different. By then, it didn't matter so much that we were from the state. We became people who were helping them and collaborating with them."[9]

Residents expressed strong support for the new approach. "The process was really interesting," one community member said, "because we could put forth our opinions and do almost everything ourselves—the land use planning and all of that." Another added that the new process was important "because we can make our own decisions, rather than having others come and impose things on us."

What exactly did Rosario Hábitat do to inspire such a different response? After the initial interventions in Corrientes and Las Flores, the program re-centered the development process around a series of participatory workshops. In these gatherings residents learn about the program, identify local priorities, decide on rules for participation, reorganize the distribution of land, select new homes, shape local development and service plans, develop micro-enterprises and cooperatives, and negotiate community concerns.

The following pages explain what the four main workshops—planning, rule-making, lot allocation, and relocation—can teach us about participation. "In these workshops," Mariana told me, "we learned how to communicate together and understand both our own teams and the residents . . . and we started with games." After describing each workshop, I discuss how staff tried to overcome the challenges in Corrientes and Las Flores by designing participation more like a game.

Engaging the Senses

In Villa Itatí, community participation began with an impossible puzzle. Itatí was one of the largest *villas* in the city, housing around 1,000 families. It straddled both sides of the train tracks and bordered a main commercial avenue. On a sunny Saturday morning, Rosario Hábitat had invited all the families in one sector of the *villa* to gather for an initial planning workshop. During these workshops, community members identify the main local problems and ways to address them. At the same time Rosario Hábitat tries to shake residents out of their routines and inspire them to participate actively.

By 10:00 around 60 people (representing almost all of the families) had streamed into the community center across the street from the *villa*. Lucia, the workshop coordinator, stood at the entrance, giving everyone a welcome packet as they entered, along with a hug or kiss. Inside the meeting room, staff were preparing and passing around *mate* tea for all to share.[10]

Rosario Hábitat

Once people had settled into rows of green plastic chairs, Lucia welcomed them with a challenge. She reminded them that they were about to embark on a journey to remake their neighborhood, and then she divided them into teams of 10. Orange-shirted staff escorted groups to tables, handing each a basket of 25 fist-size puzzle pieces. In between sips of *mate*, Lucia recited the deceptively simple instructions: to prepare for the difficult tasks ahead, each team should put together their puzzle—without saying a word. She pressed play on a boombox at her side, and *reggaetón* beats launched the game into action.

Each group flipped its pieces onto its table, revealing a fragmented cartoon scene of a neighborhood. The participants started putting together pieces, but each group got stumped. Seeing this, Lucia announced that in the second round of the challenge, players could now talk. Each team now began to debate what to do, glancing surreptitiously at the other tables. Still, each group was left with holes in its puzzle, and some pieces that did not seem to fit. A few skeptics complained that the game was impossible.

The third round revealed why they were wrong. Lucia now said that players could also communicate with members of other teams—though this was in fact not prohibited before. In a matter of seconds, people figured out the trick. Each team had a couple pieces from another team's puzzle, and vice versa. Once the teams had traded pieces and completed their puzzles, Lucia asked what had happened, and what this had to do with Rosario Hábitat. Residents jumped in with ideas: "When there was no communication, we were isolated." "There was a lack of trust in the other teams." "We need to have open communication and work together."

The next activity put these lessons to the test. In small groups, facilitators asked residents to identify the main problems in the *villa*, and solutions that Rosario Hábitat might offer. To help with such a serious task, the facilitators gave each group a thick stack of cartoon cards. Each card depicted a neighborhood scene, like in the puzzles. The facilitators asked the groups to first look at each card and write down on sheets of green paper any problems that the image suggested. A cartoon of a tiny house cramped up against a big house, for example, inspired the problem "unequal lot sizes." A picture of a dingy alley suggested "dangerous passageways" and "people irresponsible with trash."

After people taped up the problem sheets on the wall, facilitators asked them to propose solutions on sheets of orange paper. Some solutions came quickly, such as "more equal lot sizes." Others required more discussion. To deal with the alleys, some people suggested more police and education. Others disagreed, proposing wider alleys, street lights, and dumpsters.

Finally, Lucia asked each group to post its problems and solutions in columns on the front wall, and to prepare some kind of creative presentation of their main ideas. After 15 minutes of preparation, the first group led off with a Jerry Springer-esque talk show episode. First, they acted out a fight that had erupted between two guests, in which Julieta was tossing out a bunch of dirty diapers into an alley. Ana came walking along and confronted Julieta on her littering, and the scene quickly degenerated into a hair-pulling melee, complete with hollers from the audience (see figure 5.3).

Rodrigo, playing the talk show host, intervened and asked what Rosario Hábitat could do about fights like this. Group members planted in the audience called out ideas: "get trash dumpsters so that Julieta has somewhere else to put her trash," "install street lights so that neighbors could see their fight and break it up." Other groups presented TV news reports, radio call-in shows, and skits of their own. Pointing to the wall full of problems and proposed solutions, Lucia thanked everyone for participating, and said that they would meet again soon to decide how to put the solutions into action.

Figure 5.3
Skit at planning workshop: Acting out problems in the *villa*, in a planning workshop. Photo by author.

How did dozens of *villa* residents manage to lay out broad neighborhood improvement plans in just three hours? They started by playing a game. As the facilitators told me afterward, the puzzle game served three purposes. It got nearly everyone out of their seats and participating actively, making it less intimidating to speak later. The game's social nature helped people get to know their neighbors and establish a collaborative mood. The trick at the end forced them to question their perspectives and assumptions, making them more open to new ideas. While most people assumed that the game was competitive, by the end they discovered why collaboration was essential. In less than 20 minutes, the game significantly changed the workshop dynamics.

For these and other reasons discussed in chapter 4, games have become a mainstay of Rosario Habitat. These games are particularly inspired by popular education and participatory planning experiences elsewhere.[11]

Games such as the puzzle challenge, however, only tell part of the story. Staff also managed to engage residents by making the entire workshop more *like a game*, using "game mechanics" that are common in game design.[12] In the process they avoided the passive participation that undermined work in Corrientes and Las Flores.

The planning workshop in particular illustrated how three basic game mechanics—vibrant *visuals, sound effects,* and enjoyable *core mechanics*—can engage people's senses. First, rather than just using visual aids periodically to present information, the workshop fully incorporated vibrant visuals into every activity. Participants began by assembling puzzle pieces of colorful cartoons, then reviewed more cartoons, wrote on and arranged colored paper, and presented and viewed theater scenes.

Residents participated not only with their eyes, but also with their ears and bodies. The *reggaetón* music helped them push aside outside distractions and added dramatic tension to the puzzle contest. The workshop also made them move, through intrinsically enjoyable *core mechanics*—the basic actions that participants actually do.[13] Matching together puzzle pieces, flipping through cards, sticking papers on the wall, and acting are all relatively enjoyable in themselves, at least compared with typical workshop activities such as asking questions and making arguments. For many scholars, the tight linkage between engaging visuals, sounds, and actions generates the deep and meaningful experience of immersion that is common to games.[14]

But does this engaging participation really matter, or is it *just* a game? If Rosario Hábitat's goals are already set in advance, are residents just jumping through hoops to arrive at predetermined "solutions"?

Yes, the solutions are partly constrained by Rosario Hábitat's work plan, as in any development program (and as in any game). The program goals (develop basic infrastructure, support children and families, generate employment and income) are extremely broad though, encompassing most of the problems and solutions raised. While it seems that the cartoon cards might only suggest predetermined solutions, they consistently lead to new ideas as well. Resident proposals have added several components to the program, such as workshops that let families decide on floor plans for new houses, contracting of local cooperatives for construction work, and a citywide program for informal trash collectors.

Residents have not proposed deeper changes to the program, and no one that I interviewed voiced disagreement with the basic program goals and approach. In some cases this might be a sign of the agenda-setting power of the government, keeping certain questions off the table.[15] In Rosario, however, *villa* groups make vocal demands of the state all the time, organizing regular *piquetes* to block city streets (as in Las Flores). If, after the first two interventions, residents did not express major grievances during interviews or in their typical practices of public protest, it is unlikely that they were discontent with Rosario Hábitat.

Still, using colors, sounds, and movement may seem like mere window dressing for the "real" work of community participation. Indeed these techniques may not have much visible impact on the workshop results. Compared with the game mechanics discussed later, they play a rather indirect role in achieving the workshop goals.

Stimulating people's senses is essential, however, for preparing them to participate meaningfully. As the Argentine educator Mariano Algava has found, moving and engaging people's bodies inspires them to participate more actively and more creatively.[16] Once people get used to moving, speaking, listening, and looking carefully, they are more likely to carry over these habits into later activities.

When this did not happen in Corrientes and Las Flores, residents became used to participating passively—sitting in their seats and paying little attention. They signed where told and did not ask many questions. Rosario Hábitat paid a high price for this passivity, when it had to redo the entire planning process as a result.

Two years after the planning workshop in another *villa*, participants still come to the Rosario Hábitat office to follow up on the workshop, in some cases bringing the original pieces of colored paper with solutions written on them. Sometimes the action is already being implemented, and sometimes it is still in the works. Community development is a lengthy process, especially if local people are involved each step of the way. After long delays in Corrientes and Las Flores, however, Rosario Hábitat attempted to pre-empt roadblocks (both figurative and literal) through a second stage of workshops.

The Rules of the Game

After the initial planning workshops, staff hold rule-making workshops in each sector of each *villa*, using a participatory process to establish clear program rules. One Tuesday morning, I observed a rule-making workshop in Villa Itatí, at a health center recently built by Rosario Hábitat. Inside the meeting room, staff arranged 25 plastic chairs in an oval, leaving a scuffed white table in the middle. As they posted flipchart paper and maps on the walls, residents began to arrive, each one receiving a folder with handouts.

By 9:45, 20 people were waiting in their chairs, so the lead facilitator started the workshop. Despite his young face, Juan spoke with an unusually calm and clear Spanish. He explained that today the residents of *villa* sector A would start deciding which of their houses would relocate and to where, so that new roads and infrastructure could be built. Their specific tasks: pick criteria for determining who stays and who leaves, and start to map out passageways in the new block.

Paula, another facilitator, pointed to a poster on the wall, labeled *Fixed Rules*. "Eleven basic Rosario Hábitat rules are outlined here," she clarified, "and in your handouts." As she explained, passageways were necessary so that all houses would have direct and safe access to the roads. Juan went over the other rules and explained their rationales: each new lot must be at least 100 m^2 large (to ensure equality and basic living standards), no more than 30 percent of the families could move from the *villa* (to ensure that people's livelihoods were not disrupted excessively), and so forth. People asked a few questions of clarification, nodding as staff responded.

"These rules are a good start," Juan concluded, "but now it's your turn to decide on new ones." If there were three families living in a space that only fit two 100-m^2 lots, how would they decide who would relocate? Juan explained that people in other workshops had suggested several criteria for making such decisions: for example, length of tenancy, how precarious the house is, number of inhabitants, family members with disabilities, chance, and mutual agreement. Juan posted on the wall sheets of colored paper presenting these criteria.

Paula asked if anyone had other criteria to add. Yasmín said that she wanted to stay near her brother's family, so maybe they could add "family members nearby" to the list. Juan nodded and posted it on the wall. Maxi joked that "whoever serves the *mate* gets to stay." Others suggested a few more serious criteria. After 15 minutes the discussion died down, so Juan called for a vote to set the order of the criteria. Paula handed each family a paper strip with the numbers 1 to 10 printed in a column. Juan explained that everyone should think about which criteria mattered most, and then come up to the wall to label them in order of importance. After some discussions, people tore their sheets into 10 pieces and, armed with glue sticks, stuck the numbers on the criteria sheets to show their preferences (see figure 5.4). Paula counted the votes, to determine which criteria would have top priority for deciding land disputes.

Juan thanked everyone for prioritizing the criteria, and invited them up to the table in the middle of the room. A giant map lay on the table, with each family's house labeled. Their task was to suggest where passageways should go, using several long rectangular cutouts of colored transparency

Figure 5.4
Participatory rule-making: Voting on decision-making rules, in a rule-making workshop. Photo by author.

sheets. As Juan explained, each cutout represented a passageway, to scale with the map. He moved several cutouts around the map, to illustrate how they could be placed.

After Juan's demonstration, the neighbors began moving the pieces around, and new questions surfaced. Did the passageways have to be straight, like the cutouts? Yes, because otherwise they would be unsafe. Why were some cutouts wider than others? Because the width depended on how many families used the passageway to reach their house. As Mónica noticed, the cutouts were labeled with different sizes: 1.5 meters wide for access to one house, 1.8 meters for two houses, and so forth.

After 20 minutes of playing with the cutouts, participants settled on locations for two passageways. With criteria and passageways decided, Juan called the meeting to a close around 11:00.

The rule-making workshop, and others like it, helped generate and legitimate Rosario Hábitat's rules—what residents could and could not do. To do this, it used several of the same game mechanics that designers use to establish game rules: *participant-generated rules*, *multimodal presentation*, *narrative*, *just-in-time information*, and *modeling*.

First, Rosario Hábitat let *participants develop and order their own rules* for negotiating land conflicts. While most games start with fixed rules, some enable players to craft their own rules—through what Salen and Zimmerman call "transformative social play."[17] Sometimes players end up more interested in the rules they create than in the original rules.[18] This seemed to be the case in Rosario Hábitat. As Mónica boasted, "We set the rules ourselves . . . so if we complain it'll be stupid. And they have to be maintained because the agreement was collective and consensual." Sergio added that he couldn't go against the rules because "they're decisions of my neighbors in the *villa*." Small face-to-face meetings were essential for participatory rule-making, since they allowed for more comfortable dialogue and flexibility than larger or online forums.

Rosario Hábitat also imposes some fixed rules, however. Some are technical constraints for installing infrastructure, while others outline the rights of residents. The rule-making workshop did not assume that people instantly understood the rules, but rather that rules needed to be constantly communicated, explained, and reinforced. Like good games, the workshops accomplished this through *multimodal presentation* of information. As James Gee observed, games convey meaning and knowledge through images, words, sounds, and other modalities.[19] Just as board games such as *Monopoly* communicate rules (such as *collect $200 on passing Go*) by presenting them in the instructions *and* writing them on the game board, the workshop facilitators communicated rules by distributing them as handouts, writing them on the wall, and reading them aloud. When asked how clear the rules were, one participant pointed to the wall and said, "They're very clear, because they're there."

In some cases, however, the reasoning behind rules is not obvious. Many games craft *narratives* to explain why players can or cannot take certain actions, and Rosario Hábitat took a similar approach. Facilitators tried to situate and explain fixed rules within a broader story of neighborhood change. In this story, community members would try to distribute land more equally and fairly, while disrupting the neighborhood as little as possible. This narrative helped frame the rules of 100 m^2 per lot and maximum of 30 percent relocations, for example, as tools to advance common goals, rather than as arbitrary limits. One facilitator felt that this explanation helped people "accept because they understand," rather than just accept blindly.

Finally, the workshop helped participants more deeply understand the rules through *just-in-time information* and *modeling*. Games avoid overwhelming players with information, instead presenting it only at the moment when it is actually useful. Similarly the workshop explained the rules about passageway size and shape at the moment when participants were actually arranging passageways on the map. By gradually adding more information, the workshop helped participants process the rules bit by bit.

The colored passageway cutouts also served to model the rules. They provided physical models of the rules governing passageway size and shape— 1.5 m width for one family, straight lines, and so forth. Having both, Juan first moved the pieces around on the map, and likewise modeled the kinds of trade-offs and calculations that would ultimately have to be made.

By enabling participants to learn and change the rules in multiple accessible ways, Rosario Hábitat mediated between expert staff knowledge and experiential resident knowledge. This helped bridge technical "language barriers" between experts and citizens, generating more understanding of and support for the "rules of the game." At the same time this approach diffused tensions between technical constraints and local democracy, which often disrupts participatory planning.[20] In Itatí and elsewhere, staff coached a tango between top-down constraints and bottom-up democracy, syncing them together.

The experience in Itatí stands in stark contrast to the initial interventions in Corrientes and Las Flores. In these two *villas*, residents could not set rules, and staff did not present or justify rules very clearly. When they did present rules, they did not break them down into digestible chunks or model how they would be applied. Years later staff admitted that some residents in these *villas* still did not know the limits of their lots, or understand how they ended up in their new lots. Whereas in Corrientes and Las Flores, community members rejected the program rules; in Itatí and the other *villas*, residents and staff came together to agree on them. With clear rules in hand, Rosario Hábitat was ready to tackle its most difficult task: negotiating who gets what land.

Collaborative Competition

At the heart of Rosario Hábitat are two basic conflicts. First, there is conflict between residents and the municipality. City planners want some people to leave the *villa*, so that there will be space for roads and 100-m² lots, but many residents do not want to go. Then there is conflict between residents. Most want larger lots and newer houses, but there is limited land and housing available. To make matters more complicated, some people *do* want to leave (even if they do not have to), and some *do not* want to move to larger lots or newer houses (even if they can).

Building on the rule-making workshops, Rosario Hábitat tries to negotiate this web of conflicts in lot allocation (*loteo*) workshops, such as the one described at the start of this chapter. In these workshops, staff resolve disputes by blending competition and collaboration.

In Itatí, the conflicts within the program were compounded by preexisting turmoil in the *villa*. A week before the lot allocation workshops were scheduled to start, some young gang members from the *villa* robbed at gunpoint the driver of a Rosario Hábitat transport van, as the van was waiting outside the community center. A few days later, the same youth entered the center and robbed the workers there. Shots were fired, and one worker was grazed in the neck by a bullet. Needless to say, staff postponed the workshops, until they could secure police escorts into the *villa*.

When the project team and I entered the *villa* a few weeks later for the lot allocation workshop, the mood was still tense. Juan began by mentioning the attacks and pleading with residents to help maintain a safe environment. Paula emphasized that this was perhaps the most important workshop of the program. In the *villas*, land was already divided informally into lots. Through the lot allocation workshops, residents would reorganize these lots, so that new infrastructure could be built.

Juan began the first lot allocation workshop in Itatí by reviewing the program rules discussed above, and inviting everyone to gather around the map in the center of the room. Like in the prior workshop, each family's current lot was labeled on the map, and the new passageways were marked with transparency cutouts. There was also a colorful pile of smaller transparency cutouts, shaped like squares, rectangles, and Ls, as in the video game *Tetris* (see figure 5.5). As Juan explained, each piece represented a 100-m^2 lot—the dimensions were even written on the cutouts. The goal: to arrange the pieces such that each family had a 100-m^2 lot within the available terrain.

At first, people just stared. Juan picked up a yellow rectangle and placed it over Maria's tiny lot, then slid a blue square next to it, over Miguel's land. The square did not quite fit though—part of it overlapped a passageway. Juan now invited Maria and Miguel to try to rearrange their pieces, or substitute them for other shapes, so that both lots would fit within the boundaries. Otherwise, Miguel would have to leave the block and relocate. Miguel reached hesitantly for a thinner orange rectangle and tried switching it for Maria's yellow one, then shifting his blue square over into the liberated space. His move worked, but created a new problem. Now Maria's lot overlapped with Daniel's land to the north.

Figure 5.5
Lot allocation puzzle: Rearranging land lots in a lot allocation workshop. Photo by author.

Rosario Hábitat

After a few minutes of shape-swapping, it became clear that Miguel and Maria could not both fit in the block—at least not if Daniel's lot stayed as it was. It also became clear that Daniel's lot was relatively big—150 m². Miguel put a red 100-m² rectangle over Daniel's lot, and suddenly there was space for the three lots.

Picking up on the conflict, Juan asked Daniel if he could give up some space. Daniel stared down at the map and cringed, saying that he was planning to build a new bathroom in the extra space. Juan asked if they needed to use the criteria to see who had priority, but then Daniel had an idea. Pointing to his lot on the map, he looked at Miguel. "If you give me some building materials for the bathroom, I'll give you a bit more space." Miguel looked to Juan for approval, and Juan gave the okay: "The exchange of materials is up to you, but if you can reach an agreement, no problem. Agreement *is* the top criteria, no?" Conflict solved. Paula taped a piece of flipchart paper up on the wall and wrote down the agreed exchange.

Many conflicts were resolved even more easily. Often enough families would want to move out of the *villa* that no compromising was necessary. Many families could stay where they were, and others would see an empty space on the map and volunteer to move there. Some of the more complicated conflicts, though, required two or three workshops to resolve.

At this workshop all the families were able to agree on new lot locations, whether inside or outside the *villa*. After an hour and a half of playing around with the map, Juan asked everyone to review the final distribution of lots and the list of agreed exchanges on the flipchart paper. Paula added that now was the time for each person to sign both the flipchart and their new lot on the map (see figure 5.6), if they were willing to really commit to these agreements. The participants talked it over among themselves for a few minutes, and then they all signed.

The lot allocation workshops managed to negotiate key conflicts among residents, and between residents and the program. This was possible partly because earlier workshops had established norms of active participation and agreed-upon rules. With the stage thus set, the lot allocation workshops walked residents through the drama of conflict-resolution using two additional game mechanics: *magic circles* and *group vs. system* competition.

As Johann Huizinga described them, *magic circles* are play spaces that are temporarily separated from the ordinary world, within which special rules apply.[21] Just as the marked rectangle of a soccer field defines a magic circle for soccer, the puzzle map served as a magic circle for the lot allocation workshop. Conflicts that at other times led to violence could be tackled on a safer playing field, such that outcomes depended on agreed-upon

Figure 5.6
End results of the lot allocation puzzle. Photo by author.

rules rather than force. Land disputes took the form of overlapping colored puzzle pieces, which neighbors could rearrange safely.

When discussing these disputes, residents tended to point to the map, not each other. On the simplified map terrain, land inequalities were communicated more clearly. The relatively easy mechanics imposed by the magic circle (moving puzzle pieces) also helped neutralize inequalities between participants with different skills, creating more horizontal relations. As Denis Merklin has shown, poor Argentines tend to organize their participation around tactile territorial questions, which in this case were framed clearly by the lot allocation map.[22] Thanks to the mapping puzzle, a facilitator concluded, "We were able to achieve consensuses that would have been impossible otherwise."

This level of consensus was also encouraged by *group vs. system competition*, which some games use to bring a group of players together to compete against the game system. In the lot allocation workshop, neighbors struggled together against the constraints imposed by the program rules and the map itself. For one facilitator, the residents' collective quest to complete the puzzle "generates a certain intimacy . . . a group spirit."

Combined, the workshop's magic circle and group vs. system competition created what I call *collaborative competition*—competition that both requires and enhances collaboration. The workshop activities instilled a competitive drive in participants, but they also compelled people to work together if they wanted to compete successfully. As in soccer and many team sports, competition inspired and demanded closer teamwork. While planners often call for more collaborative participation, Rosario Hábitat shows that certain kinds of competition can be the friend, rather than foe, of collaboration.[23]

The lot allocation puzzle is not always successful, however. In another area, two facilitators used the same basic process, laying out a map of the block and transparency cutouts on a table and inviting residents to come up and rearrange their lots. Yet the workshop ended disastrously. A man on crutches furiously stormed out of the room (to the extent that a man on crutches can storm off anywhere) and several other residents followed, cursing the workshop for being a mess.

What happened? Though the workshop looked similar on paper, the facilitators did not use most of the game mechanics discussed earlier. To begin, they did not establish or communicate the lot allocation rules, leaving participants confused and distrustful. They then failed to manage conflict. The facilitators did not create much of a magic circle. They neither introduced themselves nor the goal of the workshop. Their map was too small for everyone to see, and so marked up with drawings that the lots were hard to distinguish. The map lay in the middle of the room on a children's table, too low for the adult participants to easily reach. The facilitators took out the colored cutouts but barely touched them, and they did not encourage participants to move them around. While in other workshops the map had brought people into a magic circle in which all could participate, in this one it became a spectacle. The residents stared down at the map, struggling to decipher it and unsure how to change it.

The facilitators also did little to foster team spirit, or group vs. system competition. They asked each family to lean down next to the map and pick its new lot individually, without reminding them about the program rules that limited their options or emphasizing the need to reach agreements together. Not surprisingly, many families picked new lots that were in conflict with their neighbors' lots. In these cases the neighbors rushed down to the map and started to argue. Since the workshop did not pose a collective problem to solve, it left neighbors pitted against each other, individual vs. individual. Staff tried to resolve the disputes, without much success. By the end of the workshop, two-thirds of the participants had already left, many without agreeing to their new land lots. After not establishing healthy or collaborative competition, staff were left with a rather unhealthy chaos.

When we returned to the office after the workshop, it became even more obvious why the workshop was dysfunctional. A couple senior staff had sat in on the workshops, to monitor. They were clearly not pleased with the facilitators: "You have to do everything more forcefully." The facilitators nodded, but didn't say much. As the discussion died down, one finally spoke up, "Can we go now, so we can get our paychecks?" As he got up and drifted out of the room, the other called out, "Don't forget about our task for tomorrow—planning the vacation schedule!"

Not everyone is suited to facilitate games or game-like workshops, just as not everyone is suited to coach a football team. These facilitators had neither the interest nor skills to pull off the lot allocation. Perhaps more facilitation training might have helped. Or perhaps not. As I learned later, staff recruitment was hit or miss in Rosario Hábitat, and some people got their jobs mainly for being good foot soldiers for the governing Socialist Party.

Even with better facilitation, the lot allocation puzzle is not always appropriate. According to Ximena and Mariana, two veteran facilitators, the rigid shapes of the puzzle pieces occasionally get in the way of creative

Rosario Hábitat

solutions. In these cases facilitators use the puzzle exercise to scope out options, and then discuss those options more with residents before making final decisions. Collaborative competition is a tool, but not an end in itself. Ultimately, results are what matter most.

Linking Participation to Outcomes

After observing the lot allocation workshop described at the start of this chapter, I did not return to Villa La Cerámica until its participatory process was ending. After several years of work, the project team had finally reached the last round of workshops. In these relocation workshops, families that could no longer fit in the *villa* were invited to select homes in a new housing development To accommodate those who are leaving their *villa*, Rosario Hábitat builds new housing developments throughout the city. The residents weigh in on where these new developments should be and then choose which one they will move to. Finally, in relocation workshops they pick their new houses.

The first relocation workshop in La Cerámica was held one evening behind a social club that bordered the new development, so the people could see their half-constructed new homes in the background. As I helped set up a ring of chairs, staff explained that this workshop was for single people and huge families, who had special relocation needs.

By 5:30, 10 residents were sitting stiffly in their chairs, representing all but one of the families. Ximena welcomed them, announcing that today they would choose from among the largest and smallest lots in the two new blocks. First, she proposed a round of introductions, asking everyone to say their name and favorite place in their house. For nearly an hour, the introductions unleashed a stream of insights, laughs, and discussions. Alberto admitted that he liked to keep to himself and was quiet, but Gigi gushed about playing music and dancing in her yard. Shaking his hips, Juan Pablo proposed that next time they do a night workshop in her yard. Carlos said nothing about his house, so Ximena asked about his favorite furniture. He sighed, "I don't really have anything," and laughed slowly. By the end, everyone had talked and met new neighbors.

Ximena now got to the point. "The idea of that exercise was to get to know each other and start to build a new neighborhood," she explained. "You could stay in this new house for life, so think about what you'd want." Next, the residents would have to decide on some rules, before picking lots. Like in the rule-making workshops, they discussed and voted on criteria for negotiating conflicts over lots. Juan Pablo then pointed to the wall and explained the maps of the new blocks and the floor plans of the new houses. Eight lots were highlighted on the map—three large and five small, some on corners or street fronts and some set back from the street.

The families now began to pick from among these options. Gigi and Hilda requested two of the neighboring setback houses, pointing out that since they were friends they should get priority, since this was one of the top criteria the group selected. No one objected, and Juan Pablo labeled the lots with their names. Carlos pleaded for another rear lot and got it, and the rest of the families picked their lots with surprising ease. In less than 10 minutes, all the lots were allocated, and staff passed out cups for a soda toast. After toasting, Juan Pablo led everyone on a tour of the new houses. The future homeowners pointed and pondered. "I could plant flowers here." "Look how wide the path is." "That'll be my room." By the time we finished, it was almost 8:30.

Impressively, all of the residents participated actively for the full three-hour meeting. Why? In part because of the game mechanics discussed earlier, but also for new reasons. The relocalization workshop, in particular, illustrated how Rosario Hábitat links participation with measurable outcomes—a key challenge of any participatory process.[24] It enabled families to see the results of their participation, by presenting *clear and measurable outcomes*, maintaining *uncertain outcomes*, breaking participation down into *levels*, and keeping score with *points*.

By definition, all games have *clear and measurable outcomes*, meaning that a player wins, loses, ties, or receives a score.[25] The clearer the potential outcomes, the greater is the motivation to play. Rosario Hábitat is fortunate that its workshops have extremely (and often literally) *concrete outcomes*. When asked why they participated, most residents said that they wanted to get paved streets, new houses, closed sewers, and other infrastructure. Scholars generally acknowledge that clientelistic processes depend on community members receiving specific and desired goods.[26] The case of Rosario Hábitat suggests that participatory democratic processes also rely on such concrete benefits.

While bricks and mortar infrastructure is an instant appeal, the program makes it more appealing with *vivid presentation of the outcomes*. In the relocalization workshop, staff posted plans for new blocks and houses on the wall, convened within sight of the houses under construction, and started by envisioning favorite house spaces. In other workshops, they displayed giant posters with photos of other *villas* before and after improvements (see

Rosario Hábitat 143

Figure 5.7
Concrete outcomes: Vivid presentation of workshop outcomes, through a "Yesterday and Today" poster. Photo by author.

figure 5.7). Tellingly, everyone I interviewed said they believed that the infrastructure would be built, though they were skeptical of other development programs. As Julia said, "I've lived in the *villa* since 1973 and many programs have come and gone, but none of them delivered. Rosario Hábitat is the only one that delivers, that is, already delivering."

Although concrete results were guaranteed, residents did not know what exactly these results would be. *Uncertain outcomes* are essential for sustaining people's attention—if the outcomes are known, people will stop playing.[27] In the relocalization workshop the families knew *that* lots would be assigned, but they did not know who would get *which* lots.

The facilitators also broke participation down into *levels*. To achieve the workshop goals, participants had to advance through a series of tasks. First, they had to envision what they valued in a house, then select decision-making criteria, then pick lots. They could not pick lots without having first agreed on decision-making criteria. Because the workshop was divided up so sharply, people had multiple opportunities to achieve intermediate objectives. Because these objectives built on each other, they generated a sense of progress, something lacking in many three-hour meetings. The whole participatory process was similarly divided into levels, such that community members had to first outline development plans, then agree on rules, then decide on new block plans.

Finally, staff used *points and scores* to quantify the results of participation. In the relocalization workshop this occurred during voting for decision-making criteria, but residents have also voted on locations for new housing developments, models for new homes, and other improvements. These vote tallies allowed people to more easily measure the impact of their participation. The quantification of lot sizes also served as a kind of score. Many residents, such as Andrea, measured the outcomes in square meters: "Now I have 36 m^2 of land . . . if they give me even five more meters, it's a miracle."

The outcomes certainly seemed more impressive than in Corrientes or Las Flores. In Corrientes, the program offered more modest improvements, making it a harder sell. In both of these *villas*, staff failed to present outcomes vividly—partly because they did not yet have photos to show of improvements in other program *villas*. Nor did staff establish a clear link between participation and outcomes. There were no clear levels of participation, and results were not measured in points. The new streets and alleys were mapped out before community meetings, leaving little room for uncertainty.

Game Design for Community Participation

At Rosario Hábitat, games offered a treasure chest of tools for community participation. *Games* such as the puzzle challenge ignited participation, built community, and opened people's minds. *Game mechanics* such as vivid visuals, sound effects, and enjoyable core mechanics activated and engaged people's senses. Participant-generated rules, multimodal presentation, narrative, just-in-time information, and modeling established and legitimated rules. Magic circles and group vs. system conflict generated healthy competition that increased collaboration. Linking participation to concrete yet uncertain outcomes, presenting these outcomes vividly, and measuring progress through levels and points provided more incentives to participate, and to keep participating.

Rosario Hábitat was much more effective when staff designed participation around these game mechanics. In Villas Corrientes and Las Flores, none of the game mechanics were used. Residents participated passively, and they did not understand or respect the rules. Participation did not seem to matter for the project outcomes, and it often devolved into violent conflict. Participation was not perfect in Villas Itatí or La Cerámica either, but the new game techniques addressed many of these initial problems.

These game mechanics are even more powerful when implemented together, as a systemic approach. When this happens, as Ximena concluded, they "build a common language." This language was clearly missing in Villas Corrientes and Las Flores, and in some later instances such as the dysfunctional lot allocation workshop. Perhaps it is no surprise that, when asked why Rosario Hábitat uses game techniques, the program director had a simple explanation: "For me, because they work, because they give results."

Rosario Hábitat's director supported this approach mainly because it helped complete development projects with strong community support, but the effects run deeper. For Alejandra, a project coordinator, the participatory workshops "build networks, between community members and institutions." From Monica's resident perspective, "Now, you leave your house and pass a neighbor in the street, and you start talking about any issue at all." The public sphere that emerged in and around the workshops created space for residents to discuss how their neighborhood and their city are governed—discussions that are essential for deepening democracy.

By learning to speak and enact a language of games, staff and residents also changed the political culture in the *villas*. When new community issues emerge, such as a program for trash scavengers or the construction of a new public plaza, staff and residents now expect participatory workshops. Unlike in the past, they start by discussing how to actively engage residents, establish rules, negotiate conflicts, and generate clear outcomes. Due to the conscious strategies of certain staff, participatory practices that were once marginal became the norm.[28]

Thanks to all this talking, residents and staff emerge from the program with new skills, knowledge, and attitudes. Residents learn about urban development and city government, and their potential to influence both. Staff become more sensitive to the needs and local knowledge of community members. Both staff and residents learn negotiation and conflict-resolution skills. Rosario Hábitat thus develops both the city *and* citizens.

In the end, the experience of Rosario Hábitat suggests that if government programs use game mechanics that engage the senses, legitimate rules, generate collaborative competition, and link participation with outcomes, then they can increase and enhance democratic participation. Without these mechanics, participation is more passive, rules are less trusted, conflict is more disruptive, and the reasons for participation are less clear. A game approach therefore helped address some of the most common challenges to making participatory democracy work.

Even if a game approach had such big effects, is this really news? In a sense, neither games nor game mechanics are particularly new. Planners and facilitators have used games in participatory processes for years.[29] Many game mechanics are similar to participatory techniques discussed elsewhere.[30]

The case of Rosario Hábitat, however, builds on these discussions in five ways. First, it suggests that games can serve as more than appetizers for the "real" meat of participation—serious discussions and decision-making. Games are not just for simulations or preparatory activities. While games may not always be appropriate, each moment of participation can and should be engaging, and game design can help.

Second, the lens of game design reveals several tools that have not surfaced in discussions about democratic participation, such as core mechanics, just-in-time information, and magic circles. Third, game mechanics offer more focused and succinct terms—such as modeling, multimodal presentation, and points—for ideas that are often discussed vaguely. Fourth, they help explain *when*, *where*, and *why* certain participatory practices work— for example, that visuals can have the most effect when fully incorporated into every meeting activity and material, since this more deeply stimulates senses. Finally, game mechanics illustrate the handicraft of democracy: how exactly facilitators of democratic processes can pursue—or undermine—theoretical ideals such as active participation and legitimate rules.

Of course, Rosario Hábitat's game mechanics are not necessarily effective at all times and in all places. Is Rosario a unique case, or could games and game mechanics also make democracy work elsewhere? Even if Rosario is not exceptional, do these participatory democratic games depend on the animated Latin cultures of countries such as Argentina? In the next chapter we find out, by traveling to the other end of the Americas—Toronto, Canada.

6 Toronto Community Housing: Game Design in Less Fertile Soils

The journey from Rosario to Toronto is 22 hours longer than I would prefer. During my research, It usually began in the morning with a doorbell buzzing through the dusty open-air patio at the heart of my Rosario apartment. Once inside the airport shuttle van, we weaved through Rosario's sprawling street grid, where traffic rules are always open to negotiation. At the city's edge, the scrap wood shacks and horse-drawn carts of a *villa miseria* faded into infinitely flat soybean fields. Several hours later, I checked in at Buenos Aires' Ezeiza airport for an overnight flight to Toronto.

In Toronto, the Airport Rocket express bus whisked me to the subway station, past Mr. Sub, Dairy Queen, and their strip mall friends. A spotless train sat waiting, and a sign inside kindly asked me to "be safe and considerate." When I surfaced a few stops later, I walked past the sushi bar, Korean BBQ joint, and Salvadoran *taqueria* to tranquil tree-lined streets, and to a decidedly less dusty apartment.

Toronto and Rosario are far apart and have little in common. So even if games can flourish in Rosario, less fertile soils might stunt their growth in Toronto. There are three good reasons why games and game mechanics might be less effective in Toronto and elsewhere in the Global North. First, Rosario's social, economic, and political conditions might be more favorable for games. Second, Argentines and other Latin Americans might be more open to play and games. Third, Rosario's programs can build on widespread play practices, while programs in the North must break with existing habits.

Faced with these obstacles, can democratic processes in the North benefit from game mechanics? Or are games and game design less useful outside Rosario? In this chapter, we start to find out, through the case of participatory budgeting (PB) at Toronto Community Housing (TCH). Each year from 2001 to 2012, the housing authority invited tenants to decide how to spend around $9 million. Similarly to Rosario Hábitat, TCH designed participation like a game. Through research over three years, I found that most of the game mechanics in PB enhanced democratic participation. In other words, *game design is not just for democratic processes in Rosario, in Argentina, or in Latin America*. Institutions in the Global North can also use game mechanics to make democratic participation more appealing and effective—though the path is not necessarily easy.

In the next section, I outline the additional obstacles to integrating games and game mechanics into democratic processes in the North. I then describe how PB spread from Brazil to Toronto, becoming a pillar of tenant engagement in Toronto's public housing authority. The third section reviews how the 2008 PB process adapted many of the game mechanics outlined in the previous chapters—and tried out new game mechanics as well. Finally, I explain how institutional changes led to a new PB process in 2009, and to new opportunities and challenges for both game design and participation.

"That Won't Work Here"

When I talk about Latin America's political games and game techniques in the United States and Canada, I often get a dismissive response: "Interesting, but that won't work here because . . .." Skeptics point to three main reasons why such games and game mechanics would flop in North America: less supportive context, less playful citizens, and less precedent for games. All three obstacles abound in Toronto.

First, Toronto is more diverse, more developed, and more conservative than Rosario, making games more challenging. Over 50 percent of Torontonians were born outside of Canada, while less than 5 percent of Rosario's residents are immigrants.[1] Rosario's cityscape is dotted with shantytowns and unpaved streets, Toronto's with glistening condo towers and gliding streetcars. Rosario is the birthplace of Che Guevara and the stronghold of Argentina's Socialist Party, while Toronto's right-wing Mayor likened community meetings to "a public lynching."[2]

Why are these conditions obstacles to games? Rosario's games and game-like processes depended on fluid communication. Because participants spoke the same language and shared roughly the same culture, they could participate more actively. In Toronto, and especially in TCH, people often speak different languages and have drastically different cultural backgrounds. Could a team of Somali refugees, Punjabi immigrants, and second-generation Jamaican-Canadians craft and understand game rules as easily as a group of Rosario's youth workers or *villa* residents?

Likewise, Rosario's programs enticed participation partly because they responded to drastic needs. *Villa* residents engaged in weeks of workshops so that they could gain water, sewage, and electricity networks. In Toronto, outcomes may be less meaningful, so the motivation to play may be less. Rosario's government officials were also more interested in exploring new approaches to participation, since they emerged out of grassroots leftist social movements. Toronto's more conservative government officials and staff are less interested in democratic participation, let alone in making it fun.

Second, for discussions about games, there may be an even deeper difference between Rosario and Toronto. Of all the peoples of the Americas, Argentines are perhaps the most flamboyant and playful, Canadians the most dour and reserved. Argentines are famous for their tango, Canadians for their earnest politeness. Argentines may be hard-wired to play, in a way that Canadians and other Northern neighbors are not.

In fact, after years of research in North and South America, I found this to be true. In the hundreds of public meetings and workshops I observed—during and outside of the book research—Latin Americans generally expressed fewer inhibitions about playing. And when I explained my book research to government officials and activists, Latin Americans were consistently more open to mixing play and games with democracy. They typically nodded knowingly, referring to examples from their own experiences. Their North American counterparts usually responded with blank stares, often followed by skepticism or by stories of games that had fizzled.

Finally, even if the conditions were ripe and the participants open-minded, facilitators in the North would have to break more sharply with established practices to incorporate games. Programs in Rosario can draw on wider norms and precedents of playful participation. But in Toronto, government employees tend to be less familiar with and enthusiastic about games, making them more likely to resist or botch games and game mechanics. Inertia is powerful. Each step down the game path may increase the likelihood of more game experiments, while a widespread aversion to games may deter programs from embarking on this path in the first place. Yet despite these obstacles, Toronto Community Housing managed to design participatory budgeting like a game.

Participatory Budgeting at Toronto Community Housing

The story of participatory budgeting dates back to 1989, in the southern Brazilian city of Porto Alegre. That year, the *Partido dos Trabalhadores* (Workers Party) won the city elections, on a campaign calling for more participatory democracy.[3] In response to demands from neighborhood associations, the new mayor opened the city budget to community participation.

Through its *orçamento participativo* (participatory budget), the administration scaled up the grassroots participation of town meetings to the city level, combining direct and representative democracy. City Hall invited citizens to decide how to spend part of the city budget, through a year-long series of neighborhood, district, and citywide assemblies. At these meetings community members and elected budget delegates identified spending priorities, deliberated on these priorities, and voted on which projects to implement. The city then turned those projects into reality. Participatory budgeting has since become an annual process, in which tens of thousands of residents decide how to spend up to a fifth of the city budget.

The results have been dramatic.[4] In 1989, only 49 percent of the population had basic sanitation service. After eight years of PB, 98 percent of households had water and 85 percent were served by the sewage system. In the same time span the city paved half of its unpaved streets and built enough new elementary and secondary schools to double the number of students. New public housing went up at increasing rates and bus companies expanded service to neglected areas. The number of neighborhood associations even increased. These changes have especially benefited poor people. Although a 2004 change in government weakened PB, the process has persisted for over two decades.

After emerging in Porto Alegre, PB was soon adopted throughout Brazil, and then elsewhere in Latin America. In the past decade it has become popular in Europe, Africa, and Asia. By 2012, over 1,500 cities were practicing it.[5] Countries such as Peru and the Dominican Republic have mandated that all local governments implement PB, and the United Nations and World Bank have named it a best practice of democratic governance.[6] States, counties, schools, housing authorities, and community associations have also used it for their budgets. PB events often include music, food, games, and other festive elements, to create a celebratory atmosphere.[7]

The first North American experiments sprouted in Canada, and outside of city hall. In 2001, Toronto Community Housing launched PB for its capital budget, empowering tenants to decide how to allocate $9 million per year, around 10 percent of the capital budget. An hour away, in the city of Guelph (population 115,000), PB grew in a coalition of grassroots neighborhood groups. Starting in 2001, the Neighborhood Support Coalition used a deliberative process to allocate roughly $250,000 annually from various government and foundation sources.[8] The Montreal borough Plateau Mont-Royal also tried PB in 2006, 2007, and 2008 for up to $1.5 million

Toronto Community Housing

of its capital budget. In 2009, I worked with Chicago Alderman Joe Moore to develop the first process in the United States, for his ward's $1.3 million discretionary budget.[9] This work inspired me so deeply that I co-founded a nonprofit organization (The Participatory Budgeting Project) to expand PB in North America. Since 2009, we have launched several other PB processes, in cities from New York to San Francisco.

Toronto, however, was the first big PB experiment in North America. Because of the demographics of the city and its housing authority, TCH's process became perhaps the most diverse in the world. Toronto is home to 2.5 million people—5.5 million in the greater metro area—and Canada's largest concentration of immigrants.[10] Not only is half of the population immigrants, but half of these have lived in Canada less than 15 years. Torontonians speak over 140 languages and dialects, and English or French is the native language for only 53 percent of the population. Nearly half of residents consider themselves visible minorities.

Like many North American cities, Toronto is increasingly rich and poor. It is the largest city in Canada, the country's economic capital, and home to the third largest financial sector in North America.[11] The city's high-income population has increased since the 1970s—but its poverty rate has grown even quicker.[12] Almost 30 percent of the city's families live in poverty, up from 16 percent in 1990.[13] Most of these families are immigrants and people of color. And for many of them, TCH is home.

TCH is the second largest public housing authority in North America, with 164,000 tenants—6 percent of the city's population.[14] Only the New York City Housing Authority is larger. Many residents are new immigrants, elderly, disabled, or living in single-parent families—some of the city's most marginalized populations. Their average household income is only around $20,000.

The authority's housing stock is vast and decaying. Its 2,000 buildings include 45,000 units in apartment towers and 11,000 in townhouses or walk-ups. Though some buildings are concentrated in large developments, most are scattered across the city—unlike the notorious public housing projects in the United States (see figure 6.1). The buildings suffer from a $300 million backlog of repairs, and over half are over 30 years old.[15]

As a public corporation, TCH operates at arm's length from the city of Toronto. Although it receives funds from the city—its sole shareholder—it is managed separately. The Board of Directors, typically composed of four city councilors and nine citizens, oversees the corporation and is accountable to the city. Its relative autonomy has allowed it to experiment with new forms of governance and participation—like in Rosario.

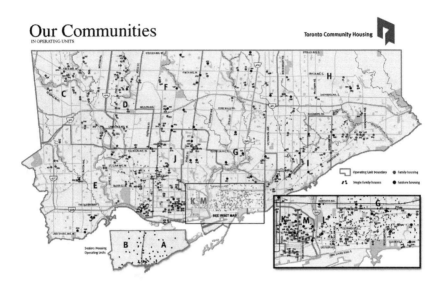

Figure 6.1
Map of Toronto Community Housing: Map of the city of Toronto divided into Toronto Community Housing's 13 Operating Units (OUs), which were established in 2008. OUs A and B at the bottom refer to the two seniors units, one unit in each half of the city. The inset at the bottom for OUs K, M, and L encompasses the downtown Toronto area. Each dot represents a public housing building. Image courtesy of Toronto Community Housing.

When PB started, however, TCH did not officially exist. The city's two housing authorities at the time—the Toronto Housing Company and the Metropolitan Toronto Housing Corporation—were merging, a process that was not finalized until January 1, 2002. In 2001, though, a few tenant engagement coordinators originally from Latin America heard about the Porto Alegre experience through contacts back home. Tenants were demanding more voice and expressing frustrations about the slow pace of repairs, and the housing authorities faced new funding cuts and difficult budget decisions. Staff thought that PB could help. Anticipating the merger, they collaborated to launch an experiment. After developing a model, staff and tenants tested it through two pilot projects, one in each of the old housing authorities. Once the companies merged, staff integrated the two processes.

Tenants began the first PB cycle in 2001 and finished in December 2003. They started by meeting in each building to choose their building's five top priorities. At each meeting, they also elected one or two delegates to represent their building in their Community Housing Unit (CHU) Council, the tenant government body in each of the city's 27 housing districts. These delegates met in their CHU Councils to decide, together with staff, how to divide the Council's funds among the priorities of each building.

Over the three years tenants allocated $18 million in capital funds for 237 infrastructure projects, such as new stoves, roof renovations, and playgrounds. Not only did spending better reflect tenant wishes, but tenants were also surprised by how much voice and authority they gained. As one tenant observed, staff "were shocked by how much we had to offer."[16] The process was a huge learning experience. Tenants gained a greater understanding of what happens in other communities, and they "learned what staff have to put up with"[17] Although most tenants started out focused on their own needs, after a few meetings many voluntarily gave up funds to support more needy communities.

After this initial success, TCH deepened the process in 2004. The next version gave more power to local housing communities and let tenants allocate $9 million each year, again just for infrastructure. Tenants decided 80 percent of the money through the CHU Councils. To allocate the other 20 percent—$1.8 million—representatives of each Council met in a city-wide assembly.[18] It was not until I first witnessed "1.8 Day," as tenants and staff call it, that I realized how much the event was like a game.

1.8 Day

In 2008 the North York Council Chamber, one of the old City Council halls in Toronto, hosted 1.8 Day. Shortly after 8 am on a Saturday morning, dozens of tenants began lining up at the registration table outside the building. Most of them awkwardly clutched poster displays, which were often as big as the tenants themselves. In a conference hall inside, the tenants arranged their displays on tables lining the walls. Each display presented the project that one CHU had proposed for funding. The tenants milled around the room, inspecting the posters and chatting.

The posters were designed to be seen. A proposal for a new handicapped-accessible playground—"Let All Children Play"—featured glossy photos of children playing, concise text boxes, and a 3D playground model made of children's toys (see figure 6.2). CHU 8's poster, crisscrossed in yellow "CAUTION" tape, warned about recent crimes in its building. Next to a bulging glass model of a security camera, built into the poster, was a proposal for new security cameras, interior lighting, and a key-card entry system.

Figure 6.2
Budget proposal display for playground improvements. Photo by author.

Foot-long swaths of yellowed peeling paint were glued to another poster, calling for a new paint job in a building.

At 9:30 am, staff called the tenants into the council chamber. The 27 delegates, one from each CHU, sat around the ring of booths at the front of the room (see figure 6.3). All but eight were women, and only seven were white. The other 15 rows of padded benches were full of alternate delegates and observers. Many tenants wore custom printed team t-shirts, with their CHU number or name on the front.

Alina, a staff coordinator, scooted up to the low podium at the center of the ring of delegates, to welcome the crowd. Short and South Asian, she spoke with an intense focus. She announced, with an exaggerated wink, that she had earned the facilitator role after winning a "tough screening process" by TCH's tenant PB Committee. "It's going to be an exciting day," Alina declared, before passing the mic to an older tenant leader in a knit white sweater. Anne spoke with more conviction than her body seemed to support. She asserted that thanks to the hard work of the

Figure 6.3
1.8 Day: Tenant delegates in the Council Chamber preparing to present their budget proposals. Photo by author.

tenants on the PB Committee, 1.8 Day was "tenant-led, tenant-run, and tenant-controlled."

Alina presented the day's agenda and rules, which were also distributed as handouts. For the next couple hours, each CHU would have five minutes to pitch its budget proposal and answer questions. When one minute remained, Alina would issue a warning. When time was up, her lovely assistant Joseph would ring the gong. Yes, the gong. Finally, after all the presentations, the delegates would vote.

To decide who would present first, Alina asked for an audience volunteer to come to the front and pick a number out of a canvas bag. A woman walked down the chamber stairs, reached her hand into the bag, rooted around, and held up a folded piece of paper. The chamber was silent. She slowly unfolded it, and shouted "CHU 21!" CHU 21's delegate rushed to the podium, accompanied by a rowdy cheer.

James, a slim Caribbean man, blasted out, "Good Morning!" The response was not lively enough for James. "I can't hear you," he teased. "I said Good Morning!" The crowd shouted back louder, and the delegate launched into his project pitch. A fluid speaker, James proposed a purging of pigeons. His high-rise was covered in moss, and pigeons were swarming the building to nibble. Even with hawks circling above, the pigeons waddled around nonstop. James performed a world-class waddle as he spoke, to the crowd's delight. The building residents, who constantly walked beneath the food-processing pigeons, were apparently less amused.

James asked for questions, and a few delegates obliged, waving yellow question cards in the air. As James clarified how and when the funding would be used, Alina interjected ominously, "One Minute." On the wall, a timer ticked down the seconds in alarm-clock red digits. Just as it reached 10, James stepped aside.

Next, CHU 22 asked for money to replace peeling paint with fresh coats. Waving a paintbrush in the air, the delegate pleaded: "Please paint your vote for CHU 22." CHU 23 made a repeat request from the previous year, for security cameras. In the past year several people had been murdered around the building, including a 16-year-old. "Without cameras," the delegate declared, "there's no justice." The other presentations breezed by, most followed by questions from the other teams.

After a short break, Janet, a ponytailed delegate wearing a baseball cap, told a tale about CHU 10. Once upon a time, in a building with shared kitchens, food was going missing. Janet raised an oversized plastic magnifying glass, bigger than her head, pretending to investigate. Searches for the culprit proved in vain. Janet's eyes gleamed as she proposed another idea: What if the building could install locks on the shared cabinets, so tenants could safeguard their food? And what if PB could fund those cabinets? The rest of the story, Janet concluded, was up to the voters.

While some presentations used poems, props, or dances, others were simple project proposals. For each, the CHU's alternate delegate held up their poster display, and paraded it around for the delegates to inspect. Only a few times did Joseph need to bang the golden gong, perched on a desk by the front row of seats. When he did, though, the tenants and staff burst out laughing.

In between laughs, the tenants debated serious issues. Many presenters used equity and democracy criteria to justify their projects: they had presented the project before but were not funded, they had the oldest security system in the city, or tenants had voted their proposal as most important. In the Q&A, delegates often asked which specific groups would most benefit from the project—the elderly, disabled, youth, and so forth.

After the presentations, lunch was served in the room next door. Teams from each CHU compared notes and starred proposals to vote for. Many entrepreneurial delegates made the rounds, lobbying and trading votes. Others grilled their peers about their projects, to decide on their final votes.

The polls opened after lunch, with each CHU's delegate voting via computer in a private room. Each delegate had 10 votes, to cast as they liked—except for their own proposal. Once the last votes were cast, everyone returned to the council chamber. To prolong the suspense, a representative from the tenant PB Committee spoke. Dressed in jeans and jean jacket, with scruffy brown hair and a goatee, Bryan asked, "Did everyone have fun today?" The response was emphatic. "Yes!" Lifting the curtain on the backstage discussions, Bryan mentioned that tenants were still debating many questions about the process. Should there be more votes per CHU? Fewer? A fixed closing time for the polls, to speed up the process?

Alina returned to the podium and asked for a drum roll. A projector lit up a screen at the front of the chamber. Alina scrolled down the projected spreadsheet, revealing the top vote-getters one by one. Of the 27 projects, 13 won funding, including re-paintings, playgrounds, security systems, CHU 10s cabinets, and CHU 21's moss eradication. The winners cheered and exchanged hugs—and some losers did too. Several delegates gathered their belongings and started to leave. But there was a problem.

The budget pot still had $113,000 left—enough to fund another project—but there was a four-way tie for 14th place. No one knew what to do. Some tenants called for another vote among the four contenders, while others argued that the remaining money should be divided up. Clusters of people started debating on the Council floor, and amid this chaos, Alina asked if the delegates wanted to vote by hand or secret ballot. The calls for hand voting won, and most of the tenants sat back down to prepare for a final round of presentations and voting.

The tied CHUs each got two minutes to present again, and then the delegates voted by hand. CHU 19's playground project won. The next day, *The Toronto Star*'s story about TCH's "ultimate reality show" started with the messy scramble for the last bit of money.[19]

Despite the confusion at the end, 1.8 Day did many things well, often using game mechanics. Organizers communicated the rules through *multimodal presentation*—on handouts and through oral explanations. The rules also felt more legitimate, since they were *generated and agreed upon by participants*. Through the PB Committee, tenant leaders had decided the plan for 1.8 Day, taking ownership over the process.

The event inspired healthy competition, over what could have been bitter battles. The ring of official seats at the front of the council chamber formed a *magic circle*, encouraging delegates to more fully step into their roles. Once inside this circle, they addressed questions directly to each other, without staff filters. The day encouraged *group vs. system competition*, as teams of tenants from each CHU competed against the constraints of a limited pot of money and limited number of votes. They could not vote for their own project, taking the edge off the competition. Perhaps as a result the tenants never downplayed other projects, and they often collaborated by trading votes. Even though real dollars were at stake, the delegates consistently played by the rules, treated each other with respect, and accepted the results. At the same time the clear sense of competition pushed them to craft more creative presentations and to work harder to attract votes.

But during the chaotic closing to the day, the competition became less productive and less healthy. The event reached its climax when the top 13 projects were announced, leaving the four-way tie as an anticlimactic nuisance for most teams. Once they saw that their building would or would not receive funds, many tenants tuned out. The more limited competition of the tie vote no longer held their attention. For the four tied groups, however, the competition became more antagonistic. They shouted over each other as Alina tried to devise a voting process. Organizers planned for group vs. system conflict, but the tie shifted the focus to a zero-sum *group vs. group* contest, in which one group's victory would clearly come at the others' expense. After the votes were cast, one loser accused fellow delegates of rigging the vote. But other losers cheered good-naturedly, and maintained their faith in the process. "We'll keep fighting," vowed Merlyn. "We're not going down that easy. We'll come back stronger."[20]

Why did most tenants accept the results, even when they lost? In part, this was because TCH clearly linked participation to outcomes. Tenants had to first progress through a series of *levels*. The building meetings, delegate elections, CHU Council meetings, and finally 1.8 Day helped tenants feel that they were advancing toward their goals. The *concrete outcomes* of building improvements also served as a guiding light, sustaining motivation during such a demanding process. "PB is the one thing," a staff coordinator told me, "that people will come out for, if nothing else. Even if there's a shooting in the building, people might not come down to a safety meeting. But if you say there's money for painting your balconies, people will come."

To further seize tenants' attention, 1.8 Day began with a dose of *chance*, as a volunteer picked the first CHU name out of a hat. The timer on the wall served as a vivid *status indicator*, measuring how quickly tenants were advancing toward the speaking time limit. Its red digits spoke louder than any facilitator could. The day ended with *points*, as votes were traded, cast, and tallied, letting people track the effects of their participation.

Finally, the event was more engaging because it appealed to the senses. The poster displays were full of *vibrant visuals*—pictures, artwork, and dazzling colors. The gong added a dramatic *sound effect*. The tenants could physically (and strategically) play with a set number of *resources*—10 votes. The *hidden information* of the vote tallies kept delegates in suspense, until staff gradually unveiled the results, one by one.

Most people left 1.8 Day smiling, whether or not their project won. But tenants and staff still had a big concern. TCH set aside $9 million annually for PB, but 1.8 Day only allocated $1.8 million. What about the other $7.2 million?

1.8 × 13 = 9

Since 2004 TCH had divvied up the other 80 percent of the $9 million among its 27 Community Housing Units. Each CHU's Council was supposed to run its own mini-PB process to allocate its funds. Some did. But in others, the situation was murky. In response, TCH decentralized PB in 2009, organizing multiple Allocation Days across the city, where tenants decided how to spend the full $9 million. This boosted participation and local buy-in, but also left staff and tenants with big challenges.

The problems with the old system started at the local level. "This is where the corruption occurred," said Rajesh, the PB Coordinator. "The priorities would be presented by staff, and they'd basically just start giving out the money through the tenant council, with whatever fashion of tenant council happened to be there that day. In some buildings, they'd make sure every building got its first priority. In others, staff would make recommendations and tenants would kind of say, 'ok, that makes sense.'"

Some local staff supported tenant participation, while others saw it as a burden imposed by head office. Many frontline workers had been at the housing authority for decades, and were allergic to change. "The Health Promotion Officers," a local staffer explained, "have an average tenure of like 25 years, and a sense of 'we'll do it our way.'" As Alina admitted, many building staff think, "Why are we bothering? We know better than tenants."

By running a central 1.8 Day, head office managed to design a deeply empowering event, but at the cost of broader participation throughout the city. Derek Ballantyne, the CEO of TCH, saw this trade-off as a fundamental flaw of PB. He complained, as a tenant participation coordinator recalled, that TCH had "created so many perks for this $1.8 million that you have people in t-shirts and doing great presentations and running around with boards, missing the opportunity to have control over the other $7.2 million."

In 2009, tenants got that opportunity. At the end of 2008, TCH reorganized its management structure, creating an opening for a new PB format. The housing authority replaced its 27 CHUs with 13 Operating Units (OUs), to cut down on middle management. Two of these OUs were dedicated to seniors housing, while the rest were divided into East, West, and Central districts (see figure 6.1). As a result the tenant PB Committee, with representatives from each CHU, suddenly became obsolete. Then, in early 2009, Ballantyne left TCH.

Tenant engagement staff lobbied to have a separate Allocation Day, modeled after 1.8 Day, in each OU. Management accepted. Like before, local staff held building meetings—over 300 total—in each building. At these meetings tenants selected their top building priorities and elected delegates. Most OUs then held delegate orientation meetings, to prepare the building delegates to present their projects and navigate the budgeting process. Finally, each OU organized an Allocation Day.

Allocating in the East

In July 2009 I attended Allocation Day for the East's Operating Units. The district managers had opted to hold the three Allocation Days on one day, under one roof. At 9:00 on a Saturday morning, I arrived at the Armenian Youth Center. Inside the modern brick building, two men in patterned African tunics beat away on wood drums slung under their shoulders, welcoming new arrivals. Down the hall, a mass of orange t-shirts, attached to staff bodies, was registering tenants at three tables. The backs of the shirts read "EA$T PARTICIPATORY BUDGETING DAY." Past the registration area was a small caféteria, with tenants and staff milling around. Three long rows of tables faced an improvised stage, and a continental breakfast spread enticed a line of attentive tenants.

At 10:00, Heather, the East Manager, welcomed us to the first East Participatory Budgeting Day. She introduced the staff scattered around the room, some of whom received rousing cheers. As Heather explained, we would all meet together in this room, then divide into smaller rooms for each OU. Michelle, the top manager in the East, offered some background on PB, going over its principles, the amount of money available in the East ($2,222,335), and how the money could be used. After 20 minutes of context, she earnestly concluded, "I wish you have a ton of fun."

Toronto Community Housing

By this point, however, most tenants seemed lulled to sleep. Then the questions started to flow. Wanda complained that she hadn't received her project quote till the day before and it looked too low—could she change it? Heather responded that she could use the most up-to-date information she had. Another tenant said that an emergency had forced her building to change its priority. Heather asked if the change was made through a building meeting (yes), and then gave the ok. Some big changes were being made very quickly.

Heather explained how the allocation process would work. Each building would have three minutes to present—no questions this year. During lunch, tenants could deliberate. After lunch, they would vote with "dotmocracy"—the same system used to select priorities at the PB building meetings. Each building would receive 15 sticker dots, each dot representing one vote. To vote for a building's project, the delegates would stick one or more dots on that building's poster. "You can do whatever you want with the dots," Heather clarified, "except sell them or put them on your own project."

Finally, Heather raised a tricky old issue—ties. "If you have three communities tied with 25 votes, what do you do?" A man called out, "Fight to the death!" Heather shot that down. She proposed three other options: (1) the building with the first name alphabetically wins, (2) split the money three ways, (3) pick the cheapest project first. Tenants interrupted with a barrage of questions, and a fourth option: a revote for the tied projects. Heather called for a show of hands, and the revote proposal won—the same one that got the 2008 1.8 Day in trouble.

I walked to the Operating Unit G room. Leroy and Betty, the two facilitators, stood at the door welcoming tenants. Leroy was a burly man in his 50s, with a bald head, glasses, and a deep Caribbean voice. He spoke and moved slowly and deliberately, while Betty waved tenants into the room warmly. Her auburn hair was tied in a ponytail, and she wore a loose gray dress. There were 20 other people in the room, representing 12 buildings. Leroy and I were the only men. Otherwise, the group was diverse, with two black hijabs, a colorful Jamaican hairwrap, a backward baseball cap, and plenty of blond, red, black, and gray heads of hair.

Betty announced that OU G would allocate $520,000. Then Leroy plodded through his talking points—the agenda, lunch, a stretch break, voting. He stood stiffly and stuck to his script, seeming uncomfortable. Betty warned that she would wave a white "30 seconds" poster when tenants approached the speaking time limit.

Leroy called the first presenters: Willowdale Building. The delegates were absent, so Leroy read their proposal from the program. On to the next building. Juanita moved to the front, and put on a show. Her building had a series of recent garage break-ins, so the tenants switched their top priority to a garage security camera. Juanita flipped through a series of colored placards, like in Bob Dylan's famous video (see figure 6.4). "Tenants' cars broken into." "Car insurance up—cameras will be cheaper!" "Priorities for us is cameras" "Cost: $35,000" The tenants cheered. Juanita sat down and let out a huge sigh. "I was nervous!"

The presentations continued, with hearty applause after each. Playgrounds, painting, and landscaping projects all grabbed the spotlight. Most people read prepared notes, with differing degrees of grace. At least half the dollar quotes in the program were incomplete or incorrect. One tenant proposed combining her first and second priorities, since both were cheap. Leroy said it was up to her, leaving it unclear what exactly tenants would vote on.

Figure 6.4
Project presentation. Photo by author.

Toronto Community Housing

Wanda and Amy were the last showstoppers. They wore team shirts and hats. The white shirts said, in handwritten Sharpie text, "Paint + Plaster." The same text was on their hats, but with an extra line: "Victory!" Wanda let loose an impassioned speech, as Amy held stark photos of peeling paint and mildew. "Our hallways are full of mold and mildew. We have not been painted or plastered in 10 years! Our children are breathing in toxins!" She spoke in a tense staccato. "Fix our walls and paint! Give it to us for the children!" The other delegates responded with wild applause and warm laughs.

The presentations ended shortly before noon, and Leroy dismissed us for lunch. Some tenants perused the posters, which were now taped up around the room.

After lunch, staff handed out sticker dots. Back in the OU G room, Betty had some news. "Don't vote yet—we have a speaker who arrived late." The last delegate was ill, so he sent a neighbor as a substitute. Tanya's hair was bundled on her head, wrapped in a green and yellow cloth. She knew nothing about PB, so Betty quickly filled her in. But Tanya's attention was mainly focused on her two young kids, who wandered around the room.

Betty asked the tenants if Tanya could present her building's project, and they agreed. Tanya pleaded for votes for kitchen improvements. The bathrooms above were leaking, damaging the ceilings. "We, as community need to come together to make sure they do the job. . . . If we fix it good one time, it'll be good. . . . So if we could voice that to them, because when we call the call center, they don't understand." Tanya wavered, unsure of her words.

It was time to vote. For the next 15 minutes, tenants circled the room, putting one dot here, two there. Some of them whispered and exchanged suspicious glances. "Ok, you did it?" "Respect, respect." "That's not nice. . . ." Juanita plopped into her chair early, fuming. "We're not thinking about the whole community! We should look at each project and consider what's needed . . . not trade votes." Coincidentally, Juanita had not attracted many votes.

In a few minutes, everyone was seated. Wanda saw that Tanya still had a sticker left, and asked if she was going to cast it. Tanya said she wouldn't bother, since one dot would not matter. On hearing this, other tenants implored her to cast her last vote. Tanya remained seated, but gave her last dot to her 8-year-old son, and told him to put it wherever. He drifted over to the poster displays, and tenants started lobbying, "Put it there!" "On the green one!" He stuck "his" dot on the green poster, and sunk back into his seat.

166   Chapter 6

At the front of the room, Sally muttered, "She's not allowed to do that. . . ." "It's no big deal," Wanda responded. "It's just one dot." But Sally kept complaining: "So anyone can just come in and puts dots wherever? If specific people are supposed to vote, why is a child going up?"

A storm erupted. Tanya leapt to her feet and shouted, "My friggin' god, I was right here! I didn't want to get up. Get over it! I mean, oh my god, it's a child! He's not going to hide it or anything." She grabbed her bag and headed toward the door, gesturing for her kids to follow. "One vote, whoopee!!!" Other people chimed in, mainly in support of Tanya.

Betty tried to make peace, searching for words. "The rules say that a presenter or alternate can cast the votes. If the presenter or alternate gives the dots to someone else and that person votes as the presenter wants, that's all right. However, it's fine to question the process . . . we're trying to follow rules." After a few minutes of debate, Tanya reluctantly sat back down.

Juanita was the next to erupt. "I have a beef with this. I don't think we should be going around and asking others to vote for our projects. That's rigging votes, when you see your fellow tenants conniving." People muttered, but there was no uproar. "We should be able to look at a community, listen, and vote on our own, without having me come to you and say vote for me and I'll vote for you. That is not a true democratic system."

Another woman proposed voting silently, one building at a time. Tanya agreed that they should not have to lobby for votes. "If we work together we get a lot more things done than fighting against each other." Lots of applause, but I was not sure for what.

Betty suggested that people take a break, as she counted the votes to see who won. In a few minutes, Leroy started writing the funded projects on the board. With the tenants now back in the room, Betty read down the list of vote totals. As she reached the end, $30,000 remained. The last project (Willowdale), had asked for $30,000. It seemed that everyone would be funded, and the tenants let loose a giant cheer.

Then Wanda pointed out a problem. Her project's official TCH-printed poster—the one that was now covered in sticker dots—had the incorrect cost. It listed the project at $20,000, instead of the $40,000 that Wanda presented in the morning. Her building got 18 votes, putting it in second place. With that many votes, should it not get the full amount requested? But if Wanda's building got full funding, Willowdale could not. Betty pointed out the irony: "You've got a last-place project that's fully funded and a second place project that isn't."

Tanya proposed that everyone compromise and take less funding, to leave enough for all. Patricia rejected the idea, explaining that projects had to be completed by the end of the year—if they did not have enough money, the building lost all the funding. Mina, a coordinator from head office who had crept into the room, presented what seemed to be the only options: (1) Wanda's building could get $20,000 and everyone else would get full funding. (2) Wanda's building could get the full $40,000, and the tenants could vote on which of the last two projects would be funded.

Wanda stood up. "Our price was wrong," she began. "It was not my fault. But I am willing to keep the $20,000." Mina again presented the two options, adding that Wanda was ok with the $20,000. This time, there was consensus: "Number one!" Wanda's building received $20,000. The tenants cheered, and at 2:40pm, everyone walked away happy. Well, almost everyone.

Eager to talk with Wanda, I lingered in the room. She was conflicted. "I gave it the best shot I could. Went for broke. I could have won. I did win, but . . .." She looked down. "I think I would have won no matter what, even with $40,000, even with $90,000. It wasn't fair. And I didn't get the quote till yesterday." But she had faith in the process, and felt that the voting itself was fair. Except for that unfortunate typo on her official poster. So after nearly winning the vote but only getting half her project's funding, would she be back next year? "Oh, I will be, I definitely will be."

Three Steps Forward, Three Steps Back

I was not sure what to make of this new Allocation Day. On one hand, dozens of public housing tenants had deeply engaged with some of the biggest questions and challenges of democracy: Who decides the rules, and who can change them? What criteria should guide decision-making? Who has the right and responsibility to participate? The tenants were learning democracy by doing.

And they were gaining power. Unlike in previous years, tenants directly and transparently decided how to spend the entire $9 million of PB money. Each of the 188 funded projects was proposed and picked by tenants.[21] And the process engaged many more tenants. Three hundred and thirty-five delegates attended Allocation Days, over six times as many as in the prior year. More than 70 percent of them participated for the first time. The 13 smaller Allocation Days, rather than one grand event for the entire city, made it easier for less experienced tenants to participate. "It was a cozier atmosphere," Alina reflected. "People who wouldn't normally feel comfortable speaking to large groups of people were able to make passionate cases for why they wanted things funded."

The 2009 PB also made staff more comfortable with the process. Since local staff ran each Allocation Day, they were forced to take more ownership over PB, and commit to it. "This was the best PB ever," said Evelyn Murialdo, Director of the Community Health Unit, "in terms of my unit not being the stars. It was the first time that field staff took a real leadership role."

But this new role created new problems. In years past, a team of passionate central staff had carefully planned 1.8 Day. There were always surprises, but in general, the day was tightly organized. Facilitators knew how to rouse participation and were comfortable using playful techniques. In 2009 teams of local staff, often with less PB experience, were responsible for managing Allocation Days. Many of these new facilitators were not as supportive of democratic participation, or of game techniques. They also had little time to gather the information and resources necessary to facilitate— such as accurate project quotes and complete handouts.

The field staff generally rose to the occasion. On evaluation forms, most delegates said they enjoyed the day. But because staff were less prepared, the rules were often less clear. Staff asked tenants to propose their building's top three priorities but only vote on the number one priorities. Many tenants were confused about the point of the other priorities, justifiably so. Some staff said there would be a second round of voting, but the funding pot was too small to even cover the first round's proposals. No OUs actually voted on second or third priorities. It was also unclear if there would be sanctions for buildings that did not send a delegate—would they be disqualified?

In the end, staff had to issue too many rulings—arbitrary interpretations of the rules. Had tenants been more involved in writing the rules, perhaps the rules would have been less puzzling. The tenant PB Committee was disbanded in 2008, however, and was not replaced. In its absence, staff across the city had not agreed on—or written down—a clear set of rules. "I guarantee," reflected one tenant, "that if I call and ask for the rules . . . I'd wait a while and they wouldn't have it. . . . If rules are not concrete, they're going to be broken."

The rules were especially unclear and inconsistent for the meetings prior to Allocation Day. At the building meetings many staff still referred to PB as 1.8 Day, often offering vague explanations of what projects were eligible and what would happen to the priorities. "They just asked us what we wanted," Frank recalled from his building meeting. "I live in a building

Toronto Community Housing

where three-quarters of the people are Orientals and a lot don't speak English, and they just thought they were sort of giving their opinions."

Unclear rules sometimes led to unhealthy competition. Like at 1.8 Day, most tenants were able to negotiate their differences and compete for funds while maintaining a strong community bond. But staff had still not figured out how to deal with tie votes for the last bit of funding—a common occurrence. Each OU handled the challenge differently, often leading to bitter debates at the end. More important, the dotmocracy voting rules were only loosely enforced. Some tenants openly admitted that they voted for themselves, despite the rules. Tenants who were not delegates—or even adults—cast votes. Not surprisingly, delegates who did not bend these rules, such as Sally and Juanita, were upset.

Unprepared staff, unclear and inconsistent rules, and unhealthy competition fueled some of the big problems that, as I explained in chapter 1, are common in games. When the rules were hazy, some staff manipulated participation. Betty, for example, encouraged Tanya to deliver a special presentation right before the voting, giving her proposal a boost. "There's always the issue with staff not being neutral enough," Rajesh said, speaking from his experience as the PB Coordinator. In one OU, for example, a tenant proposed that if a building was not represented by a delegate at Allocation Day, it should not receive votes. Staff agreed, and announced this as a new rule. "Staff shouldn't respond saying that's fine," Rajesh argued. "Endorsing it gave it the staff approval that it didn't need." Bob, a delegate, complained that staff "changed some priorities to suit themselves. In our building, fixing the gardens was voted the second priority, but this just disappeared. I asked the supervisor what happened and he didn't have an answer. They just didn't want the gardens to go through." Thirteen percent of delegates said their Allocation Day priorities did not reflect discussions at their building meeting.

Staff were not the only manipulators. Some tenants gamed the system, taking advantage of unprepared staff and unclear rules to gain benefits for their buildings. They combined projects, switched priorities, and changed quotes, often bending the rules. In most cases these changes responded to new conditions on the ground, and they seemed to be in the best interest of their buildings. But regardless, these tenants gained an extra—and perhaps unfair—advantage over their peers who stuck strictly to the rules.

In the end, were the decisions fair? Over 90 percent of delegates said so. Even though, unlike in OU G, many buildings did not receive funding. Staff and tenants generally understood that the results were as fair as the funding constraints allowed. "If we fund 20 projects and don't fund 19 that's fine," a local staffer said. "It's part of any budget process."

The tenants who cried foul were most concerned with vote trading and cheating. Like Juanita, they complained that delegates were winning funding based mainly on how aggressively they lobbied and traded votes, rather than how important their project was. Delegates who were new to the process or who lacked the confidence to negotiate often went home empty-handed. Most staff were skeptical that they could curb vote trading and lobbying. "I'm not sure you can avoid that," Heather said. "What other process do we have in society where people don't do that?"

A few tenants worried that the results were biased toward the most popular or charismatic presenters. "Those who have good charisma," one delegate fretted, "those who buddy-buddy, have a better chance of winning. I say this as someone who has these charms and who has won today. What about those who do not speak good English, who are shy, etc.?"

Finally, the PB process was also less fun than in years past, partly because it was decentralized to local staff and counted on less support from energetic central staff. During the presentations at 1.8 Day, the gong and timer added laughs and dramatic tension. Betty's bland "30 seconds" sign did neither. Vibrant visuals and sound effects may be harder to reproduce when events are spread out. After all, TCH only had one gong. Dotmocracy offered a fun way to vote—an enjoyable core mechanic—but cheating made it less fun.

In Toronto, as in Rosario, designing democracy like a game was not easy. In 2009 central staff managed to diffuse participatory democracy and game mechanics more broadly across the housing authority. But local staff were not always able or eager to follow head office's lead.

Growing Games in the North

Since 2001 Toronto Community Housing has shown that game design can enhance democratic participation outside of Latin America. True, governments in the Global North face more obstacles to designing participation like a game. Social, economic, and political conditions may be less conducive. Citizens tend to be less inclined to play. And game approaches must break more sharply with norms of participation. Yet despite these challenges, most game mechanics had similar effects in Toronto and Rosario.

At 1.8 Day, TCH dished up heaping portions of game mechanics, and most tenants left happy. Staff communicated rules through multimodal presentations, and made them more legitimate by letting tenants craft them. The event brought tenants into the magic circle of the Council

Toronto Community Housing

chambers, and structured healthy competition by pitting groups against the constraints of the system. Even losers accepted the results, since levels, concrete outcomes, status indicators, chance, and points forged a clear link between tenant participation and budget allocation. The day was more engaging because of vibrant visuals, sound effects, resources, and hidden information.

In 2009 the housing authority replicated 1.8 Day across the city, creating new opportunities and challenges. The new process boosted participation, tenant power, and field staff buy-in. But it also left PB with less prepared staff, less clear rules, and less healthy competition. These shortcomings enabled some staff and tenants to manipulate the process, sometimes leading to unfair outcomes. They also made PB less enjoyable. Could game design address these problems?

7 My Game Design Experiment

In the last chapter we saw that game mechanics can be introduced into democratic processes even in the unfertile soils of Toronto. Yet we also saw how difficult this approach was, as head office staff struggled to embed new participatory practices throughout the housing authority. Knowing that game mechanics work is not enough. If game design is to have more impact on democracy, governments and organizations need effective strategies for applying it.

To identify such strategies, I ran an experiment. Over two years I led a *participatory evaluation* at Toronto Community Housing, in which I worked with a team of tenants to evaluate and improve participatory budgeting. We studied game design and tried to instill game mechanics in the PB process, in order to address the problems raised in the last chapter. I also tried model the change we were seeking, by designing the evaluation around games and game mechanics.

The participatory evaluation showed how games—not just game mechanics—can work in democratic processes in the Global North. While TCH did not include games in PB meetings, in the evaluation we played games in nearly every workshop. In the process we learned an immense amount about the challenges of designing games for democracy—and how to overcome these challenges. Unstable players and conditions, frequent interruptions, and scant preparation time sometimes wreaked havoc with our games. But we found ways to preempt and alleviate these problems: setting aside more time for design and playtesting, relying on simple materials and flexible activities, and spending more time modeling gameplay during workshops.

We also demonstrated how to redesign a democratic process to make it work more like a game—and showed that such a redesign improves the quality of participation. During the evaluation, we used games and game-like activities to reach broad agreement on key changes to the 2009 PB process. By implementing many of these changes in 2010, staff were able to address key problems and increase tenant satisfaction with the process. The participatory evaluation showed that carefully crafted games and game-like activities make democratic participation more enjoyable and productive.

The next section explains why we launched a participatory evaluation and how it worked. I then describe several games and game mechanics that we used to engage tenants and staff, and what they taught us about game-based participation. Finally, I discuss how the evaluation attempted to redesign the PB process based on the lessons of game design.

Participatory Evaluation of Participatory Budgeting

In 2009, when I did the bulk of my research at TCH, I faced a daunting logistic challenge. Most of the Allocation Days were happening on the same day, at the same time, in locations hours apart. Even with my research assistant, Joanna, there was no way we could observe most of the meetings. But I had heard that each would be distinct, so I did not want to miss out. When I raised this problem with staff, we devised a creative solution.

To cover more ground—and make the research more useful to TCH—I would work with a team of tenant researchers. Through a *participatory evaluation*, we would study PB together. And based on our research and the lessons of game design, we would propose improvements.

When planning the evaluation, we drew on broader lessons from participatory action research. This research approach, as Yoland Wadsworth explains, "involves all relevant parties in actively examining together current action in order to change and improve it."[1] Since the 1980s, development programs across the world have incorporated participatory action research methods into evaluation processes.[2]

Based on these experiences, participatory evaluation offers several benefits, when done well.[3] It inspires new observations and ideas, by bringing together different perspectives and interpretations. It focuses evaluation questions and tools, by creating more opportunities for staff and participants to indicate what information they are interested in and anticipate using. It helps prevent misunderstandings and generate sounder conclusions, as evaluators are constantly checking their ideas with staff and participants. And it makes evaluation more useful, by generating more support for recommendations. When staff and participants play an active role in evaluation, they are more likely to believe in its findings and take action in response.

My Game Design Experiment

The participatory evaluation also let me put game design into practice. As part of the research, I planned and facilitated 17 workshops with tenant researchers and staff. In these workshops, I tried out many of the games and game mechanics used in Rosario, and designed new games and game-like activities.

First, Joanna and I met with the tenant researchers to collectively learn about PB and tenant participation, design research methods, and collect data. Then we all observed building meetings, delegate orientation sessions, and Allocation Days—39 events in all. At these events we interviewed 55 tenants. We also carried out a survey of 464 tenant delegates and interviewed 16 staff members. After this field research, we met again to analyze the data and develop recommendations. In workshops with staff, we reviewed and revised the recommendations, to build broad agreement around next steps. Finally, we compiled each year's findings and recommendations in a report, which served as a guide for the next PB cycle.

Soon after starting the research in June 2009, TCH hired me to facilitate two years of participatory evaluation. The first year was closely aligned with my book research, while in 2010 there was less of an explicit game focus.

Twelve tenants participated the first year and 13 the second year, with some overlap. The tenant researchers included youth and seniors, immigrants and non-English speakers, and people with physical and mental health issues. Their highest level of education ranged from middle school to law school. Some researchers had full-time office jobs, while others could not use email.

So how did we engage this diverse lot of tenants in studying and improving PB? With games, of course.

Designing My Own Games

During the two years of participatory evaluation, we used dozens of games and game-like activities. Below, I review only a few examples, to draw out lessons for democratic participation.

Each year, we started the first workshop with a hodgepodge of around a dozen tenants, sitting around a conference room table and looking at us expectantly. Some faces we recognized, others we did not. Some tenants knew each other, others did not. Some were good friends, others *definitely* were not.

Before we could work together, we had to turn these dozen individuals into a team. We began with a Theater of the Oppressed game called *Good Day*.[4] I asked everyone to find someone—preferably a stranger—shake their hand, and exchange names. Still holding on to that hand, each person had to then shake hands and exchange names with someone else. The goal: to introduce yourself to everyone in the room, while always clasping someone's hand. I had already played the game at a Theater of the Oppressed event in Rosario, so I was curious to see how it played in Toronto.

The tenants started slowly, rising to their feet and shaking a neighbor's hand. Next they began stretching and hopping to reach another hand, then another, and another. As bodies twisted, faces began to smile, then laugh together. The game worked. But why? Partly, as game designer Jane McGonigal points out, because touching people is one of the fastest ways to build social bonds.[5] According to McGonigal, touching causes the body to release oxytocin, a chemical that makes people like and trust each other. Acting silly in front of others has a similar effect.[6] The game was fun because we touched and made fools of ourselves.

To learn more about our fellow researchers, we moved on to one of my favorite popular education games—*School Bus*. "It's the end of the school day," I explained, "and you walk outside. But you don't know what bus to get on. I'll tell you where the buses are going, and you'll run to catch the bus that matches you." I would ask a question and pose three or four possible answers, then assign each answer to a virtual bus in a different part of the room.

First, I asked, "Where were you born?" Tenants born in Toronto were to move to the bus by the door, elsewhere in Ontario to the front board, elsewhere in Canada to the back wall, and outside Canada to the window. Next, "How long have you been at TCH?" "When was the last time you went to a public meeting?" And a few other questions. After each one, the tenants sprinted to a virtual bus in a particular corner of the room. When they arrived, I asked them to look around, to see how their peers responded. Often they interjected to explain their answers.

Good Day and *School Bus* helped animate the tenants and build a team. They forged new bonds, lightened the mood, and activated people's bodies—in less than five minutes and with no materials or set-up. *Good Day* broke down barriers by connecting people physically. *School Bus* revealed commonalities and differences, offering insight into what each person brought to the table. Both games relied on inherently fun *core mechanics*— twisting your body and running across the room.

As *School Bus* made apparent, some tenants had more experience with participation, research, and PB than did others. After reviewing the research plan, we wanted to pool together the diverse tenant experiences and develop a common body of knowledge. So we played *Jeopardy*. Before the

My Game Design Experiment

workshop, I posted four columns of colored paper on the wall. The top row listed categories: PB at TCH, PB around the World, The Practice of PB, and Participatory Evaluation. The next four rows of paper were labeled with point amounts—from 100 to 400.

The tenants divided into three teams: Lions, Tigers, and Bears. The basic rules were the same as on TV. When a team picked a point amount (such as PB at TCH for 300), I flipped the sheet of paper on the wall to reveal an answer (for example, "How long the first PB cycle at TCH lasted"). If the team posed the right question (for example, "What is 3 years?"), it selected again. Despite this *reinforcing feedback loop*, teams guessed wrongly often enough that they each took several turns. As a *balancing feedback loop*, I asked that a new tenant from each team pick the point amount each turn, to discourage any one person from dominating.

While we played, the tenants were glued to the game. They whispered covertly, strategized about point amounts, and cheered when they posed the right questions. When we reviewed at the end of the workshop, they remembered almost all the information—especially for the questions they got wrong! *Jeopardy* requires substantial preparation and setup, but I've found it easy to adapt the basic skeleton of the game to virtually any subject. And because most people already know the game, they tend to jump in quickly.

Ironically, the biggest wrench in our game of *Jeopardy* was another game. Halfway through, we were interrupted by a pair of portly seniors kindly informing us that we would have to vacate the room ASAP. We were meeting in the rec room of a TCH residential building, and apparently, it was BINGO Night. Staff had double booked. After a fruitless debate, we stripped all the flipcharts and papers from the wall, and relocated to the tiny reading room downstairs. Its walls were lined with bookcases, so we could not set up the *Jeopardy* materials and finish the game.

Unfortunately, this was not an uncommon occurrence. When working with cash-strapped local agencies such as TCH—and even more cash-strapped tenants—plans are always subject to change. Other workshop activities were interrupted by lost keys, broken video projectors, missing interpreters, bedbug scares, and AA meetings. These surprises present a challenge for games. Many games rely on particular equipment or spaces, and changes in the environment can make the game unplayable. If you're kicked off the basketball court, it's hard to play basketball. To prepare for disruptions, we tried to always have backup activities ready, to plan multiple variations of each game, and to use materials that could be quickly set up and moved.

After learning basic information on PB and tenant participation, we began to develop research methods and materials. First, we identified research indicators—what signs we would look for—to evaluate the quality of PB. With guidance, the tenants brainstormed dozens of indicators, from "number of tenants participating" to "whether cost estimates for projects are presented" to "whether tenants think the process is fair." After revising the indicator list for a couple weeks, however, the tenants were still unsure how they would spot wild indicators in the field.

To help the researchers situate abstract knowledge (indicators) in concrete practice (PB meetings), I prepared a *Matching Puzzle*. I divided the tenants into two teams and dumped two stacks of paper cards—one orange, one blue—onto their tables (see figure 7.1). On each blue card, an indicator was written (such as "whether tenants think the process is fair," "info

Figure 7.1
Indicator matching puzzle: Staff and tenant researchers matching research indicators with real-world examples. Photo by author.

My Game Design Experiment

presented in multiple formats"). On each yellow card was an example of an indicator in practice (such as "in an interview a tenant complains that the voting was rigged," "staff give tenants a handout with the rules and read the handout aloud"). The goal was to arrange the cards on the table so that each blue card was matched with the most appropriate orange card. Each team would get one point for every correct match.

The game worked wonderfully, in a sense. The tenants became deeply absorbed, debating the practical meaning of each indicator. They learned what they might look for when doing field research, and finally "got" many of the indicators. Despite repeated requests to wrap up, they begged me to let them keep playing. But there were two problems.

First, the puzzle was harder than expected. Of course, the matches were all clear to me. Not so for the tenants. I had planned a half hour for the activity, but after 45 minutes the teams were only halfway done the puzzle. Second, there were more possible matches than I had realized. When we reviewed the teams' matches at the end and tallied points, the tenants suggested many correct matches that had escaped me. For example, I matched the indicator "visual aids" with the example "Staff display photos from last year's allocation day at a building meeting," but a tenant (correctly) thought that it could also pair with "There is a flipchart with ground rules for the meeting on the wall." I clarified that they had to find the *best* match, but still, they had a right to complain when some of their matches weren't considered the best.

These are typical problems of game design, and there is a typical solution—*playtesting*. Wrinkles always surface during initial prototypes of a game, and designers iron them out by testing the games and making adjustments. Unfortunately, game designers usually have more time and budget for playtesting than facilitators do. In Toronto we only had a couple days between workshops to design activities, and a limited budget for preparation.

Even with such constraints, a few minutes playtesting games with a friend or coworker is wise—it can save hours of grief later. And when budgets are modest, games should be too. Intricate games can be highly effective, but only if there are enough resources to design them properly. In the case of the puzzle game, I could have used fewer cards to make the game quicker and easier, and written the examples so that they only matched one indicator well.

Regardless, we needed more than indicators and methods to do research. The tenants also needed research skills. To sharpen their observation skills, we played a game that I called *What Changed?* Before workshops, I always prepare the room—rearranging chairs and tables, posting flipcharts and signs, distributing handouts, and so forth. At the start of one workshop, I divided the tenants into three teams, and asked each team to list as many things as possible that I had changed in the room.

Suddenly, the researchers looked around the room differently, examining everything around them. After a few minutes, the teams had full lists written on flipchart paper. As we tallied the points from each team, the tenants realized how much work goes into facilitation, and what they should look for at the PB meetings. Of course, several tenants interpreted the same change in different ways, highlighting how there is no single objective viewpoint, and how important it is to write clear field notes. One tenant's "set up chairs" was another's "arrange chairs in circle around table."

The tenants went out into the field to observe building meetings, and then we met again to debrief. I wanted the researchers to openly share what they had learned, but in a safe space where they would not be judged. I recruited Sheila to lend a hand. Sheila was a new tenant who would be joining the research team, and she needed a crash course in what we had learned. Oh, and Sheila was imaginary.

To start the exercise *Help Sheila*, I put an empty chair at the front of the room and pointed to it. "This," I announced, "is Sheila." "Hi Sheila!" the tenants called out. I explained that Sheila was nervous about the research and desperate for advice, and asked if the tenants could share a few suggestions and lessons learned. Angela recommended to "pay attention to body language." Dionne advised, "Don't let what you know interfere with what you're observing." For Simone, the key was to "Keep moving . . . don't stay in one spot. See the room from different angles." Sheila was not the only one learning, as the tenants shared and absorbed different perspectives and research skills.

So far the workshop games were mainly educational. But after observing dozens of PB meetings, interviewing just as many tenants and staff, and surveying hundreds of tenants, we needed to move beyond learning. We needed to decide what findings and recommendations to present. To synthesize the piles of field notes, interview notes, and surveys, we tried our luck at dating.

I adapted a *Speed Dating* exercise from popular educator Gilda Haas (aka Dr. Pop), to enable tenants to quickly share and extract research data.[7] We first reviewed some past findings and discussed how to write new ones. I then asked each tenant to flip through their notes and write down on a My Findings handout their top findings for each stage of PB.

My Game Design Experiment

When their sheets were filled in, we divided into two groups. In each group, pairs of researchers interviewed each other about their findings. The first researcher tried to explain her findings, while her partner wrote down the most important points, as he understood them, on a Team Findings handout. To get the story right, the partner often had to ask questions of clarification. After five minutes, I yelled "Switch!" The researchers now had to find new group members to interview, writing down their new dates' findings elsewhere on their Team Findings handouts.

Finally, we asked each group to talk about their dates, and pick out the take-home points. On flipchart paper, Joanna and I wrote down the top findings that had survived three rounds of refining and vetting: a researcher's My Findings handout, their dates' Team Findings handouts, and the group discussion. At the next workshop, we reviewed the top findings and repeated the *Speed Dating* exercise to develop recommendations.

There was one awkward moment during the speed dates. In Joanna's group, some of the tenants were becoming distressed by the brisk pace of the exercise. By the time they figured out what to say, they had to switch. Why was their response different? Because that group included the oldest tenant researchers and a non–English speaker, slowing down the discussions. Fortunately, Joanna picked up on this tension and suggested extending the times for her group. By adapting the rules to the participants, we fixed the problem and made the exercise more inclusive.

Finally, after presenting our findings and recommendations at a workshop with staff, we wanted to reach agreement on which recommendations to implement. We divided into several mixed groups of staff and tenants, and asked each group to review, revise, and agree on one category of recommendations (such as building meetings, outreach). To make this process quicker and more fun, we passed out three cards to each person: green, yellow, and red.

We asked the group members to review the recommendations in their category one by one. After reading a recommendation, each person should hold up a card to indicate their opinion. If they agreed fully, the green card. If they totally disagreed, the red card. If they had mixed feelings, the yellow card. If there were only green cards, the group approved the recommendation and could move on quickly. If only red cards, the recommendation was tossed. If a mix, the people with the red or yellow cards explained their qualms, and the others tried to address them. The groups kept voting and filtering opinions until they reached consensus, often rewriting the recommendations and adding new ones.

We had already used the colored cards with tenants, so most of them took to the exercise. Some staff, however, were reluctant. When Joanna and I, as facilitators, had fun with the cards, holding them up high and pleading to see people's colors, tenants and staff followed suit and raised their cards. Enthusiastically modeling the activity was essential for enticing others to take part. When they did, we moved more quickly through the recommendations, and we moved more in general. The physical activity and vibrant colors helped keep people alert and engaged.

Over two years of participatory action research, the tenant researchers were able to participate more actively and democratically thanks to the eight games and game-like activities described above—and others. *Good Day* and *School Bus* built trust and team spirit, while letting us learn more about each other. *Jeopardy, Matching Puzzle, What Changed?*, and *Help Sheila* enabled the researchers to understand different perspectives, learn new knowledge and skills, and apply this knowledge and skills practically. *Speed Dating*, and *Green Yellow Red Cards* helped us synthesize opinions and reach decisions. All of the games activated people's minds and bodies, and made participation more fun.

But game design was hard. Changing conditions and interruptions sometimes made play impossible. Games often did not play as planned— they took longer, were more difficult, or led to problematic player actions. We had little time to test games before workshops, and some people were reluctant to play.

To address these challenges, we tried to playtest games in advance, even if only briefly. We prepared backup activities and different versions of each game, in case we had to change plans. We used simple materials that could be easily assembled and moved, and learned to set aside more time for game design. When confronted with new challenges in the middle of games, we adjusted the rules, to make the games work for everyone. When people hesitated to play, we modeled the activities more enthusiastically and assertively.

Despite the bumps in the road, the tenants thanked us for the games. "I used to look at games as a waste of time," Patricia said after the research, "but now I see their use." Several tenants said that they started recreating our workshop games in other meetings that they organized. "Games help," Lorraine concluded, "to ease whatever tension and anxiety you came with . . . you're more able to participate because then you can think clearly." We were glad the tenants had fun, but this was not our main goal. The real test was whether games and game mechanics could make PB work better.

My Game Design Experiment

Leveling Up

While playing games in research workshops, the tenants learned about game design. We discussed many of the game mechanics described in chapter 3, and some tenants tried designing their own games for our final workshops with staff. While conducting research, we asked the tenants to look for ways that game mechanics could improve PB. Using the lens of game design, we devised recommendations for how to establish clearer and more consistent rules, to foster collaborative competition, to link participation with outcomes, and to make PB more engaging. After proposing a laundry list of recommendations in 2009, we tracked whether they were followed in 2010.

From a game design perspective, perhaps the biggest problem in the 2009 PB cycle was unclear and inconsistent rules. Staff followed different rules in different locations, and often failed to communicate or explain them clearly to tenants. Our research team proposed how game mechanics could remedy the situation:

- At all meetings, present rules orally, on handouts, and on flipcharts. (*multimodal presentation*)
- Before building meetings, prepare and distribute a PB brochure and other basic materials in multiple languages, so that tenants can process the rules in advance. (*multimodal presentation*)
- During building meetings, distribute building improvement plans, explanations and photos of capital and operating costs, menus of common project costs, and lists of past budget priorities—so that tenants can refer to this information precisely when they are deciding priorities. (*just-in-time information*)
- Sign a one-page agreement with each delegate describing the position. (*multimodal presentation*)
- Hold trainings for delegates on public speaking, preparing project proposals, and budgeting, to communicate the rules in more ways. (*multimodal presentation*)
- Provide delegates with displays and other materials from the previous year, to model how to prepare their own presentation materials. (*modeling*)
- Create a new PB Steering Committee to help plan the process and set the rules. (*player-generated rules*)
- Make the rules consistent across the city—so that the rules are less open to interpretation and judgment calls. (*minimize rulings*)
- Organize trainings and preparation meetings for local staff—so that they can present the rules more consistently and less ambiguously. (*minimize rulings*)

Clearer and more consistent rules, however, were not always enough. To address the unhealthy competition that sometimes surfaced, basic rules and activities had to change. The 2008 and 2009 PB Allocation Days were ill-prepared to deal with tie votes, and in 2009 dotmocracy voting fueled bitter feelings. To fix these problems, we proposed steering the type of conflict toward group vs. system, and away from the more antagonistic group vs. group conflict. In other words, we hoped to focus tenants' attention on fitting the many proposals into the limited pot of money, so that they would feel less like they were pitted directly against each other. We also suggested preparing clear contingency plans for when this was impossible.

Our main recommendations for encouraging healthy competition were as follows:

• Allow each delegate to cast 15 votes—in 2009 some Allocation Days had used 10, others 12. The more votes in the system, the less likely ties were, and so the less likely that teams of tenants would be pitted directly against each other. (*discourage group vs. group conflict*)

• Use electronic voting or paper ballots to secretly cast all votes at once—rather than publicly casting (or not casting) sticker votes on each building's poster, which encouraged teams to pressure and spy on each other. (*discourage group vs. group conflict*)

• Outline a clear process for resolving ties before the voting, in case teams were forced to compete directly in a final tie vote. (*establish clear group vs. group protocol*)

Though unclear rules and unhealthy competition were the two main challenges, we also saw other room for improvement. While the results of PB were crystal clear for tenant delegates, most tenants were oblivious to the outcomes. Many had no idea that PB existed, or that it could bring concrete improvements to their buildings. To boost their interest, we proposed three ways to make the outcomes more visible and measurable:

• Publicize completed PB projects with ceremonies and announcements. (*measurable outcomes*)

• Have delegates report back to their buildings and tenant councils about PB. (*measurable outcomes*)

• Send the PB results to the TCH Board of Directors to publicize. (*measurable outcomes*)

Finally, we noticed that in parts of the city, PB had become less fun and engaging when it was decentralized. Energetic head office staff were no longer in charge, and most local staff were not as passionate about leading

My Game Design Experiment

exciting events. Some districts, however, were trying creative ways to make participation fun, so we suggested replicating and adding to their box of tricks:

- Use pictures and graphics in handouts and presentation materials. (*vibrant visuals*)
- Decorate Allocation Days with colors, balloons, and special t-shirts. (*vibrant visuals*)
- Play music at Allocation Days. (*sound effects*)
- Vote via dotmocracy at all building meetings. While dotmocracy seemed ill-suited for the high-stakes elections of Allocation Days, it offered a more accessible and fun way to start prioritizing projects at building meetings. (*enjoyable core mechanics*)
- Allow time for Q&A after each Allocation Day presentation. Listening to dozens of presentations in a row is not fun, and another activity could break the monotony. (*enjoyable core mechanics*)

So what impact did all these recommendations have? In 2010, during the following PB cycle, TCH fully or partly implemented 18 of the 20 recommendations above. Some of the most important recommendations were followed entirely. The Allocation Days switched to paper ballots, rather than dotmocracy. Staff presented clear procedures for resolving tie votes—before the voting. Delegates had time for Q&A after each presentation.

Other recommendations were adopted in altered form, or in some parts of the city more than in others. More staff modeled poster and presentation examples from the prior year. More rules and information were distributed before and during building meetings—often through handouts, posters, and oral presentations. More Allocation Days featured music and decorations.

Of course, some of these changes might have occurred without us. Several staff, however, said that they used the final evaluation report as a guide for planning the next year's process. Considering the feedback from staff and the slow pace of change before the evaluation, it seems we made an impact. This was largely because we worked hard to build staff buy-in. The two final evaluation workshops that we held, to revise and finalize the report, were the main forum for staff and tenants across the city to discuss PB. At these workshops, staff and tenants reached agreements on all the recommendations (player-generated rules), so both sides became more invested in the process.

According to our surveys of tenant delegates, the changes addressed some key problems of the 2009 PB. Only 1 percent of tenant delegates said the purpose and rules of Allocation Day were not clear in 2010, down from 10 percent in 2009. Only 5 percent said they did not have enough time or support to prepare for Allocation Day in 2010, down from around 30 percent in 2009. Thanks to clearer and more consistent rules, TCH cut in half the number of delegates who said their proposals on Allocation Day were different from the ones that tenants had selected in their building meeting. Tenant delegates' overall rating of PB jumped 20 percent.

Tenants liked the process more partly because it was more fun. "It's nice to have a good time," one tenant remarked. "We don't have to be so hard-nosed all the time . . . let the community have fun." Staff generally agreed. "Fun doesn't mean belittling," Alina said, "fun just means engaging. I know that if I have to go to something boring, I'm going to choose not to go. I'm going to find something else." Most local staff recognized that fun and games were not always appropriate and needed to be handled with care, but also that they could make participation more effective. "Everything doesn't have to be so serious," Heather argued. "And I'm not saying that housing and where people live isn't serious. But sometimes we get so bogged down in the seriousness of it that we can't problem solve."

In 2010 we evaluated the process again, to solve another batch of problems. With a new team of researchers, we made another round of recommendations. Many of the new suggestions were also implemented. A key one, unfortunately, was not. Since giving birth to PB, TCH had done little to spread the news. Not only were many tenants unaware of this ambitious effort at democracy and transparency, but so were most local politicians and community organizations. In 2009, we suggested that staff invite elected officials, community organizations, and media to observe Allocation Days. In 2010, we made this a formal recommendation. But TCH did little external outreach either year. Staff were stretched thin already, and outreach fell by the wayside.

The lack of public outreach came back to bite in 2011.[8] In late February, TCH's auditor released a controversial report on the authority's finances. The media dished out juicy details, such as a $40,000 staff Christmas party, $1,000 chocolates, and shady contracting deals with China. Beyond PB, TCH's budget had been spared public scrutiny. A few staff had taken advantage—albeit at a relatively modest scale, when compared with the luxuries and creative accounting of most corporations.[9] Nevertheless, Rob Ford, the city's right-wing mayor and an advocate of privatizing public housing, demanded that the TCH board and CEO step down immediately.

They resisted, but Ford swept through City Council, riding his wave of post-election popularity. At 11:57pm on March 9, after two full days of debates and tenant protests, the Council approved Ford's proposal.[10] The TCH board was ousted. Case Ootes, one of Ford's right-hand men, was installed as sole interim director. Ootes promptly purged the CEO. Ford even used political pressure to force former CEO Derek Ballantyne out of his post-TCH job. The following year, the new TCH administration scaled back on PB.

During the public debates, no city councilors cited TCH's transparent PB process or tenant participation system, as points in favor of the authority's board. But should we have expected anything else? After all, the councilors were never really invited to the game, not even to observe from the sidelines.

Learning by Playing

When TCH replicated 1.8 Day across the city in 2009, it expanded tenant participation and power, but also created new challenges. Local stuff struggled to take on new responsibilities, communicate the rules to tenants, and guide the delegates through healthy competition. To identify solutions to these problems, I facilitated a diverse group of tenant researchers through a participatory evaluation.

As we researched how to improve PB, we studied game design and played games. By playing dozens of games and incorporating game mechanics into workshop activities, we built trust and team spirit, learned about each other and different perspectives, and developed and applied new skills and knowledge. We even managed to synthesize the researchers' opinions and make decisions with staff about changes to the PB process.

But we faced many challenges along the way. When designing games and game-like activities, we had to cope with unstable players and conditions, frequent interruptions, and scant preparation time. Fortunately, we found ways to overcome most of these challenges: setting aside more time for design and playtesting, relying on simple materials and flexible activities, and modeling gameplay.

Not only did the participatory evaluation use games and game mechanics to engage tenants, but it also helped redesign the broader PB process to do the same. Through the evaluation, we reached broad agreement on changes to the 2009 PB process. After TCH implemented most of our recommendations, PB worked better.

When we carefully crafted games and game-like activities for the evaluation, the researchers learned more and enjoyed the work more. When TCH mixed more game mechanics into PB, tenants participated more smoothly and left more satisfied. It paid to play.

But in Toronto as in Rosario, using game design for democratic participation was not easy. Sometimes, games and game mechanics solved old problems but sparked new ones. In the next chapter, I reflect on the experiences in Rosario and Toronto, to propose tools and strategies for navigating the field of game design more safely. With a clearer lay of the land, could we steer a more rewarding course, while avoiding the landmines?

8 Conclusion: A Toolbox for Fixing Democracy

In the past four chapters, we met city builders and puzzle masters, speed daters and blind painters, anti-oppression jokers, and dotmocratic voters. Before that, we learned about game designers and the tricks of their trade. So what, in the end, does all this mean for democracy?

At the beginning of the book, I posed two questions: *Can games make democratic participation more appealing? If so, how?* After years of research, I believe the answer to the first question is a firm yes. Most of the time, in the programs I studied, games and game mechanics made participation more enjoyable and attractive. In many cases they also made it more effective, transparent, and fair.

The second question, of course, is the tricky one. In this chapter, I review *how* game design can make participation more appealing. I propose that democratic processes include five kinds of games: animation, team-building, capacity-building, analysis, and decision-making. I also suggest that governments and organizations design these processes more like a game, by drawing on 26 *game mechanics* that engage the senses, to establish legitimate rules, generate collaborative competition, link participation to measurable outcomes, and create experiences designed for participants.

In the next section, I outline the main roles of *games* for democratic participation. I then show how each of the *game mechanics* introduced in chapter 3 can be mixed into democratic processes. The following two sections assess the dangers of games and game mechanics, and propose strategies for overcoming these challenges.

Finally, based on all these lessons learned, I suggest that we rethink democracy and games. I argue that governments and organizations should make participation more fun, to increase citizen engagement and trust in democracy, and to empower people to democratically decide more issues that affect their lives. To accomplish this, we should directly—and carefully—include games and game mechanics in democratic processes, not only through digital technologies but also in face-to-face interactions.

Games in Democratic Processes

The most obvious way to harness the power of games is to directly include them in democratic processes. Each of the programs I studied involved games to some extent. The City of the Children and Theater of the Oppressed programs inserted games in workshops and meetings. Rosario Hábitat did as well, but less often. Though Toronto Community Housing did not include games in participatory budgeting, I used them in the participatory evaluation. These games helped facilitators activate people's bodies, build teams and capacities, analyze information, and make decisions.

Animation games transformed passive observers into active participants, usually at the beginning of meetings and workshops. Citizens typically arrive at public meetings in a state of passivity, accustomed to sitting in their chairs, watching, and listening. To get people out of their seats and moving around, the City of the Children and Theater of the Oppressed workshops played games of *Stop*. The game challenged people to walk and greet people in more animated ways. Likewise, the *Good Day* handshake game that we played in Toronto forced tenants to stand, clasp hands, and twist their way around the room. In both cases, people were visibly more awake and energetic after a few minutes playing, and they then spoke and acted more fluidly later.

Team-building games integrated active individuals into collaborative teams. People often engage as individuals, with particular interests and demands. But to deliberate and make democratic decisions, they need to work together, at least somewhat. The City of the Children instilled team spirit through the *Newspaper Game*. The young councilors learned that to stay alive, they had to stand together on sheets of newspaper, clinging to each other for support. Rosario Hábitat's *puzzle challenge* taught *villa* residents that they had to communicate clearly within *and* across groups to find the missing puzzle pieces—and to fix neighborhood problems. After these games, players spoke and listened more openly, letting others talk and building on their ideas more than before.

Capacity-building games armed people with the skills and knowledge necessary to work together. Democracy is a demanding exercise, requiring capacities that are often underdeveloped or neglected. Citizens need

Conclusion

to listen and observe critically, speak clearly, and negotiate wisely. They also need technical information, and knowledge about their neighbors and communities. During the participatory evaluation in Toronto, we included capacity-building games in almost every workshop. *What changed?* taught tenants to hone their observation skills, as they scoured the room for changes we had made during setup. By playing *Jeopardy*, tenants processed and applied new knowledge about participatory budgeting, tenant participation, and evaluation.

Analysis games offered accessible ways to understand complex systems, by breaking these systems into manageable chunks. Democratic processes ask people to assess problems with complex causes and propose solutions with complex effects. To meet these challenges, participants need to unravel complexity. The Theater of the Oppressed game *Image of the Word* showed how actors could break down abstract concepts and complicated laws into simple bodily poses. Each person presented part of the concept or law, and together they created a full and legible image. In Toronto, we used the *Matching Puzzle* to break down another daunting topic—research indicators. Only by mixing and matching indicators with real-world examples did the tenants grasp how our indicators played out in practice.

Decision-making games enabled players to harness their new knowledge, skills, and understandings to reach concrete decisions. Even with clear analysis, people rarely agree entirely. Yet they need to transcend or negotiate different opinions if democratic processes are to have an impact. After our field research for the participatory evaluation in Toronto, for example, we had piles of data and diverse opinions about what it meant. Through *Speed Dating*, the tenants decided which data were most relevant, agreeing on a common list of findings and recommendations. In the Theater of the Oppressed workshops, participants identified tricky practical problems from their workplaces, and then decided on solutions through Forum Theater games. In these games, spect-actors squared off against other actors, trying to make their solution work while the actors tried to maintain the oppression. When the actors won, the group rejected the solution. When the spect-actor won, the group endorsed it.

These five categories—animation, team-building, capacity-building, analysis, and decision-making—are not mutually exclusive. Many games, including several mentioned above, served multiple purposes. But as useful as the games were, people could not play *all* the time. Each process mixed games into other activities. To make these other activities more enjoyable and effective, facilitators often built them around game mechanics.

Game Mechanics in Democratic Processes

Game mechanics, as we learned in chapter 3, are the rules, structures, elements, and processes that designers use to shape gameplay. But they are not just for game designers. In Rosario and Toronto, facilitators also used game mechanics, to shape participation. These design tools helped negotiate conflict, establish rules, clarify outcomes, and boost engagement. Below, I review the key game mechanics used, along with examples of how they played out.

Conflict and Collaboration

Conflict Type: Designers structured different types of conflict, to shape the basic relations between players and the game. Sometimes, conflict was *individual vs. individual.* In Rosario Hábitat, facilitators asked two *villa* residents to individually place their lots on the same part of the map, putting them into direct conflict with each other (this did not work so well!). At TCH, individual tenants ran against each other to win election as a budget delegate for their building. In some Rosario Hábitat workshops, facilitators imposed *individual vs. system* conflict, asking a *villa* resident to individually place her lot on the map, so that it fit in the limited space available.

The most collaborative types of conflict involved groups. The Theater of the Oppressed workshops used *individual vs. group* conflict, with individual spect-actors intervening in Forum Theater skits to overcome an oppressive situation, while other actors tried to maintain the oppression. The two processes at TCH involved *group vs. group* conflict. During PB, a tie vote between three groups' proposals resulted in a head-to-head re-vote. The participatory evaluation featured many group competitions, such as when three teams of tenants competed to identify the most changes to the room, in the game *What Changed?* TCH and Rosario Hábitat also used *group vs. system* conflict. At Rosario Hábitat, *villa* residents worked together to fit their lots into the limited map space while sticking to the program rules. At TCH, each team of tenants tried to win funding before the pot of money ran out.

Magic Circles: Several programs created artificial play spaces that were temporarily separated from the outside world. The puzzle map of Rosario Hábitat's lot allocation workshop displaced conflict onto a safe map space, where residents could rearrange puzzle pieces according to agreed-upon rules. The ring of official seats in the City Council chamber at TCH's 1.8 Day created a special space for tenants to present and debate proposals.

Balancing and Reinforcing Feedback Loops: Facilitators rarely designed processes to balance or reinforce player performance. One exception was the

Jeopardy game during the participatory evaluation at TCH. During the game we *balanced* unequal player performance by asking a new tenant from each team to pick the point amount each turn, to deter any one person from dominating. The game also *reinforced* performance by allowing teams that guessed right to pick the next category and point amount.

Rules
Multimodal Presentation: Most of the programs communicated rules in multiple formats to help participants understand them. At Rosario Hábitat and TCH, for example, rules were regularly posted on the wall, distributed via handouts, and read aloud. Rosario Hábitat also inscribed the rules about lot and passageway size onto colored cutouts, in the lot allocation mapping puzzle.

Just-in-Time Information: Many workshops presented rules and information at the precise moment when they were useful for a player. At Rosario Hábitat, facilitators presented rules about passageway shape and size at the moment when residents arranged passageway cutouts on the map. At TCH's building meetings, many staff shared building plans at the moment when tenants began debating which projects to propose, to frame these discussions.

Modeling: Most of the programs demonstrated or walked participants through actions that they would soon need to undertake, or rules they would need to follow. At TCH, staff distributed old poster displays to show tenant delegates how to prepare their own. Rosario Hábitat's colored passageway cutouts served as physical scale models of the rules governing passageway size—straight lines, 1.5 meters wide for access to one house, and so on. These techniques helped people understand how rules translated into practice.

Player-Generated Rules: Participants could sometimes write the rules, making them seem more legitimate. In Toronto, the tenant PB Committee developed the 1.8 Day rules in advance. In Rosario Hábitat's workshops, *villa* residents decided on criteria for negotiating land conflicts.

Sanctions: The programs rarely imposed penalties or other enforcement for rule violations. When they did, controversy often ensued—such as when TCH staff and tenants in one community decided that if a delegate did not show up to present her building's proposal, the project should not be funded.

Rulings: Ambiguous or incomplete rules sometimes forced staff to act as judges, declaring whether and how a rule applied. At TCH, for example, staff had to rule on whether a child could cast a vote and whether a tenant delegate could combine two project proposals. These sudden—and often arbitrary—rulings fueled skepticism and mistrust for some people.

Outcomes

Clear Goals and Objectives: To let participants know what they were supposed to be doing, the programs generally presented clear goals and objectives. Rosario Hábitat staff told residents that the lot allocation goal was to arrange house lots on the map. At TCH, the PB goal was equally clear: decide which projects will win funding.

Measurable Outcomes: Staff in Rosario and Toronto planned for concrete and measurable outcomes—money, infrastructure, policies, and positions. For example, $20,000 for building repairs at TCH, paved streets and new houses at Rosario Hábitat, a new set of rules for the TCH PB process, and new tenants chosen as building delegates. Rosario Hábitat used vivid imagery to make outcomes even more tangible, such as through "Yesterday and Today" posters on the walls, showing pictures of *villas* before and after interventions.

Uncertain Outcomes: The programs often kept outcomes uncertain, so that participants could not know in advance who would win what. At Rosario Hábitat, for example, each family knew it would get a new lot, but none knew *which* lot—until the end of the relocalization workshop.

Chance: Staff never left major results to chance, but sometimes they used chance to make minor choices. At TCH's PB Day, for example, a volunteer picked a building name out of a hat, to determine who would present first. Chance helped keep some outcomes uncertain, while adding drama.

Points: Several programs let people measure their progress toward goals through a numerical score. In Rosario, *villa* residents voted on decision-making criteria, and the criteria with the most points became top priorities. Some residents also tracked how many square meters they would win with their new lots. In Toronto, tenants voted for project proposals, and the proposals with the most votes won funding.

Status Indicators: At TCH, staff used status indicators to signal tenants' progress at PB allocation days, such as through a timer on the wall counting down the seconds remaining in the five-minute presentation time.

Levels: Some programs broke participation down into stages, requiring that people complete a set of tasks before moving to the next stage. Rosario's *villa* residents, for example, had to first select decision-making criteria, before they were allowed to pick lots. TCH tenants had to progress through building meetings, delegate elections, tenant council meetings, and finally 1.8 Day, in order to win funding.

Engagement

Vibrant Visuals: Facilitators often weaved engaging images, graphics, and other visual effects throughout workshops. They filled rooms with cartoon puzzle pieces and cards, colored paper signs, spectacular poster displays, and custom designed t-shirts, catching people's eyes and enveloping them in the event activities.

Sound Effects: Occasionally, meetings used sound or music to immerse players in activities. During Rosario Hábitat's puzzle challenge, facilitators blasted *Reggaetón* music to energize players. In Toronto, staff struck a gong when a delegate's speaking time ran out, sparking laughter and focusing attention.

Enjoyable Core Mechanics: During the most engaging workshops, the most common activities were inherently enjoyable. People stretched and acted during Theater of the Oppressed, stuck papers on walls and matched puzzle pieces in Rosario Hábitat, and placed sticker dots on voting sheets at TCH.

Choice Points: The programs gave participants regular opportunities to make decisions that affected the course of the process. At Rosario Hábitat, for example, residents identified criteria, ranked the criteria, arranged passageways on the map, arranged housing lots, and decided on locations for relocated homes. The parade of decisions kept people engaged.

Resources: Some meetings provided people with scarce items that they could use to achieve goals. *Villa* residents could play with the resources of passageway and lot cutouts, while TCH tenants could strategize over how to allocate their 10 votes. These resources made participation more complex and interesting.

Hidden Information: Staff rarely hid information from players, in order to gradually reveal it later. Perhaps the only example was at TCH, where staff kept the final PB vote tally secret, until revealing the winning proposals one by one. This generated anticipation and suspense.

Characters: Theater of the Oppressed made the most use of characters. People cast themselves as apathetic office workers, rebellious teachers, and other characters in Forum Theater skits, letting them experiment with new roles and empathize with other perspectives. In the participatory evaluation in Toronto we used Sheila, an imaginary tenant researcher, to tease out tenants' lessons learned in the game *Help Sheila.*

Narrative: Staff sometimes built narrative elements into participation, to situate it within a broader story. In Theater of the Oppressed, actors presented a story of a sex education conflict in a Catholic School. Rosario Hábitat facilitators told a broader long-term story of neighborhood change and improvement, to explain each step of the participatory process. In both of these Rosario programs, narrative added deeper meaning to individual actions.

Metagaming: The programs rarely organized related activities outside of games or game-like processes. The closest case was the tenant committee at TCH that discussed the PB process and proposed changes. During the participatory evaluation, we also proposed that TCH celebrate completed projects at regular report-back meetings and ceremonies, to engage more tenants in PB outside of the process itself.

In the end, the five programs used all the game mechanics discussed in chapter 3, though some more than others. Though 26 game mechanics is a lot, facilitators need many tools to deal with the challenges of the trade. Each game mechanic improved the quality of participation at some point. When I interviewed staff at each program, I shared the list of game mechanics and asked whether they were relevant for their workshops and meetings. Most facilitators welcomed the array of ideas. "The list is great," a TCH staffer told me. "You should go through something like this before you plan a meeting."

But even if staff reviewed lists of games and game mechanics when planning events, they would not necessarily use these tools wisely. As we saw in the last four chapters, games and game-like activities can backfire.

Five Lurking Dangers

In the introduction, I posed five potential dangers of using games and game-like activities for democratic participation. For the programs I researched, games never led to the most feared danger—violence. The others—unfair outcomes, lack of fun, trivialization, and manipulation—caused some problems, though only in limited circumstances. These problems did not seem more common than in other democratic processes, but they still tarnished participation on some occasions.

Violence: None of the games led to violence, for a simple reason: Like most games, they were not violent. Staff did not ask participants to engage in any violent activities. Even when the subject matter was violent—such as child abuse in the Theater of the Oppressed workshops—the real life portrayals of violence were restrained. They were also nothing to laugh at. Perhaps because the games were all face to face, they did not seem to desensitize people to violence.

In Rosario Hábitat, game mechanics actually turned violent community resistance into productive collaboration. By funneling conflict through safe spaces, clear rules, and playful activities, facilitators opened space for democratic deliberation and decision-making.

Unfair Outcomes: The programs did not seem to end in many unfair outcomes, at least according to the people involved. In interviews and surveys the vast majority of participants and staff said that the results were fair. Why? Since they were so actively involved, they were able to scrutinize decision-making and understand the reasons behind disagreeable outcomes. If a *villa* resident lost land in a lot allocation workshop, she knew why and knew that the outcome was based on criteria that she had approved.

Even if people thought the outcomes were fair, this does not necessarily mean that they were. Some *villa* residents and TCH tenants went home winners more because of their charisma or negotiation skills than their needs. Others left without their fair share because of inconsistencies in the rules—such as Wanda's underfunded wall repairs at TCH. Yet these instances were rare, and did not seem more common than in other democratic processes. If anything, the relatively transparent rules of the Rosario and Toronto programs helped level the playing field, keeping powerful players from reaping undue benefits.

Lack of Fun: Not only were the programs generally fair, but they were also generally fun. Or at least *more* fun than pursuing similar goals through more traditional means. Many participants explicitly said that they had fun, especially for the City of the Children, Theater of the Oppressed, TCH's 1.8 Day, and the participatory evaluation. Even when discussing laws, budgets, and research, they had a good time. No topic was too dry to play with. The games and game-like activities were not always raucously fun, but they still seemed more enjoyable than typical meeting activities

Yet certain workshops were less fun than others. Some Children's Council meetings involved more fidgeting than laughs. Some Rosario Hábitat workshops deteriorated into painful shouting matches. And when TCH decentralized its PB process, many of the Allocation Days felt less exciting. What did these non-fun events share in common? Without fail, they involved fewer games and game mechanics than other program events.

Trivialization: While too few games and game mechanics can suck the fun out of events, if facilitators spend too much time delivering fun and games, they could trivialize serious political issues. Fortunately, with only a few exceptions, participants did not say that the games or game-like activities felt trivial or inappropriate. They did not always welcome these activities at first, but after diving in, they generally recognized that games could help tackle serious problems. In fact, oversimplification of complex real-world issues—whether into condensed skits or colored puzzle pieces—was key to letting people engage with these issues in meaningful ways.

In one case, though, play and games trivialized participation in the eyes of outsiders. The City of the Children's Plaza Dreams program failed to impact public policy because city officials and planners found it trivial. And with good reason. The abstract paintings and poetry that emerged from the program's workshops were not substantial enough to contribute meaningfully to urban planning decisions. Because facilitators rigidly separated play from work, they did not engage participants in the serious questions that needed to be addressed, around issues such as accessibility, environmental impacts, and safety.

Manipulation: Since the facilitators had so much power, they could have manipulated participants to achieve certain results. I found that at most events, facilitators strove to be neutral, deferring to participant opinions. They posed questions and prodded people to ask their own questions, and they changed plans in response to feedback. Games and game mechanics helped bridge language barriers between experts and citizens, making complex policy issues more accessible to community members. Once people understood the issues, they could engage more actively and keep a watchful eye on staff. Often they challenged facilitator instructions or assumptions, steering activities in new directions.

But staff manipulation was sometimes a problem, in particular at TCH. Some local staff coerced tenants into proposing or approving certain projects. At other times they liberally interpreted voting or discussion rules, changing the results in meaningful ways. These abuses were not pervasive, though they were common enough to worry tenants and head office staff. They persisted largely when the rules of the process were not clearly established or enforced. Yet despite these problems, local staff manipulation at TCH had been even more widespread for spending decisions *before* PB. If anything, incorporating game mechanics into PB helped uncover and stamp out abuses.

In the end, game design rarely caused major problems. But in some limited instances it generated unfair outcomes, trivialized serious issues, failed to make participation more fun, and enabled manipulation.

These problems seemed to surface most under two conditions—when there was not enough support from decision makers up above or capacity from facilitators on the ground. In Rosario, many city officials did not believe the City of the Children's playful methods generated serious policy proposals. Program staff alienated decision makers by insisting on the

Conclusion 199

purity of children's play, and by refusing to consider adult concerns such as safety and cost. It should be no surprise, then, that the program's budget was sliced in half, and that almost none of its proposed plazas have been built. Likewise managers in some TCH communities did not see the value of active tenant engagement, and so they tried to manipulate or subvert it.

Elsewhere in TCH, and in some Rosario Hábitat projects, reluctant or unprepared facilitators were the problem. Not everyone is cut out to design and lead fun workshops, especially without much preparation or training. Many facilitators seemed uncomfortable playing with puzzle pieces, or unable to clearly communicate rules. Even the best designed plans would not work in their hands. Games are like jokes—a lot depends on the delivery.

Games and game mechanics depend on political will and capable facilitators, but these preconditions are not set in stone. To some extent, designers and advocates can accommodate—and build up—limited political support and facilitator skills. Even if top officials are not keen on games, some staff may be. The Theater of the Oppressed group got hundreds of youth workers to play by going through mid-level contacts at the Department of Children. Once positive feedback from the first workshops filtered up through the Department, officials decided to extend the program.

Even without capable facilitators, institutions can find ways to make games work. First, they can contract out, hiring people who have the right skills. This strategy worked well for the Department of Children, when it contracted the services of the Rosario Theater of the Oppressed Group. Second, old facilitators can often learn new tricks, if they are taught. When Rosario Hábitat's workshops flopped at first, it organized a series of facilitator trainings, bringing in participatory planners from Mexico to model games and playful techniques. Finally, management can recruit and hire more capable facilitators. Community engagement managers at TCH spent years bringing in local staff with more enthusiasm and experience in grassroots participation, building up a critical mass of skilled facilitators. This enabled head office to eventually decentralize PB. In the end, games and game mechanics can only be effective tools if decision makers believe in them and facilitators know how to use them.

Five Winning Strategies

The programs in Rosario and Toronto managed to avoid the dangers above when they systematically weaved together games and game mechanics.

There are no simple or universal recipes, but the programs generally fared better when they tried to engage the senses, establish legitimate rules, generate collaborative competition, link participation to measurable outcomes, and design for participants.

Engage the Senses: Democratic processes usually focus on engaging people's minds, through presentations and discussions. But words alone rarely captivate attention. To engage participants more fully, facilitators in Rosario and Toronto animated their bodies and senses. They used animation games to get people moving, and kept them moving through later games. When not playing games, they designed participation around enjoyable and physical core mechanics, such as acting out scenes and arranging items on walls and maps.

Facilitators also engaged people's eyes and ears. Rather than just use a few PowerPoint presentations or handouts, they filled workshops with vibrant visuals—ornate posters, colored paper, cartoon cards, gigantic maps, transparency cutouts, and custom-made t-shirts. Workshop spaces kept participants' eyes glued to the action. Meanwhile, sound effects such as music and gongs penetrated people's ears, making them listen more attentively. By engaging people through actions, visuals, and sounds, facilitators generate deep and meaningful experiences of immersion, which are common to games. By moving beyond words, they also made participation more accessible to people with different linguistic abilities.

When workshops engaged people's senses, they tended to be more fun. When they did not—such as in some Children's Council and Rosario Hábitat meetings—people grew bored or frustrated. Once participants were more alert, they also scrutinized the programs more closely, keeping a watchful eye for signs of manipulation and unfair outcomes.

Establish Legitimate Rules: Rules are one of the main tools for governing, whether in constitution, laws, ordinances, regulations, or other agreements. They are also one of the main sources of conflict, when people doubt or contest them. When rules are seen as illegitimate—or when they are not understood—they become a nightmare to implement and enforce. The 2000 US presidential election of Bush vs. Gore is a prime example. Unclear and misunderstood voting rules confounded voters and election officials, leaving the country with what many saw as an illegitimate government. Unfortunately, while democratic processes usually present rules, they rarely establish these rules as clear and legitimate. They often assume that once rules are made public, it is the public's responsibility to learn and follow them.

Game designers, in contrast, assume that it is the *designer's* responsibility to make rules understood, and that merely presenting rules does not suffice. Like game designers, the designers of the most successful Rosario and Toronto workshops used a variety of techniques to establish clear rules. They communicated rules multimodally—orally, on handouts, and on posters—so people could process them in more ways. They shared rules at the moment when they came into force, presenting them just-in-time. And they modeled rules, through demonstrations and by inscribing the rules in materials such as maps and puzzle pieces.

The rules felt more legitimate when they were clear *and* when participants could directly craft them. Rosario Hábitat and TCH allowed residents to decide many rules themselves, building their buy-in and ownership over the process When participants had more control over the rules, it was easier to prevent staff manipulation. Participatory rule-making made players into co-designers, diluting the power of staff and limiting their ability to abuse this power.

Thanks to these game mechanics, facilitators rarely struggled to enforce or apply the rules, through sanctions and rulings. Clear and legitimate rules cut down on manipulation and unfair outcomes, by making it harder for people to sidestep or lose faith in the rules. And they made participation more enjoyable. When people had set parameters for what to do, they could focus more on enjoying their actions and worry less about ambiguities.

Generate Collaborative Competition: By nature, politics involves bringing together individuals and groups with different interests and perspectives. During policy-making, however, political players often refuse to work together or fail to reach agreements. Initial conflicts persist, or become even more antagonistic. Many democratic processes seek to minimize conflict by shunning any kind of competition. Others, such as the Brooklyn hearing in chapter 1, naturally invite competition, yet do little to make it healthy or collaborative. Game designers, however, recognize that competition makes people care more about playing and try harder to succeed—and that it can even *encourage* collaboration.

Like most democratic processes, the Rosario and Toronto programs inherently involved conflict and competition. People entered with different opinions, and often with conflicting interests. Yet many facilitators managed to generate productive and collaborative competition. They often began with team-building games, to develop a spirit of group collaboration and healthy competition. Capacity-building, analysis, and decision-making games then built more collaborative competition into later workshops.

More fundamentally, facilitators structured safe spaces for group competition. They erected magic circles around spaces of participation—so that conflicts could play out more safely within the confines of maps and stages. They encouraged groups to work together to overcome systemic challenges and limitations, through group vs. system conflict structures. And they focused attention on shared principles and criteria, so that conflicts felt less divisive.

By accepting and structuring conflict, programs can make participation more enticing, productive, and fun. Conflict creates a compelling sense of drama, which grabs people's attention and makes them work harder to achieve goals. By presenting a clear and constantly evolving challenge, conflict also makes participation more rewarding and engaging.

Link Participation to Measurable Outcomes: One of the top challenges of democratic participation is finding ways to connect input from citizens with policy outputs.[1] When this connection is strong, public knowledge and expertise can be translated into appropriate policies. People feel that they are being listened to, and that officials are truly representing their views. In most public consultations, however, there is little clear connection between inputs and outputs. Community members voice their opinions, but then officials make decisions behind closed doors. As a result people often feel that their interests are being ignored and that policy decisions are illegitimate, or they tune out entirely. When people cannot measure how their participation made a difference, public meetings tend to attract "professional citizens"—people who participate because they enjoy meetings, whether or not they have an impact.

Game mechanics can build a bridge between inputs and outputs. In fact this connection is arguably the main goal of game design—to create meaningful experiences in which there is a clear relationship between player actions and game outcomes. Games entice a much wider range of players by letting them constantly track their progress toward goals and outcomes. They make participation worth the effort.

The most successful processes in Rosario and Toronto did the same by combining game mechanics such as levels, status indicators, and points. TCH's 1.8 Day, for example, required tenant delegates to advance through multiple levels of meetings and voting, measured the status of their presentations with a wall timer, and invited them to assign points to project proposals. Many of the programs labored to provide clear goals, and to make potential outcomes seem concrete *and* uncertain—specific enough to matter, yet not predetermined. As a result people better understood how they could bring about certain outcomes—but only if they stayed involved.

By offering something to play for, the programs made participation more enticing and less trivial. The meaningful and winnable rewards at the end of the tunnel compelled people to push forward. Even when Rosario Hábitat asked *villa* residents to play with puzzle pieces, or when TCH staff banged a gong, participation felt serious. People always knew that there was something to win, and they could see the direct results of their participation. When designers connect activities to clear outcomes, participation becomes seriously engaging.

Design for Participants: Governments and organizations usually design public processes for themselves. They hope to collect information, recruit supporters, comply with requirements, achieve their goals, or enhance their image. Fulfilling the needs and desires of participants is usually a secondary priority. For game designers, in contrast, the player is the primary concern. If designers do not make players happy, people will not play their games, and they will be out of a job well before the next election. Good designers therefore design games around players. "The primary role of the designer," Fullerton writes, "is as an advocate for the player."[2]

The programs in Rosario and Toronto practiced participant-centered design in two main ways. First, they planned for diverse players, creating clear opportunities for different kinds of people to participate in different ways. At TCH, for example, outgoing tenants could present proposals, crafty tenants could prepare display boards, and analytical tenants could negotiate and allocate votes. Tenants could present their projects in whatever style suited them—song, skit, story, or traditional presentation. Instead of imposing a single way to participate, programs can open up multiple avenues for people to get involved, according to each individual's skills and interests.

Second, the programs often used iterative design—regularly redesigning activities in response to feedback. In our participatory evaluation in Toronto, we asked for written and oral feedback at the end of most workshops, and then adjusted the next workshop's plan accordingly. Before playing new games, we tried to playtest them (though not often enough), to see how they would work with actual human beings. When a game or activity was not working properly, we tweaked the design as people played. We assumed that our initial plan was only a starting point, making adjustments when necessary—while still pursuing our broader goals. Some democratic processes do likewise, though often they are less flexible.

When the programs accommodated different playing styles and regularly (but not constantly) tweaked their designs, participants left satisfied. People with very different abilities stayed engaged in PB and the participatory evaluation, and found meaningful ways to participate. Rosario Hábitat turned violent protesters into happy homeowners, by adjusting its process through iterative design. Such dynamic systems, with countless moving parts, rarely work with rigid designs. But if governments are willing to design—and redesign—democratic processes around participants, the moving parts are more likely to work in harmony.

While planners, facilitators, and organizers may not be familiar with the language and mechanics of game design, some of them are already employing similar techniques. Many of the games and game mechanics have emerged organically over time as tricks of the democratic trade. What game design offers, however, is a more expansive set of tools and clearer strategies for how to use them effectively.

Rethinking Democracy and Games

If game design can help engage people in democracy, we should think differently about democracy, and about games. To fix democracy, we should try to make it fun. And to make democracy fun, we should use games in new ways.

At the beginning of the book, I presented three big problems for democracy: citizens are engaging in democracy less, trusting it less, and granting it less power. Making democracy more enjoyable can help address each problem.

By offering a more attractive supply of democracy, governments can boost citizen demand for engagement. Most opportunities for democratic participation are rather unappealing. But when they are enjoyable, as in Rosario and Toronto, people take interest. Participation is still not at the top of most people's agendas, but it is farther from the bottom.

Engagement not only becomes attractive, but also more accessible. As Boaventura de Sousa Santos and Leonardo Avritzer have argued, democracy can be more popular if it relies on forms of communication and interaction that are familiar to ordinary people.[3] For most citizens, playing games is more familiar and comfortable than making deputations, deliberating on policy proposals, or other typical forms of engagement. By grounding participation in accessible activities, governments and organizations can

Conclusion

reach beyond the usual suspects, and keep people engaged. In Rosario and Toronto, barely any participants dropped out, once they saw how user-friendly the programs were.

If democracy is appealing, people will also trust it more. When democracy is an unpleasant civic chore, it is usually left to politicians and professional citizens. Other people see that decision makers do not reflect the broader community, and they become cynical. But when they can form positive associations with democracy—as something fun and engaging—people are likely to believe in its merits. Most participants in Rosario and Toronto said they supported and had faith in the democratic processes I studied, even when they were skeptical of government more broadly.

By making participation fun, we can deepen democracy's power. Increasing engagement enables more people to democratically decide more issues that affect their lives. Once people are engaged in and trust democracy, they are more likely to grant it more power. In Rosario and Toronto, when participation became enjoyable and meaningful, staff and community members pushed to expand democratic decision-making further. They opted to make a greater number of policy and budget decisions through democratic means. People generally want more of a good thing.

Games can help make democracy a good thing—especially if we use them in new ways. As described in chapter 3, game designers are developing serious games about social issues, and activists are mixing play with politics. These efforts have raised awareness about certain causes, and engaged people in community organizing and social movements.

But games can play even deeper roles. To begin, serious games can become more serious. Governments, organizations, and game designers can not only develop games about politics, but also embed games directly in political processes. These games encourage players to transform their knowledge and creativity into concrete political action. This has been happening for decades in Latin America, and such games can give democracy a boost elsewhere too.

Game mechanics can also make participation more game-like, even when games are not appropriate. The same structures, processes, and features that make games engaging can be integrated into democratic processes, to make democracy engaging. Game mechanics should be used with care, however. Haphazardly sprinkling them into events rarely works, but carefully weaving together clusters of mechanics can have deep effects on participation.

These deep effects do not depend on digital technology. They depend on good design. Game design can—and should—reshape democratic processes offline as well as online. Too often, governments look to tech tools as magic bullets, assuming that innovation requires new technology. Rather than layering isolated digital tools on top of dysfunctional political processes, we should redesign democracy. We should reconsider how political decisions are made, and how we could turn democratic decision-making into a game worth playing. Starting with this design challenge, we might choose to integrate digital technology, but only when it is the most effective tool for the task at hand.

If anything, digital games and mechanics are supportive additions to—rather than replacements for—in-person meetings. Governments and organizations do not have the resources to develop elaborate digital games for most issues, nor do they need to. Though digital tools are becoming more prevalent, most organizing still happens offline. Face-to-face interaction creates a social contract, which encourages players to respect the rules and play fair.[4] It also tends to forge stronger social ties, which often compel people to take bold and meaningful action.[5] And even as the Internet and digital technology become increasingly accessible, higher socioeconomic groups still use them more often and more proficiently.[6] Video games are a valuable tool, but they are not our salvation. If anything, they are supportive additions to—rather than replacements for—in-person meetings.

Finally, while the programs I discussed in this book take place at the local level, games and game mechanics can also be scaled up. Local workshops and meetings can be—and have been—multiplied to allow participation at larger scales. Several Latin American counties and states have extended participatory budgeting beyond the municipal level, for example, by holding assemblies in each town and city and recruiting budget delegates to aggregate the results across localities.[7] They have leveraged the power of face-to-face interaction to engage local people in regional budget decisions. In Bolivia, Theater of the Oppressed groups have used forum theater games to help citizens rewrite their national constitution.[8] While these experiences deal with large-scale policies and issues, they still engage people locally. Meaningful democratic deliberation is rare without some degree of intimate face-to-face participation.

Digital games and game mechanics could also help accommodate more people across more dispersed locations, but with risks. Their technical nature places more power in the hands of expert designers, making it more difficult (though not impossible) for participants to craft rules. If they do

Conclusion

not involve human interaction, they are also less able to negotiate deep conflicts or build trusting relationships between participants and organizers. These risks could be minimized by combining the reach of digital game tools with the depth of face-to-face engagement.

As powerful as digital and nondigital games may be, their impact depends on political will. For now, the strongest political players are often opposed to genuinely democratic games, for quite rational reasons. They benefit from weak democracy, so why should they empower the gaming masses? If anything, they are more inclined to design shallow games that give only the illusion of power. Partly because these trivial or manipulative efforts are so common, many officials and organizations that believe in empowerment remain skeptical of games.

This skepticism is healthy. Games and game design do not necessarily make the world better, no matter how many times their boosters declare so. As we saw in Rosario and Toronto, games and game mechanics can mask or reinforce power inequities. They can lead to unfair outcomes. And they can be so trivial as to have no meaningful impact. Political games can do as much harm as good, if they are not grounded in a solid understanding of both politics and game design.

But if used wisely, game design can transform democracy. Despite its many merits, democracy is not the most enticing pastime for most people. As so many other parts of our lives—from entertainment and social media to business and education—are becoming more deeply engaging, democratic participation is falling even further behind. Too often it is boring, pointless, or painful. When democracy is unappealing, it attracts a rather unrepresentative lot—political junkies, passionate extremists, and other usual suspects. When participation is narrow, decisions tend to benefit the few rather than the many. And when decisions are biased, democratic institutions lose trust, engagement, and power.

By making democracy fun, we can make it work. Democratic participation can and must be more than a civic chore. Some leaders get it—the City of the Children visionary Chiqui González, the planners at Rosario Hábitat, and the participatory budgeting coordinators at Toronto Community Housing, to name just a few. They understood that if we want government to truly represent and serve the people, we need new ways to reach beyond the usual suspects. If we want more people to contribute to their community and government, we need to give them new reasons to participate. And if we want participation to be more meaningful, we need to design democracy as a more enjoyable experience, as a game worth playing.

Thousands of Drops in the Bucket

In the six years that it took to research and write this book, the landscape of political games has shifted. In 2007, there were a few thickets of interesting games scattered about. Now, scores of governments and organizations are aspiring to grow democratic games, for urban planning, community organizing, budgeting, and other issues. But we still have a long way to go, especially outside of Latin America. Even in Latin America, political games grew out of decades of organizing and experimentation. Whether the rest of the world manages to replicate—or surpass—these efforts depends on *how* games are used.

If games and game mechanics are haphazardly added to democratic processes, they may enable unfair outcomes and manipulation, or make participation seem trivial or not much fun. But if they are carefully blended together, they can address some of the most pressing problems of democracy. In this book I have offered a few pointers for how to mix games and game mechanics into democracy. Others will no doubt invent more recipes for democratic games.

In fact this task is already underway. In May 2010, I returned to Rosario for a short visit, six months after completing my research there. As soon as I arrived, the director of the city's participatory budgeting program wrote that he wanted to show me a new initiative. I had researched Rosario's PB several years earlier, but it had recently fallen on hard times. The city's financial troubles and the broader economic crisis had led to project delays, and fewer people were turning out.

In 2009, I had facilitated a couple workshops for city staff on "Game Design for Democratic Participation," and apparently the PB office had put the workshop lessons into practice. To engage more residents, they had designed a new voting process: *bolivoto*.[9] Or in more proper Spanish, it is *voto bolita* (marble vote).

During the voting period the city placed rows of freshly painted orange pipes upright in bustling public places. Each pipe was labeled with the name and description of a project proposed for funding. At a nearby table, staff passed out voting cards and handfuls of marbles to registered voters, each marble representing one vote. To vote for a project, people dropped a marble in its pipe.

The *bolivoto* made voting fun. People eagerly lined up to vote, drawn by the vibrant orange pipes, the fun core mechanic of dropping marbles, and the satisfying clunk of the marble hitting bottom. Thanks partly to the

Conclusion

attention generated by the *bolivoto*, PB participation skyrocketed. Around 33,000 people voted in 2010, three times as many as in the prior year.[10]

As a souvenir, the PB director gave me one of the voting cards—a marble attached to a beige slip of paper. He promptly pointed to the bottom of the paper. Flashing a wide smile, he acknowledged that staff had borrowed a certain phrase from my book. The slogan of the *bolivoto* campaign was printed beneath the marble: "*haciendo más divertida la democracia*"—making democracy more fun.

Notes

Chapter 1

1. For background on the Atlantic Yards development and this public hearing, see Norman Oder, "AY Supporters Out in Force at Epic Hearing, but Opponents Go the Distance," *Atlantic Yards Report*, August 24, 2006, http://atlanticyardsreport.blogspot.com/2006/08/ay-supporters-out-in-force-at-epic.html; Andy Newman, "Raucous Meeting on Atlantic Yards Plan Hints at Hardening Stances," *New York Times*, August 24, 2006, http://www.nytimes.com/2006/08/24/nyregion/24yards.html; "How to Rig a Public Hearing—Coverage of the Scam Atlantic Yards," *DEIS Proceedings*, 2006, http://www.themusicdrop.com/fbr/deis_hearing_show_web_1.mov.

2. When I refer to citizens, I mean the inclusive "small c" notion of community members, not the exclusive legal category.

3. Wilde allegedly said, "The problem with socialism is that it takes up too many evenings."

4. Iris Marion Young, *Inclusion and Democracy* (Oxford: Oxford University Press, 2002), 16.

5. Josh Lerner, "Communal Councils in Venezuela: Can 200 Families Revolutionize Democracy?" *Z Magazine* 20, no. 3 (2007): 45–49.

6. Jane McGonigal, *Reality Is Broken: Why Games Make Us Better and How They Can Change the World* (New York: Penguin, 2011), 51.

7. Amanda Lenhart et al., *Teens, Video Games, and Civics* (Washington, DC: Pew Internet/American Life Project, September 16, 2008).

8. McGonigal, *Reality Is Broken*, 62.

9. This definition follows closely that of Carole Pateman in Carole Pateman, *Participation and Democratic Theory* (New York: Cambridge University Press, 1970).

10. Matt Leighninger, *The Next Form of Democracy: How Expert Rule Is Giving Way to Shared Governance . . . and Why Politics Will Never Be the Same* (Nashville: Vanderbilt University Press, 2006); Cheryl King, Kathryn Feltey, and Bridget O'Neill Susel, "The Question of Participation: Toward Authentic Public Participation in Public Administration," *Public Administration Review* 58, no. 4 (1998): 317–26; Raymond Burby, "Making Plans That Matter: Citizen Involvement and Government Action," *Journal of the American Planning Association* 69, no. 1 (2003): 33–49.

11. Colin Hay, *Why We Hate Politics* (Oxford: Polity, 2007), 13. OECD stands for the Organization for Economic Co-operation and Development.

12. Ibid., 21.

13. Robert D. Putnam, *Bowling Alone: The Collapse and Revival of American Community* (New York: Simon and Schuster, 2001); Hay, *Why We Hate Politics*.

14. Putnam, *Bowling Alone*.

15. Theda Skocpol and Morris P. Fiorina, *Civic Engagement in American Democracy* (Washington, DC: Brookings Institution Press, 1999); Hay, *Why We Hate Politics*; Pippa Norris, *Democratic Phoenix: Reinventing Political Activism* (Cambridge, UK: Cambridge University Press, 2002).

16. Norris, *Democratic Phoenix*.

17. Theda Skocpol, *Diminished Democracy: From Membership to Management in American Civic Life* (Norman: University of Oklahoma Press, 2004).

18. Arend Lijphart, "Unequal Participation: Democracy's Unresolved Dilemma," *American Political Science Review* 91, no. 1 (1997): 5–6.

19. Archon Fung, "Varieties of Participation in Complex Governance." *Public Administration Review* 66, Special Issue (December 2006): 66–75.

20. Lijphart, "Unequal Participation."

21. Zoltan Hajnal, *America's Uneven Democracy: Race, Turnout, and Representation in City Politics* (Cambridge, UK: Cambridge University Press, 2010); Morris Fiorina, "Extreme Voices: A Dark Side of Civic Engagement," in *Civic Engagement in American Democracy* (Washington, DC: Brookings Institution Press, 1999).

22. Vivien Lowndes et al., *Enhancing Public Participation in Local Government* (London: UK Department of the Environment, Transport and the Regions, 1998).

23. Fung, "Varieties of Participation in Complex Governance," 74.

24. John Dewey, *The Public and Its Problems* (New York: Holt, 1927).

25. Sidney Verba, Kay Lehman Schlozman, and Henry Brady, *Voice and Equality: Civic Voluntarism in American Politics* (Cambridge: Harvard University Press, 1995).

Notes to Pages 9–11 213

26. Rogers M. Smith, "Putting the Substance Back in Political Science," *Chronicle of Higher Education*, April 5, 2002 (sec. Chronicle Review), http://chronicle.com/article/Putting-the-Substance-Back-in/35557/.

27. Pew Research Center, *Distrust, Discontent, Anger and Partisan Rancor* (Washington, DC: Pew Research Center, April 18, 2010), http://www.people-press.org/2010/04/18/distrust-discontent-anger-and-partisan-rancor/.

28. Hay, *Why We Hate Politics*, 38.

29. Russell J. Dalton, *Democratic Challenges, Democratic Choices: The Erosion of Political Support in Advanced Industrial Democracies* (Oxford: Oxford University Press, 2004).

30. Paul Reynolds, "Survey Reveals Global Dissatisfaction," *BBC*, September 15, 2005, sec. Europe, http://news.bbc.co.uk/2/hi/europe/4245282.stm.

31. Hay, *Why We Hate Politics*, 1.

32. Pierre Rosanvallon, *Counter-democracy: Politics in an Age of Distrust* (Cambridge, UK: Cambridge University Press, 2008).

33. Hay, *Why We Hate Politics*.

34. Lawrence Walters, James Aydelotte, and Jessica Miller, "Putting More Public in Policy Analysis," *Public Administration Review* 60, no. 4 (2000): 349–59.

35. OECD, *Focus on Citizens: Public Engagement for Better Policy and Services*, OECD Studies on Public Engagement (Paris: OECD, 2009).

36. Hay, *Why We Hate Politics*.

37. Benjamin R. Barber, *Strong Democracy: Participatory Politics for a New Age* (Los Angeles: University of California Press, 2003).

38. Young, *Inclusion and Democracy*; Barber, *Strong Democracy*; Boaventura de Sousa Santos, ed., *Democratizing Democracy: Beyond the Liberal Democratic Canon* (New York: Verso, 2007); Lani Guinier and Gerald Torres, *The Miner's Canary: Enlisting Race, Resisting Power, Transforming Democracy* (Cambridge: Harvard University Press, 2003).

39. Hay, *Why We Hate Politics*, 155.

40. Reynolds, "Survey Reveals Global Dissatisfaction."

41. Joseph Alois Schumpeter, *Capitalism, Socialism and Democracy* (New York: Harper, 1975); Norberto Bobbio, *The Future of Democracy* (Minneapolis: University of Minneapolis Press, 1984); Adam Przeworski, Ian Shapiro, and Casiano Hacker-Cordón, "Minimalist Conception of Democracy: A Defense," in *Democracy's Value* (Cambridge, UK: Cambridge University Press, 1999).

42. Pateman, *Participation and Democratic Theory*; Barber, *Strong Democracy*; Archon Fung and Erik Olin Wright, eds., *Deepening Democracy: Institutional Innovations in Empowered Participatory Governance* (New York: Verso, 2003).

43. Jane Mansbridge, *Beyond Adversary Democracy* (Chicago: University of Chicago Press, 1983).

44. Alexis de Tocqueville, *Democracy in America* (New York: Harper Perennial, 1966); Pateman, *Participation and Democratic Theory*; Jane Mansbridge, "Does Participation Make Better Citizens?" *The Good Society* 5, no. 2 (1995): 1–7; Josh Lerner and Daniel Schugurensky, "Who Learns What in Participatory Democracy? Participatory Budgeting in Rosario, Argentina," in *Democratic Practices as Learning Opportunities*, ed. Ruud van der Veen, Danny Wildemeersch, Janet Youngblood, and Victoria Marsick (Rotterdam: Sense Publishers, 2007), 85–100.

45. Francesca Polletta, *Freedom Is an Endless Meeting: Democracy in American Social Movements* (Chicago: University of Chicago Press, 2002); Eddie Yuen, "Introduction," in *Confronting Capitalism: Dispatches from a Global Movement*, ed. Eddie Yuen, Daniel Burton-Rose, and George Katsiaficas (Brooklyn: Soft Skull Press, 2004); David Solnit, ed., *Globalize Liberation* (San Francisco: City Lights Books, 2004); Leighninger, *The Next Form of Democracy*.

46. Carolyn Lukensmeyer, *Bringing Citizen Voices to the Table: A Guide for Public Managers* (San Francisco: Jossey-Bass, 2013); Susan Clark and Woden Teachout, *Slow Democracy: Rediscovering Community, Bringing Decision Making back Home* (White River Junction, VT: Chelsea Green, 2012); "Healthy Democracy," 2013, http://healthydemocracy.org/; "The Center for Deliberative Democracy," 2013, http://cdd.stanford.edu/polls/; "The World Café," 2013, http://www.theworldcafe.com/; "Future Search Network," 2013, http://www.futuresearch.net/; Leighninger, *The Next Form of Democracy*; Tina Nabatchi et al., eds., *Democracy in Motion: Evaluating the Practice and Impact of Deliberative Civic Engagement* (Oxford: Oxford University Press, 2012).

47. "Right to the City," 2013, http://www.righttothecity.org/; "MoveOn.Org," 2013, http://front.moveon.org/; Sue Branford and Jan Rocha, *Cutting the Wire: The Story of the Landless Movement in Brazil* (London: Latin American Bureau, 2002); "Occupy Wall Street," 2013, http://occupywallst.org/; Heather Gautney et al., *Democracy, States, and the Struggle for Global Justice—Google Books* (New York: Routledge, 2009); Polletta, *Freedom Is an Endless Meeting*; Hilary Wainwright, *Reclaim the State: Adventures in Popular Democracy* (London: Verso, 2003); Santos, *Democratizing Democracy*.

48. "National League of Cities: Democratic Governance and Civic Engagement," 2013, http://www.nlc.org/find-city-solutions/center-for-research-and-innovation/governance-and-civic-engagement/democratic-governance-and-civic-engagement; "Red FAL: Forum of Local Authorities for Social Inclusion and Participatory

Democracy," 2013, http://www.redfal.org/; "Columbia Institute," 2013, http://www.columbiainstitute.ca/.

49. Putnam, *Bowling Alone*.

50. Skocpol and Fiorina, *Civic Engagement in American Democracy*.

51. Putnam, *Bowling Alone*.

52. Dalton, *Democratic Challenges, Democratic Choices*; Pippa Norris, *Critical Citizens: Global Support for Democratic Government* (Oxford: Oxford University Press, 1999).

53. Paul R. Abramson, John Herbert Aldrich, and David W. Rohde, *Change and Continuity in the 2004 and 2006 Elections* (Washington, DC: CQ Press, 2007); Putnam, *Bowling Alone*.

54. Abramson, Aldrich, and Rohde, *Change and Continuity in the 2004 and 2006 Elections*.

55. Raymond Wolfinger and Steven Rosenstone, *Who Votes?* (New Haven: Yale University Press, 1980), 3.

56. Hay, *Why We Hate Politics*.

57. Ibid.

58. Anthony Downs, *An Economic Theory of Democracy* (New York: Harper, 1957).

59. OECD, *Focus on Citizens*.

60. Young, *Inclusion and Democracy*, 16.

61. Mary Ryan, *Civic Wars: Democracy and Public Life in the American City during the Nineteenth Century* (Berkeley: University of California Press, 1997); Michael McGerr, *The Decline of Popular Politics: The American North, 1865–1928* (New York: Oxford University Press, 1986); E. M. Addonizio, D. P. Green, and J. M. Glaser, "Putting the Party Back into Politics: An Experiment Testing Whether Election Day Festivals Increase Voter Turnout," *PS: Political Science and Politics* 40, no. 4 (2007): 721–27.

62. Michael A. Neblo et al., "Who Wants to Deliberate—And Why?" *American Political Science Review* 104, no. 03 (2010): 566–83.

63. Tracy Fullerton, *Game Design Workshop: A Playcentric Approach to Creating Innovative Games*, 2nd ed. (New York: Morgan Kaufmann, 2008), 312.

64. Raph Koster, *A Theory of Fun for Game Design* (Scottsdale, AZ: Paraglyph Press, 2005), 40.

65. Ibid.

66. Marc LeBlanc, "8KindsOfFun.com," 2010, http://algorithmancy.8kindsoffun.com/.

67. Mihaly Csikszentmihalyi, *Flow: The Psychology of Optimal Experience* (New York: Harper Collins, 1991).

68. Andrew Boyd and Stephen Duncombe, "The Manufacture of Dissent: What the Left Can Learn from Las Vegas," *Journal of Aesthetics and Protest* 1, no. 3 (2004): 46.

69. Volkswagen, "The Fun Theory," 2010, http://www.thefuntheory.com/.

70. Carlos Forment (Carlos Forment, "The Democratic Dribbler: Football Clubs, Neoliberal Globalization, and Buenos Aires' Municipal Election of 2003," *Public Culture* 19, no. 1 (2007): 85.) makes a similar point, suggesting that sports franchises sometimes serve as models of and for government.

71. Katie Salen and Eric Zimmerman, *Rules of Play: Game Design Fundamentals* (Cambridge: MIT Press, 2004), 80.

72. Fullerton, *Game Design Workshop,* 2nd ed., 312.

73. Peter Warman, *Newzoo Games Market Report: Consumer Spending on Key Platforms and Business Models* (Amsterdam: Newzoo, May 2010) ; McGonigal, *Reality Is Broken*, 3.

74. McGonigal, *Reality Is Broken*, 3.

75. Victoria Rideout, Ulla Foehr, and Donald Roberts, *Generation M2: Media in the Lives of 8- to 18-Year-Olds* (Menlo Park, CA: Kaiser Family Foundation, January 2010).

76. The Entertainment Software Association, "Industry Facts," 2011, http://www.theesa.com/facts/index.asp.

77. Rideout, Foehr, and Roberts, *Generation M2*.

78. Entertainment Software Association, "Industry Facts."

79. Rideout, Foehr, and Roberts, *Generation M2*.

80. *Playing and Reality* (London: Tavistock, 1971).

81. James Paul Gee, *What Video Games Have to Teach Us about Learning and Literacy*, 2nd ed. (Palgrave Macmillan, 2007); Stuart Brown and Christopher Vaughan, *Play: How It Shapes the Brain, Opens the Imagination, and Invigorates the Soul* (New York: Penguin, 2010).

82. Brown and Vaughan, *Play*.

83. Richard Blunt, "Do Serious Games Work? Results from Three Studies," *eLearn Magazine*, December 1, 2009, http://elearnmag.acm.org/featured.cfm?aid=1661378.

84. Alex Dobuzinskis, "Global Movie Box Office Nears $30 Billion in 2009," *Reuters*, March 10, 2010, http://www.reuters.com/article/2010/03/10/us-boxoffice-idUSTRE 62955520100310; McGonigal, *Reality Is Broken*, 4; John Gaudiosi, "New Reports

Forecast Global Video Game Industry Will Reach $82 Billion by 2017," *Forbes Tech*, July 18, 2012, http://www.forbes.com/sites/johngaudiosi/2012/07/18/new-reports-forecasts-global-video-game-industry-will-reach-82-billion-by-2017/.

85. PricewaterhouseCoopers, "Back on Track—Think Global, Win Local to Succeed in the Global Sports Market," May 26, 2010.

86. AT&T, "AT&T Announces the Eighth Season of 'American Idol' Smashes All-Time Record for Fan Engagement through Text Messaging," May 22, 2009, http://www.att.com/gcn/press-room?pid=4800&cdvn=news&newsarticleid=26832. One caveat: In *American Idol*, people can vote more than once, the number of votes is greater than the number of voters.

87. Tom Chatfield, *Fun Inc.: Why Games Are the 21st Century's Most Serious Business* (London: Virgin Books, 2010).

88. Amanda Schaffer, "Why Video Games Really Are Linked to Violence," *Slate*, April 27, 2007, http://www.slate.com/articles/health_and_science/medical_examiner/2007/04/dont_shoot.html.

89. Douglas Gentile and Craig Anderson, "Violent Video Games: Effects on Youth and Public Policy Implications," in *Handbook of Children, Culture, and Violence*, ed. N. Dowd, D. G. Singer, and R. F. Wilson (Thousand Oaks, CA: Sage, 2006), 225–46; Craig Anderson, Douglas Gentile, and Katherine Buckley, *Violent Video Game Effects on Children and Adolescents* (Oxford: Oxford University Press, 2006).

90. Kristin Kalning, "Does Game Violence Make Teens Aggressive?" *Msnbc.com*, December 8, 2006, http://www.nbcnews.com/id/16099971/ns/technology_and_science-games/.

91. Christopher Ferguson, "Video Games and Youth Violence: A Prospective Analysis in Adolescents," *Journal of Youth and Adolescence* 40, no. 4 (2010): 377–91.

92. January 2009 *Personality and Social Psychology Bulletin*, Andrew Przybylski,.

93. P.W. Singer, "Meet the Sims . . . and Shoot Them: The Rise of Militainment," *Foreign Policy*, April 2010, http://www.foreignpolicy.com/articles/2010/02/22/meet_the_sims_and_shoot_them.

94. Ibid.

95. Keith Button, "A 'subtle' Approach: Soldiers Learn Nuances of Foreign Cultures through Video Gaming," *Training and Simulation Journal*, October 1, 2009.

96. American Public Media, "Budget Hero," 2008, http://www.marketplace.org/topics/economy/budget-hero.

97. Lev Semenovich Vygotsky, *Mind in Society: The Development of Higher Psychological Processes* (Cambridge: Harvard University Press, 1978).

98. Robert Dahl, "The Concept of Political Power," *Behavioral Science* 2, no. 3 (1957): 201-215.

99. Peter Bachrach and Morton Baratz, "The Two Faces of Power," *American Political Science Review* 56, no. 4 (1962): 947–52; Stephen Lukes, *Power: A Radical View* (London: Macmillan, 1974).

100. "Gamification Blog," 2011, http://www.gamification.co/; David Helgason, "2010 Trends," *Unity Technologies Blog*, January 14, 2010, http://blogs.unity3d.com/2010/01/14/2010-trends/.

101. "Epic Win—Level up Your Life," January 30, 2010, http://www.rexbox.co.uk/epicwin/.

102. Sebastian Deterding, "Pawned. Gamification and Its Discontents," September 24, 2010, 40–41, http://www.slideshare.net/dings/pawned-gamification-and-its-discontents.

103. Richard H. Thaler and Cass R. Sunstein, *Nudge: Improving Decisions about Health, Wealth, and Happiness* (New Haven: Yale University Press, 2008).

104. Max Horkheimer and Theodor W. Adorno, *Dialectic of Enlightenment: Philosophical Fragments* (Stanford: Stanford University Press, 2002); Guy Debord, *Society of the Spectacle* (London: Rebel Press, 1983).

105. Auyero *Poor People's Politics: Peronist Survival Networks and the Legacy of Evita* (Durham, NC: Duke University Press, 2000).

106. Debord, *Society of the Spectacle.*

107. Deterding, "Pawned. Gamification and Its Discontents," 42–44.

108. Gustave Le Bon, *The Crowd: A Study of the Popular Mind* (New York: Macmillan, 1897).

109. Deterding, "Pawned. Gamification and Its Discontents"; John Pavlus, "Sixty-two Reasons Why 'Gamification' Is Played Out," *Co.Design*, November 8, 2010, http://www.fastcodesign.com/1662656/sixty-two-reasons-why-gamification-is-played-out; Bobby Schweizer, "The Difference between Newsgames and Gamification," *Newsgames*, December 3, 2010, http://newsgames.gatech.edu/blog/2010/12/the-difference-between-newsgames-and-gamification.html.

110. McKenzie Wark, *Gamer Theory* (Cambridge: Harvard University Press, 2007), 21.

111. Russell Davies, "Playful," *Russell Davies*, November 9, 2009, http://russelldavies.typepad.com/planning/2009/11/playful.html.

112. Michael Agger, "How Video Games Can Make Us Heroes," *Slate*, January 24, 2011, http://www.slate.com/articles/arts/books/2011/01/how_video_games_can_make_us_heroes.html.

Notes to Pages 22–29

113. Mathew Kumar, "GDC: Will Wright's Perspectives on Play," *Edge Magazine*, March 16, 2010, http://www.edge-online.com/features/gdc-will-wrights-perspectives -play/.

114. Deterding, "Pawned. Gamification and Its Discontents," 21.

115. McGonigal, *Reality Is Broken*; Gene Koo, "Video Games and Democratic Participation," *Valuable Games*, April 21, 2009, http://blogs.law.harvard.edu/games/2009/04/21/video-games-and-democratic-participation/; Jesse Schell, "'Design outside the Box' Presentation," February 18, 2010, http://www.g4tv.com/videos/44277/DICE-2010-Design-Outside-the-Box-Presentation/; Byron Reeves and J. Leighton Read, *Total Engagement: Using Games and Virtual Worlds to Change the Way People Work and Businesses Compete* (Cambridge: Harvard Business Press, 2009); Helgason, "2010 Trends."

Chapter 2

1. Andrew Colman, *Game Theory and Its Applications in the Social and Biological Sciences* (New York: Routledge, 1995), 6.

2. Marcia Stepanek, "Game Theory," *Stanford Social Innovation Review*, July 12, 2010, http://www.ssireview.org/blog/entry/game_theory/ .

3. See, among many other examples, a speech in Tampa, Florida, by Barack Obama, "Obama's Speech in Tampa, Florida," *RealClearPolitics*, October 20, 2008, http://www.realclearpolitics.com/articles/2008/10/obamas_speech_in_tampa_florida.htm.

4. Huizinga and Caillois did not distinguish between play and games. All definitions were reviewed in Salen and Zimmerman, *Rules of Play: Game Design Fundamentals*, 75–79, and originally published earlier in Clark Abt, *Serious Games* (New York: Viking Press, 1970), 6–7; Roger Caillois, *Man, Play, and Games*, trans. Meyer Barash (Chicago: University of Illinois Press, 2001), 9–10; Johan Huizinga, *Homo Ludens: A Study of the Play Element in Culture* (Boston: Beacon Press, 1955), 13; Greg Costikyan, "I Have No Words and I Must Design," *Interactive Fantasy*, no. 2 (1994); Bernard Suits, *Grasshopper: Games, Life, and Utopia* (Orchard Park, NY: Broadview Press, 2005), 54–55; Chris Crawford, *The Art of Computer Game Design* (New York: McGraw-Hill, 1984); Elliot Avedon and Brian Sutton-Smith, eds., *The Study of Games* (New York: Wiley, 1971), 405.

5. *Rules of Play: Game Design Fundamentals*.

6. Ibid., 80.

7. Ibid., 304. Salen and Zimmernan's definition covers the broadest meanings of play, such as the play of gears in a car, and so does not dictate that play be enjoyable. Since I only discuss human play, I add that play must be enjoyable. For humans, moving freely around a confined space is generally not playful unless the person enjoys the activity in some sense.

8. Ibid., 72–73.

9. Arthur Jacobson. "Origins of the Game Theory of Law and the Limits of Harmony in Plato's Laws," *Cardozo Law Review* 20, May–July (1999): 1335–55.

10. Plato, *The Dialogues of Plato*, trans. J Hayward (Chicago: University of Chicago Press, 1952), Book X, 903.

11. Nicholas Howe, "Metaphor in Contemporary American Political Discourse," *Metaphor and Symbol* 3, no. 2 (1988): 87–104; Joseph N. Cappella and Kathleen Hall Jamieson, *Spiral of Cynicism: The Press and the Public Good* (Oxford: Oxford University Press, 1997).

12. Thomas Patterson and Philip Seib, "Informing the Public," in *The Press*, ed. Geneva Overholser and Kathleen Hall Jamieson (Oxford: Oxford University Press, 2006), 195.

13. Benjamin Shepard, *Play, Creativity, and Social Movements* (New York: Routledge, 2009).

14. *Rules for Radicals* (New York: Vintage Books, 1972).

15. "Religion's Answer to the Problem of Evil," in *The Papers of Martin Luther King Jr.*, Volume I: Called to Serve, January 1929–June 1951 (Berkeley: University of California Press, 1992), 428.

16. Sherry Arnstein, "A Ladder of Citizen Participation," *Journal of the American Institute of Planners* 35, no. 4 (1969): 216–24.

17. Joseph N. Cappella and Kathleen Hall Jamieson, "News Frames, Political Cynicism, and Media Cynicism," *Annals of the American Academy of Political and Social Science* 546 (July 1996): 71–84; Cappella and Jamieson, *Spiral of Cynicism*; Shanto Iyengar, Helmut Norpoth, and Kyu S. Hahn, "Consumer Demand for Election News: The Horserace Sells," *Journal of Politics* 66, no. 1 (February 2004): 157–75.

18. Howe, "Metaphor in Contemporary American Political Discourse."

19. *Democracy and the Market* (Cambridge, UK: Cambridge University Press, 1991), 10.

20. Abigail De Kosnik, "Participatory Democracy and Hillary Clinton's Marginalized Fandom," *Transformative Works and Cultures* 1 (2008), http://journal .transformativeworks.org/index.php/twc/article/viewArticle/47.

21. Walter Lippmann, *Public Opinion* (New York: Harcourt, Brace, 1922); Stephen Duncombe, *Dream: Re-imagining Progressive Politics in an Age of Fantasy* (New York: New Press, 2007), 102.

22. Martin J. Osborne and Ariel Rubinstein, *A Course in Game Theory* (Cambridge: MIT Press, 1994), 2.

Notes to Pages 33–34

23. Martin J. Osborne, *An Introduction to Game Theory* (Oxford: Oxford University Press, 2004).

24. Downs, *An Economic Theory of Democracy*; Mark Lichbach, *The Rebel's Dilemma* (Ann Arbor: University of Michigan Press, 1998); Herbert Gintis et al., *Moral Sentiments and Material Interests: The Foundations of Cooperation in Economic Life* (Cambridge: MIT Press, 2005); Kristen Monroe, Michael Barton, and Ute Klingemann, "Altruism and the Theory of Rational Action: Rescuers of Jews in Nazi Europe," *Ethics*, no. 101 (1990): 103–22.

25. William Poundstone, *Prisoner's Dilemma* (New York: Doubleday, 1992), 407.

26. John Aldrich, "Rational Choice and Turnout," *American Journal of Political Science*, 37, no. 1 (1993): 246–78; Gary Cox, "Centripetal and Centrifugal Incentives in Electoral Systems," *American Journal of Political Science*,34, no. 4 (1990): 903–35; Gary Cox, *Making Votes Count* (Cambridge, UK: Cambridge University Press, 1997); Gary Cox, "Electoral Rules and the Calculus of Mobilization," *Legislative Studies Quarterly* 24, no. 3 (1999): 387–420.

27. Monroe, Barton, and Klingemann, "Altruism and the Theory of Rational Action: Rescuers of Jews in Nazi Europe," *Ethics* 101, no.1 (1990): 103–22; Rajiv Sethi and E Somanathan, "Norm Compliance and Strong Reciprocity," in *Moral Sentiments and Material Interests: On the Foundations of Cooperation in Economic Life*, ed. Herbert Gintis et al. (Cambridge: MIT Press, 2003); Paul Whiteley, "Rational Choice and Political Participation—Evaluating the Debate," *Political Research Quarterly*, no. 48 (1995); James Andreoni, "Cooperation in Public-Goods Experiments: Kindness or Confusion?" *American Economic Review* 85, no. 4 (1995): 891–904; Ernst Fehr and Bettina Rockenbach, "Detrimental Effects of Sanctions on Human Altruism," *Nature*, no. 422, no. 6928 (2003): 137–40; Thomas Palfrey and Jeffrey Prisbrey, "Anomalous Behavior in Public Goods Experiments: How Much and Why?" *American Economic Review* 87, no. 5 (1997).

28. Monroe, Barton, and Klingemann, "Altruism and the Theory of Rational Action: Rescuers of Jews in Nazi Europe ," *Ethics* 101, no.1 (1990): 103–22.

29. Barry Hindess, *Choice, Rationality, and Social Theory* (London: Unwin Hyman, 1988); Theodore Lowi, "The State in Political Science: How We Become What We Study," *American Political Science Review*, 86, no. 1 (1992): 1–7; Bernard Berelson, Paul Lazarfeld, and William McPhee, *Voting* (Chicago: University of Chicago Press, 1954); Monroe, Barton, and Klingemann, "Altruism and the Theory of Rational Action: Rescuers of Jews in Nazi Europe"; Herbert Simon, "Human Nature in Politics: The Dialogue of Psychology with Political Science," *American Political Science Review*, no. 79 (1985).

30. Robert Jackson, "Rationality and Political Participation," *American Journal of Political Science*, 37, no. 1 (1993): 279–90.

31. George Steinmetz, "Positivism and Its Others in the Social Sciences," in *The Politics of Method in the Human Sciences: Positivism and Its Epistemological Others,* ed. George Steinmetz (Durham: Duke University Press, 2005): 1–56.

32. Ibid.; Sonia Amadea, *Rationalizing Capitalist Democracy: The Cold War Origins of Rational Choice Liberalism* (Chicago: University of Chicago Press, 2003); Joan Scott, "The Evidence of Experience," *Critical Inquiry,* no. 17 (1991): 733–97.

33. Whiteley, "Rational Choice and Political Participation—Evaluating the Debate"; Jane Mansbridge, ed., *Beyond Self-Interest* (Chicago: University of Chicago Press, 1990); Jeff Goodwin, James Jasper, and Francesca Polletta, eds., *Passionate Politics: Emotions and Social Movements* (Chicago: University of Chicago Press, 2001).

34. Poundstone, *Prisoner's Dilemma.*

35. Elisabeth Wood, *Insurgent Collective Action and Civil War in El Salvador* (Cambridge, UK: Cambridge University Press, 2003); Karl-Dieter Opp, "Postmaterialism, Collective Action, and Political Protest," *American Journal of Political Science,* 34, no. 1 (1990): 212–35.

36. Monroe, Barton, and Klingemann, "Altruism and the Theory of Rational Action: Rescuers of Jews in Nazi Europe"; Andreoni, "Cooperation in Public-Goods Experiments: Kindness or Confusion?"

37. *Pathologies of Rational Choice Theory: A Critique of Applications in Political Science* (New Haven: Yale University Press, 1994).

38. Salen and Zimmerman, *Rules of Play: Game Design Fundamentals,* 80.

39. Games for Change, "Games for Change Website," 2009, http://www.gamesforchange.org/.

40. Poundstone, *Prisoner's Dilemma.*

41. Celia Pearce et al., "Sustainable Play: Toward a New Games Movement for the Digital Age," *Games and Culture* 2, no. 3 (2007): 261–78; Salen and Zimmerman, *Rules of Play: Game Design Fundamentals,* 256–57.

42. Games for Change, "Games for Change Website."

43. *Ayiti: The Cost of Life,* http://ayiti.globalkids.org/game/.

44. Street Football World, "Streetfootballworld Website," 2010, http://www.streetfootballworld.org/.

45. Joseph Kahne, Ellen Middaugh, and Chris Evans. "The Civic Potential of Video Games" (Chicago: The John D. and Catherine T. MacArthur Foundation), September 7, 2008.

46. Gee, *What Video Games Have to Teach Us about Learning and Literacy*; Kurt Squire, "From Content to Context: Video Games as Designed Experiences," *Educational Researcher* 35, no. 8 (2006).

Notes to Pages 36–40

47. Salen and Zimmerman, *Rules of Play: Game Design Fundamentals*, 305.

48. "The ReDistricting Game," 2009, http://www.redistrictinggame.org/.

49. Chris Swain, "Pre-launch Trip to Washington," *Buzz about the ReDistricting Game*, May 23, 2007, http://redistrictinggame.blogspot.com/2007/05/jonathan-aronson-and-i-went-to.html; Chris Swain, "The ReDistricting Game Being Used in PA Lobbying Effort," *Buzz about the ReDistricting Game*, March 30, 2008, http://redistrictinggame.blogspot.com/2008/03/redistricting-game-being-used-in-pa.html.

50. Auyero *Poor People's Politics: Peronist Survival Networks and the Legacy of Evita* presents perhaps the most intimate depiction of this clientelism.

51. McGerr, *The Decline of Popular Politics: The American North, 1865–1928*; Ryan, *Civic Wars: Democracy and Public Life in the American City During the Nineteenth Century*.

52. Phillip Converse, "Change in the American Electorate," in *The Human Meaning of Social Change*, ed. Angus Campbell and Phillip Converse (New York: Sage, 1972): 263–337; Jerrold Rusk, "The Effect of the Australian Ballot Reform on Voting: 1876–1908," *American Political Science Review*, 64, no. 4 (1970): 1220–38. Other factors also contributed greatly to high turnout, in particular the corruption enabled by public (not secret) ballots and the smaller voter pool before women were enfranchised.

53. Addonizio, Green, and Glaser, "Putting the Party Back into Politics."

54. "Limits of Political Engagement in Antebellum America: A New Look at the Golden Age of Participatory Democracy," *The Journal of American History* 84, no. 3 (1997): 855–85.

55. James C. Scott, *Weapons of the Weak: Everyday Forms of Peasant Resistance* (New Haven: Yale University Press, 1987).

56. *Rabelais and His World* (Indianapolis: Indiana University Press, 1984).

57. T. V. Reed, *The Art of Protest: Culture and Activism from the Civil Rights Movement to the Streets of Seattle* (Minneapolis: University of Minnesota Press, 2005), 2.

58. Carlos Forment, *Democracy in Latin America: 1760–1900*, vol. 1 (Chicago: University of Chicago Press, 2003), 206; John Lowell Lewis, *Ring of Liberation: Deceptive Discourse in Brazilian Capoeira* (Chicago: University of Chicago Press, 1992); Ciudades Educadoras América Latina, *Montevideo Ciudad Educadora: Identidad, cultura y participación a través de la música* (Rosario, Argentina: Ciudades Educadoras, 2002).

59. Juana Córdova, "El Año viejo. Un Medio de expresión popular," *Revista Artesanías de América, CIDAP*, 2001.

60. James C. Scott, *Domination and the Arts of Resistance: Hidden Transcripts* (New Haven: Yale University Press, 1992).

61. Benjamin Shepard, "If I Can't Dance: Play, Creativity, and Social Movements" (City University of New York, Graduate Faculty in Social Welfare, 2006), 37.

224   Notes to Pages 40–42

62. Michael Demming, *The Cultural Front: The Laboring of American Culture in the Twentieth Century* (New York: Verso, 1996).

63. L. M. Bogad, *Electoral Guerrilla Theater: Radical Ridicule and Social Movements* (New York: Routledge, 2005).

64. Reed, *The Art of Protest: Culture and Activism from the Civil Rights Movement to the Streets of Seattle*, 1.

65. Shepard, "If I Can't Dance: Play, Creativity, and Social Movements," 117; Abbie Hoffman, "Museum of the Streets," 1980, http://theanarchistlibrary.org/library/Abbie_Hoffman__Museum_of_the_Streets.html.

66. Carol Hanisch, "A Critique of the Miss America Protest," in Notes from the Second Year: Women's Liberation, ed. Shulamith Firestone and Anne Koedt (New York: The New York Radical Women, 1968), 86–88.

67. Shepard, "If I Can't Dance: Play, Creativity, and Social Movements," 163.

68. Benjamin Shepard and Ronald Hayduk, *From ACT UP to the WTO: Urban Protest and Community Building in the Era of Globalization* (New York: Verso, 2002); Shepard, "If I Can't Dance: Play, Creativity, and Social Movements."

69. Shepard and Hayduk, *From ACT UP to the WTO: Urban Protest and Community Building in the Era of Globalization*.

70. Shepard, "If I Can't Dance: Play, Creativity, and Social Movements," 23.

71. Andrew Boyd, "Irony, Meme Warfare, and the Extreme Costume Ball," in *From ACT UP to the WTO: Urban Protest and Community Building in the Era of Globalization*, ed. Benjamin Shepard and Ronald Hayduk (New York: Verso, 2002): 245–53; Billionaires For Bush, "Billionaires For Bush Website," 2009, http://www.billionairesforbush.com/.

72. Shepard, "If I Can't Dance: Play, Creativity, and Social Movements," 54.

73. Shepard, "If I Can't Dance: Play, Creativity, and Social Movements."

74. James Jasper, *The Art of Moral Protest: Culture, Biography, and Creativity in Social Movements* (Chicago: University of Chicago Press, 1997), 8.

75. Wini Brienes, *Community and Organization in the New Left: 1962–1968* (South Hadley, MA: Praeger, 1982); Reed, *The Art of Protest: Culture and Activism from the Civil Rights Movement to the Streets of Seattle*; Shepard, "If I Can't Dance: Play, Creativity, and Social Movements."

76. Duncombe, *Dream*, 67–70.

77. Yuen, "Introduction," xv.

78. Shepard, "If I Can't Dance: Play, Creativity, and Social Movements."

Notes to Pages 42–45

79. Yuen, "Introduction," xvii.

80. Shepard, "If I Can't Dance: Play, Creativity, and Social Movements," 857.

81. Boal, *Legislative Theater: Using Performance to Make Politics* (New York: Routledge, 1998), 16, similarly proposed to "make 'theatre as politics,' instead of simply making 'political theatre.'"

82. Paulo Freire, *Pedagogy of the Oppressed* (New York: Continuum, 1970).

83. Centro Ecuménico de Educación Popular, *Técnicas Participativas Para La Educación Popular* (Buenos Aires: Editorial Lumen Humanitas, 1996); Mariano Algava, *Jugar y Jugarse: Las Técnicas y la dimensión lúdica de la educación popular* (Rosario, Argentina: Ediciones América Libre, 2006).

84. Mariano Algava, "Cuando el pueblo se juega (juego, subjetividad y Realidad)," in *Pedagogía de la Resistencia: Cuadernos De Educación Popular*, ed. Claudia Korol (Buenos Aires: Asociación Madres de Plaza de Mayo, 2004), 239.

85. Rick Arnold and Bev Burke, *A Popular Education Handbook* (Toronto: OISE, 1982); Rick Arnold, Barndt Deborah, and Bev Burke, *A New Weave: Popular Education in Canada and Central America* (Toronto: OISE, 1985); Centro Ecuménico de Educación Popular, *Técnicas participativas para la educación popular*. Rosa Parks had been trained at the Highlander Center before she sparked the bus boycott, and Project South was the lead organizer of the first US Social Forum, in 2007.

86. Augusto Boal, *Theater of the Oppressed* (New York: Theater Communications Group, 1979).

87. Augusto Boal, *Games for Actors and Non-Actors*, trans. Adrian Jackson (New York: Routledge, 2002).

88. Ibid., 244.

89. Boal, *Legislative Theater: Using Performance to Make Politics*.

90. Augusto International Theater of the Oppressed Organization, "Theatre of the Oppressed Website," 2010, http://www.theatreoftheoppressed.org.

91. Kheir Al-Kodmany, "Visualization Tools and Methods for Participatory Planning and Design," *Journal of Urban Technology* 8, no. 2 (August 2001): 1–37; Ernesto Arias, "Bottom-up Neighbourhood Revitalisation: A Language Approach for Participatory Decision Support," *Urban Studies* 33, no. 10 (December 1996): 1831–1848; Heather Urie, "Trying to Entice Public to Meetings, Boulder Offers Prizes," *Boulder Daily Camera*, October 17, 2010, http://www.dailycamera.com/ci_16339442.

92. Involve, *Not Another Consultation! Making Community Engagement Informal and Fun* (London: Local Government Improvement and Development, November 2010), http://www.local.gov.uk/web/guest/health/-/journal_content/56/10171/3510888/ARTICLE-TEMPLATE.

93. JoAnn Greco, "Can Do in San Juan's Cano," *Planning*, April 2009.

94. Stephanie Guilloud and William Cordery, "Fundraising Is Not a Dirty Word: Community-Based Economic Strategies for the Long Haul," in *The Revolution Will Not Be Funded: Beyond the Non-profit Industrial Complex*, ed. INCITE! Women of Color against Violence (Cambridge, MA: South End Press, 2007).

95. Rebecca Abers, *Inventing Local Democracy: Grassroots Politics in Brazil* (Boulder, CO: Lynne Rienner Publishers, 2000); Gianpaolo Baiocchi, "Participation, Activism, and Politics: The Porto Alegre Experiment," in *Deepening Democracy: Institutional Innovations in Empowered Participatory Governance*, ed. Archon Fung and Erik Olin Wright (New York: Verso, 2003): 45-76; Gianpaolo Baiocchi, *Militants and Citizens: The Politics of Participatory Democracy in Porto Alegre* (Stanford: Stanford University Press, 2005); Boaventura de Sousa Santos, "Participatory Budgeting in Porto Alegre: Toward a Redistributive Democracy," *Politics and Society* 26, no. 4 (1998): 461–510.

96. Giovanni Allegretti and Carsten Herzberg, "Participatory Budgets in Europe: Between Efficiency and Growing Local Democracy," *The Transnational Institute Briefing Series*, Amsterdam: The Transnational Institute, 2004; Gianpaolo Baiocchi, ed., *Radicals in Power. The Workers' Party and Experiments in Urban Democracy in Brazil* (London: Zed Books, 2003); Josh Lerner, "Let the People Decide: Transformative Community Development through Participatory Budgeting in Canada," *Shelterforce*, 2006; Josh Lerner and Donata Secondo, "By the People, For the People: Participatory Budgeting from the Bottom Up in North America," *Journal of Public Deliberation* 8, no. 2 (2012), http://www.publicdeliberation.net/jpd/vol8/iss2/art2/; Gianpaolo Baiocchi and Ernesto Ganuza, "The Power of Ambiguity: How Participatory Budgeting Travels the Globe," *Journal of Public Deliberation* 8, no. 2 (2012), http://www.publicdeliberation.net/jpd/vol8/iss2/art8/.

97. Lerner, "Communal Councils in Venezuela: Can 200 Families Revolutionize Democracy?"; T. M. Isaac and Patrick Heller, "Democracy and Development: Decentralized Planning in Kerala," in Deepening Democracy: Institutional Innovations in Empowered Participatory Governance, ed. Archon Fung and Erik Olin Wright (New York: Verso, 2003), 77–110.

98. Abt, *Serious Games*; Costikyan, "I Have No Words and I Must Design."

99. Boal, *Games for Actors and Non-Actors*; Arnold, Deborah, and Burke, *A New Weave: Popular Education in Canada and Central America*; Baiocchi, "Participation, Activism, and Politics: The Porto Alegre Experiment."

100. *Games for Actors and Non-Actors*, 15, xxiv.

101. Algava, *Jugar y jugarse: Las Técnicas y la dimensión lúdica de la educación popular*; Inés Moreno, *El Juego y los juegos* (Buenos Aires: Lumen Hvmanitas, 2005); Gilda Haas, "Gilda's Gaming Adventure," *Dr. Pop*, April 13, 2010, http://drpop.org/2010/04/gildas-gaming-adventure/.

102. Salen and Zimmerman, *Rules of Play: Game Design Fundamentals*; Katie Salen and Eric Zimmerman, eds., *The Game Design Reader: A Rules of Play Anthology*, 2nd ed. (Cambridge: MIT Press, 2006); Fullerton, *Game Design Workshop*.

Chapter 3

1. This game-playing vignette is adapted from Edward Castronova, "Virtual Worlds: A First-Hand Account of Market and Society on the Cyberian Frontier," CESifo Working Paper Series, SSRN (Social Science Research Network) no. 618 (December 2001).

2. Ibid.

3. Game design might offer other lessons for nondemocratic politics, but those are beyond the scope of this book.

4. Salen and Zimmerman, *Rules of Play: Game Design Fundamentals*, 80.

5. Ibid., 32–33.

6. Fullerton, *Game Design Workshop*, 2nd ed., 2.

7. Constance Steinkuehler, "The Mangle of Play," *Games and Culture* 1, no. 3 (2006): 199.

8. Salen and Zimmerman, *Rules of Play: Game Design Fundamentals*, 66–67.

9. Farmer and Morningstar, in Salen and Zimmerman, *The Game Design Reader*.

10. Jia Wu, *Global Video Game Market Forecast* (Strategy Analytics, February 5, 2010), http://strategyanalytics.com/default.aspx?mod=ReportAbstractViewer&a0=5282; Dobuzinskis, "Global Movie Box Office Nears $30 Billion in 2009."

11. For reviews of these debates, see Jesper Juul, *Half-Real: Video Games Between Real Rules and Fictional Worlds* (Cambridge: MIT Press, 2005); Salen and Zimmerman, *The Game Design Reader*; Salen and Zimmerman, *Rules of Play: Game Design Fundamentals*.

12. Daniel Benmergui, *personal communication*, November 6, 2009.

13. Daniel Benmergui, *personal communication*, November 6, 2009.

14. Richard Bartle, "Hearts, Clubs, Diamonds, Spades: Players Who Suit MUDs," *MUSE Ltd.*, 1996, http://www.mud.co.uk/richard/hcds.htm.

15. Fullerton, *Game Design Workshop*, 2nd ed.

16. Salen and Zimmerman, *Rules of Play: Game Design Fundamentals*, 11–13.

17. Clive Thompson, "Halo 3: How Microsoft Labs Invented a New Science of Play," *Wired*, September 2007, http://www.wired.com/gaming/virtualworlds/magazine/15-09/ff_halo?currentPage=all.

18. Doug Church, "Formal Abstract Design Tools," *Gamasutra*, July 16, 1999, http://www.gamasutra.com/view/feature/3357/formal_abstract_design_tools.php.

19. D. Cook, "What Are Game Mechanics?" *Lost Garden*, October 23, 2006, http://www.lostgarden.com/2006/10/what-are-game-mechanics.html.

20. Sus Lundgren and Staffan Björk, "Game Mechanics: Describing Computer-Augmented Games in Terms of Interaction," in *Terms of Interaction. Proceedings of TIDSE 2003*, 2003, 45–56, http://citeseerx.ist.psu.edu/viewdoc/summary?doi=10.1.1.13.5147.

21. Aki Järvinen, *Games Without Frontiers: Theories and Methods for Game Studies and Design* (Tampere: Tampere University Press, 2008), 254.

22. Miguel Sicart, "Defining Game Mechanics," *Game Studies* 8, no. 2 (2008), http://gamestudies.org/0802/articles/sicart.

23. Fullerton, *Game Design Workshop, Second Edition*, 33.

24. Ibid., 29.

25. Staffan Björk and Jussi Holopainen, "Games and Design Patterns," in *The Game Design Reader*, ed. Katie Salen and Eric Zimmerman (Cambridge: MIT Press, 2006), 421.

26. Church, "Formal Abstract Design Tools."

27. Richard Rouse III, *Game Design Theory and Practice* (Plano, TX: Wordware Publishing, 2005), 310.

28. Marc LeBlanc, "Tools for Creating Dramatic Game Dynamics," in *The Game Design Reader*, ed. Katie Salen and Eric Zimmerman (Cambridge: MIT Press, 2006), 438–59.

29. Ibid.

30. Fullerton, *Game Design Workshop*, 2nd ed., 42.

31. Salen and Zimmerman, *Rules of Play: Game Design Fundamentals*.

32. LeBlanc, "Tools for Creating Dramatic Game Dynamics."

33. Salen and Zimmerman, *Rules of Play: Game Design Fundamentals*, 250.

34. Jason Corace, *personal communication*, March 9, 2009.

35. Mattia Romeo, *personal communication*, March 17, 2009.

36. Salen and Zimmerman, *Rules of Play: Game Design Fundamentals*, 250.

37. Huizinga, *Homo Ludens: A Study of the Play Element in Culture*, 10.

38. Salen and Zimmerman, *Rules of Play: Game Design Fundamentals*, 94–95.

39. Suits, *Grasshopper: Games, Life, and Utopia*, 48–55.

40. Juul, *Half-Real*.

41. Salen and Zimmerman, *Rules of Play: Game Design Fundamentals*, 224–25; Fullerton, *Game Design Workshop*, 2nd ed., 132–33.

42. Csikszentmihalyi, *Flow: The Psychology of Optimal Experience*.

43. Salen and Zimmerman, *Rules of Play: Game Design Fundamentals*, 225.

44. Ibid., 351.

45. Gee, *What Video Games Have to Teach Us about Learning and Literacy*, 67.

46. Salen and Zimmerman, *Rules of Play: Game Design Fundamentals*, 224–25; Fullerton, *Game Design Workshop*, 2nd ed., 132–33.

47. LeBlanc, "Tools for Creating Dramatic Game Dynamics."

48. Salen and Zimmerman, *Rules of Play: Game Design Fundamentals*.

49. Fullerton, *Game Design Workshop*, 2nd ed., 30.

50. Erik Erikson, *Childhood and Society* (New York: Van Nostrand Reinhold, 1985), 212.

51. Stephen Sniderman, "Unwritten Rules," *The Life of Games*, October 1999, http://www.gamepuzzles.com/tlog/tlog2.htm.

52. Salen and Zimmerman, *Rules of Play: Game Design Fundamentals*, 128–29.

53. Sniderman, "Unwritten Rules."

54. Jo (aka Joreen) Freeman, "The Tyranny of Stucturelessness," in *Radical Feminism*, ed. Anne Koedt, Ellen Levine, and Anita Rapone (New York: Quadrangle, 1973), http://www.jofreeman.com/joreen/tyranny.htm.

55. Suits, *Grasshopper: Games, Life, and Utopia*, 45.

56. Linda Hughes, "Beyond the Rules of the Game: Why Are Rooie Rules Nice?" in *The Game Design Reader*, ed. Katie Salen and Eric Zimmerman (Cambridge: MIT Press, 2006), 514.

57. Fullerton, *Game Design Workshop*, 2nd ed., 71.

58. Gee, *What Video Games Have to Teach Us about Learning and Literacy*, 110.

59. Ibid., 113.

60. Ibid., 136.

61. Hughes, "Beyond the Rules of the Game: Why Are Rooie Rules Nice?"

62. Salen and Zimmerman, *Rules of Play: Game Design Fundamentals*, 282, 285.

63. Bernard DeKoven, "Changing the Game," in *The Game Design Reader*, ed. Katie Salen and Eric Zimmerman (Cambridge: MIT Press, 2006), 532.

64. Lerner and Secondo, "By the People, for the People: Participatory Budgeting from the Bottom up in North America."

65. Salen and Zimmerman, *Rules of Play: Game Design Fundamentals*, 276–77.

66. Sniderman, "Unwritten Rules."

67. Fullerton, *Game Design Workshop, Second Edition*, 60–65.

68. Salen and Zimmerman, *Rules of Play: Game Design Fundamentals*, 342.

69. Church, "Formal Abstract Design Tools," 372.

70. Salen and Zimmerman, *Rules of Play: Game Design Fundamentals*, 80.

71. LeBlanc, "Tools for Creating Dramatic Game Dynamics."

72. Fullerton, *Game Design Workshop*, 2nd ed., 32.

73. LeBlanc, "Tools for Creating Dramatic Game Dynamics."

74. Brian Sutton-Smith, *The Ambiguity of Play* (Cambridge: Harvard University Press, 1997), 71; Caillois, *Man, Play, and Games*.

75. Jason Corace, *personal communication*, March 9, 2009.

76. Fullerton, *Game Design Workshop*, 2nd ed., 336.

77. Ken Birdwell, "The Cabal: Valve's Design Process for Creating Half-Life," *Gamasutra*, December 10, 1999, http://www.gamasutra.com/view/feature/3408/the_cabal _valves_design_process_.php.

78. Gee, *What Video Games Have to Teach Us about Learning and Literacy*.

79. Henry Kenkins, "'Complete Freedom of Movement': Video Games as Gendered Play Space," in *The Game Design Reader*, ed. Katie Salen and Eric Zimmerman (Cambridge: MIT Press, 2006), 330–63.

80. Axel Stockburger, "Listen to the Bulk of the Iceberg," in *Space Time Play: Computer Games, Architecture and Urbanism: The Next Level* (Boston: Springer, 2007).

81. Csikszentmihalyi, *Flow: The Psychology of Optimal Experience*; Salen and Zimmerman, *Rules of Play: Game Design Fundamentals*, 315; Brenda Laurel, *Computers as Theater* (Reading, MA: Addison-Wesley Professional, 1991), 161.

82. Salen and Zimmerman, *Rules of Play: Game Design Fundamentals*, 316–17.

83. Andrew Rollings and Ernest Adams, *On Game Design* (Indianapolis: New Riders, 2003), 38.

Notes to Pages 75–82

84. Gee, *What Video Games Have to Teach Us about Learning and Literacy*, 105.

85. Fullerton, *Game Design Workshop,* 2nd ed., 318.

86. Ibid., 334–35.

87. Ibid., 30.

88. Costikyan, "I Have No Words and I Must Design."

89. Ibid., 199.

90. LeBlanc, "Tools for Creating Dramatic Game Dynamics."

91. Fullerton, *Game Design Workshop,* 2nd ed.; Katherine Isbister, *Better Game Characters by Design: A Psychological Approach* (San Francisco: Morgan Kaufmann, 2006).

92. Martın Hand and Karenza Moore, "Community, Identity and Digital Games," in *Understanding Digital Games,* ed. Jason Rutter and Jo Bryce (London: Sage Pubications, 2006), 166–83.

93. Church, "Formal Abstract Design Tools."

94. Fullerton, *Game Design Workshop,* 2nd ed., 104.

95. LeBlanc, "Tools for Creating Dramatic Game Dynamics," 457.

96. Greg Costikyan, "Where Stories End and Games Begin," *Game Developer* (September 2000): 44–53.

97. (Markku Eskelinen, "The Gaming Situation," *Game Studies* 1, no. 1 (2001), http://www.gamestudies.org/0101/eskelinen/.)

98. Henry Jenkins, "Game Design as Narrative Architecture," in *First Person: New Media as Story, Performance, and Game,* ed. Noah Windrip-Fruin and Pat Harrigan (Cambridge: MIT Press, 2004),118–30; Michael Mateas and Andrew Stern, "Interaction and Narrative," in *The Game Design Reader*, ed. Katie Salen and Eric Zimmerman (Cambridge: MIT Press, 2006): 642–69.

99. Jenkins, "Game Design as Narrative Architecture"; Mateas and Stern, "Interaction and Narrative."

100. Rogers M. Smith, *Stories of Peoplehood: The Politics and Morals of Political Membership* (Cambridge, UK: Cambridge University Press, 2003).

101. Salen and Zimmerman, *Rules of Play: Game Design Fundamentals.*

102. Tom Chick, "Shoot Club: The DOOM 3 Review," in *The Game Design Reader,* ed. Katie Salen and Eric Zimmerman (Cambridge: MIT Press, 2006), 156–69; Salen and Zimmerman, *The Game Design Reader,* 5.

103. Gee, *What Video Games Have to Teach Us about Learning and Literacy*, 5.

104. Koster, *A Theory of Fun for Game Design*.

105. Kahne, Middaugh, and Evans, "The Civic Potential of Video Games."

106. Gee, *What Video Games Have to Teach Us about Learning and Literacy*; James Paul Gee, *Good Video Games + Good Learning* (New York: Peter Lang, 2007); Koster, *A Theory of Fun for Game Design*; Eric Klopfer, Scot Osterweil, and Katie Salen, *Moving Learning Games Forward* (Cambridge: Educational Arcade, 2009), http://education .mit.edu/papers/MovingLearningGamesForward_EdArcade.pdf; "Games Learning Society Website," 2010, http://www.gameslearningsociety.org/; Eric Klopfer, *Augmented Learning: Research and Design of Mobile Educational Games* (Cambridge: MIT Press, 2008); Kurt Squire and Henry Jenkins, "Harnessing the Power of Games in Education," *Insight*, 2004; Janna Jackson, "Game-based Teaching: What Educators Can Learn from Videogames," *Teaching Education* 20, no. 3 (2009): 291; Marc Prensky, *Digital Game-Based Learning* (New York: McGraw-Hill, 2001).

107. Klopfer, Osterweil, and Salen, *Moving Learning Games Forward*. Starting in 2006, the Games, Learning and Society group "Games Learning Society" website has brought together academics, designers, and educators to discuss both approaches through annual conferences and other discussions. See Ibid.

108. "Quest to Learn" website, 2010, http://q2l.org/.

109. Stefanie Olsen, "Educational Video Games with a Mix of Cool and Purpose," *New York Times*, November 1, 2009, http://www.nytimes.com/2009/11/02/ technology/02games.html; "Institute of Play," 2010, http://www.instituteofplay .com/; "Games for Learning Institute," 2010, http://g4li.org/; "The Education Arcade," 2010, http://www.educationarcade.org/.

110. John C. Beck and Mitchell Wade, *The Kids Are Alright: How the Gamer Generation Is Changing the Workplace* (Cambridge: Harvard Business Press, 2006).

111. John Seely Brown and Douglas Thomas, "You Play World of Warcraft? You're Hired!," *WIRED*, April 2006, http://www.wired.com/wired/archive/14.04/learn .html.

112. Gagandeep, "PSP To Instill 'Team Play' in Hilton Garden Inn," *Gaming Blog*, September 29, 2008, http://www.gamingblog.org/psp-to-instill-team-play-in-hilton -garden-inn.html; Luke Plunkett, "The McDonalds Nintendo DSi," *Kotaku*, April 19, 2010, http://kotaku.com/5520108/the-mcdonalds-nintendo-dsi.

113. Katherine Mangan, "Future Business Leaders Cut Loose at MIT," *Chronicle of Higher Education*, April 3, 2011, sec. Graduate Students, http://chronicle.com/article/ At-MIT-Future-Business/126981/.

114. John Seely Brown and Douglas Thomas, "Breakthrough Ideas for 2008: The Gamer Disposition," *Harvard Business Review* (February 2008), http://blogs.hbr.org/ cs/2008/02/the_gamer_disposition.html.

Notes to Pages 84–89 233

115. John Hagel and John Seely Brown, "How World of Warcraft Promotes Innovation," *Bloomberg Businessweek*, January 14, 2009, http://www.businessweek.com/stories/2009-01-14/how-world-of-warcraft-promotes-innovationbusinessweek-business-news-stock-market-and-financial-advice.

116. Brown and Thomas, "Breakthrough Ideas for 2008: The Gamer Disposition."

117. Hagel and Brown, "How World of Warcraft Promotes Innovation."

118. Friedrich von Borries, Steffen P. Walz, and Matthias Böttger, *Space Time Play: Computer Games, Architecture and Urbanism* (Boston: Springer, 2007); J. C. Hubers et al., eds., *Game Set and Match* (Delft: Faculty of Architecture, DUT, 2004); Kas Oosterhuis and Lukas Feireiss, eds., *Game Set and Match II: On Computer Games, Advanced Geometries, and Digital Technologies* (Rotterdam: Episode, 2006).

119. Borries, Walz, and Böttger, *Space Time Play: Computer Games, Architecture and Urbanism*; Hubers et al., *Game Set and Match*; Oosterhuis and Feireiss, *Game Set and Match II: On Computer Games, Advanced Geometries, and Digital Technologies*.

120. Play Stations: Neil Leach, in conversation with the editors of STP: (328).

Chapter 4

1. María del Carmen Fernández, "Con los Niños, para todos," in *Experiencia Rosario*, ed. United Nations Development Program (Rosario, Argentina: United Nations Development Program, 2006), 177.

2. Daniel Chavez and Benjamin Goldfrank, *The Left in the City: Participatory Local Governments in Latin America* (London: Latin American Bureau and Transnational Institute, 2004); Evelina Dagnino, Alberto Olvera Rivera, and Aldo Panfichi, *La Disputa por la construcción democrática en América Latina* (Mexico City: Centro de Investigaciones y Estudios Superiores en Antropología Social, 2006); Abal Medina and Juan Manuel, *Participación y control ciudadano* (Buenos Aires, Argentina: Editorial Prometeo, 2009); Yanina Welp and Serdült Uwe, eds., *Armas de doble phyllo: La Participación ciudadana en la encrucijada* (Buenos Aires: Prometeo Libros, 2009); Andrew Selee and Enrique Peruzzotti, eds., *Participatory Innovation and Representative Democracy in Latin America* (Baltimore: Johns Hopkins University Press, 2009); Santos, *Democratizing Democracy*.

3. Baiocchi, *Militants and Citizens: The Politics of Participatory Democracy in Porto Alegre*; Abers, *Inventing Local Democracy: Grassroots Politics in Brazil*; Santos, "Participatory Budgeting in Porto Alegre: Toward a Redistributive Democracy."

4. Eduardo Canel, *Barrio Democracy in Latin America: Participatory Decentralization and Community Activism in Montevideo* (State College: Pennsylvania State Press, 2010); Benjamin Goldfrank, "The Fragile Flower of Local Democracy: A Case Study of Decentralization/participation in Montevideo," *Politics and Society* 30, no. 1

(2002): 51; Daniel Chavez, *Polis and Demos: The Left in Municipal Governance in Montevideo and Porto Alegre* (Maastricht, Netherlands: Shaker Publishing, 2004).

5. Michael Coppedge, "The Dynamic Diversity of Latin American Party Systems," *Party Politics* 4, no. 4 (October 1, 1998): 547–68.

6. Edward L. Gibson, ed., *Federalism and Democracy in Latin America* (Baltimore: Johns Hopkins University Press, 2004).

7. Municipalidad de Rosario, "Indicadores demográficos," 2011, http://www .rosario.gov.ar/sitio/caracteristicas/indicadores.jsp?nivel=Ciudad&ult=Ci_3.

8. Municipalidad de Rosario, "Origen de Rosario," 2011, http://www.rosario.gov.ar/ sitio/caracteristicas/historia/historia1.jsp; Michael Johns, "The Urbanisation of a Secondary City: The Case of Rosario, Argentina, 1870–1920," *Journal of Latin American Studies* 23, no. 03 (1991): 489–513.

9. Juan García, interviewed by Howard Richards; personal communication with Howard Richards, July 2006.

10. Florencia Almansi, "Rosario's Development; Interview with Miguel Lifschitz, Mayor of Rosario, Argentina," *Environment and Urbanization* 21, no. 1 (April 2009): 19–35; Lerner and Schugurensky, "Who Learns What in Participatory Democracy? Participatory Budgeting in Rosario, Argentina"; Lylia Maxera, ed., *Innovación y espacio local: En la Gestión municipal de la ciudad de Rosario (1995–1999)* (Rosario, Argentina: Universidad Nacional de Rosario, 1999); Municipalidad de Rosario, *Experiencia Rosario: Políticas para la gobernabilidad* (Rosario, Argentina: United Nations Development Program, 2006).

11. Guillermo Zysman, "Eramos tan pobres," *Rosario 12* (Rosario, Argentina, May 22, 2008), http://www.pagina12.com.ar/diario/suplementos/rosario/9-13644-2008 -05-22.html.

12. Almansi, "Rosario's Development; Interview with Miguel Lifschitz, Mayor of Rosario, Argentina"; Municipalidad de Rosario, *Experiencia Rosario: Políticas para la gobernabilidad.*

13. Francesco Tonucci, *La Ciudad de Los Niños: Un Modo nuevo de pensar la ciudad* (Buenos Aires: Editorial Losada, 1996).

14. Ibid., 79. All quotes in this and other Spanish-language sources were translated by the author.

15. Carla Teppa, *Proyecto la Ciudad de las Niñas y los niños* (Rosario, Argentina: Municipalidad de Rosario, 2009), 18.

16. Much of the basic information below about the project is drawn from Teppa, *Proyecto la Ciudad de las Niñas y los niños.*

17. Ibid., 19.

18. *Juego* means both play and game in Spanish, but when used broadly in its singular form, it refers more to play.

19. Del Carmen Fernández, "Con los niños, para todos," 181.

20. Teppa, *Proyecto La Ciudad de las Niñas y los niños*, 35.

21. Del Carmen Fernández, "Con los niños, para todos," 177.

22. The story of the monument is based on the archival registry of activities of the City of the Children program.

23. Some names of individuals and locations in the programs I discuss have been changed, to protect confidentiality when attributed comments or actions might lead to reprimands from coworkers or neighbors.

24. María Paula Ballesteros, "Los Chicos quieren saber de qué se trata" (Universidad Nacional de Rosario, 2009).

25. Chiqui González, "Políticas de infancia: El Paisaje de La Ciudadanía," in *Experiencia Rosario*, ed. Municipalidad de Rosario (Rosario, Argentina: United Nations Development Program, 2006).

26. Boal, *Theater of the Oppressed*.

27. Boal, *Games for Actors and Non-Actors*.

28. Ibid., 106.

29. Brown and Vaughan, *Play*, 161.

30. Alison Kadlec, "Play and Public Life," *National Civic Review* 98, no. 4 (2010): 3–11.

31. Borries, Walz, and Böttger, *Space Time Play: Computer Games, Architecture and Urbanism*.

32. Brown and Vaughan, *Play*.

33. Scott, *Domination and the Arts of Resistance*.

34. Atul Gawande, *The Checklist Manifesto* (New York: Metropolitan Books, 2009), 108.

35. Ibid.

36. Algava, *Jugar y jugarse: Las Técnicas y la dimensión lúdica de la educación popular*.

37. Brown and Vaughan, *Play*, 48.

38. Teppa, *Proyecto la Ciudad de las Niñas y los niños*, 27.

39. Ana Valderrama, "Sueños De Plaza," *Matéricos Periféricos* no. 10 (2009): 48–61.

40. The Trust for Public Land, "NYC Playgrounds Program," 2009, http://www.tpl.org/what-we-do/where-we-work/new-york/ny-city-playgrounds.html.

41. Municipalidad de Rosario, "Presupuesto participativo joven," 2011, http://www.rosario.gov.ar/sitio/desarrollo_social/juventud/pp_joven_anteriores.jsp.

42. Tonucci, *La Ciudad de los Niños: Un Modo nuevo de pensar la ciudad*, 61.

43. Archon Fung, *Empowered Participation: Reinventing Urban Democracy* (Princeton: Princeton University Press, 2006).

44. González, "Políticas de infancia: El Paisaje de la ciudadanía," 170.

45. Del Carmen Fernández, "Con los Niños, para todos."

46. González, "Políticas de infancia: El Paisaje de la ciudadanía," 170.

Chapter 5

1. Fung and Wright, *Deepening Democracy*; Santos, *Democratizing Democracy*; Andrea Cornwall and Vera Schatten Coelho, *Spaces for Change? The Politics of Citizen Participation in New Democratic Arenas* (London: Zed Books, 2007).

2. Gee, *What Video Games Have to Teach Us about Learning and Literacy*, 216.

3. Florencia Almansi, "Regularizing Land Tenure within Upgrading Programmes in Argentina: The Cases of Promeba and Rosario Habitat," *Environment and Urbanization* 21, no. 2 (September 2009): 389–413.

4. Ana Maria Rodriguez and Adriana Salomón, "The Rosario Habitat Experience: Project Management Applied to Government," *PM World Today* XI, no. 11 (November 2009): 1–9.

5. Almansi, "Regularizing Land Tenure within Upgrading Programmes in Argentina: The Cases of Promeba and Rosario Habitat"; Rodriguez and Salomón, "The Rosario Habitat Experience: Project Management Applied to Government."

6. La Capital, "Rosario Hábitat beneficiará a 600 familias en Molino Blanco," *La Capital* (Rosario, Argentina, December 16, 2003).

7. "Erradican a 200 familias en Villa la Lata y Abren Calles," *La Capital*, August 13, 2003, http://archivo.lacapital.com.ar/2003/08/13/ciudad/noticia_27064.shtml.

8. Alberto Ford and Martín Carné, "Desafíos de la participación en la implementación de políticas públicas," in *Construyendo confianza: Hacia un nuevo vínculo entre estado y sociedad civil*, vol. 2, ed. Alejandro Belmonte (Buenos Aires: Fundación CIPPEC / Subsecretaría para la Reforma Institucional y Fortalecimiento de la Democracia de la Nación de Argentina, 2009), 49–80; Fung and Wright, I.

9. For example, residents were responsible for building their own new bathrooms, using materials provided by the program. In the first two sectors of Las Flores they demanded that staff deliver the materials directly to each house. Afterward, they agreed to coordinate distribution themselves, after staff dropped off the materials in a central location.

10. *Mate* is a tea-like beverage that is ubiquitous in Argentine. It is consumed communally, by passing around a *mate* gourd filled with the *mate* herb and constantly replenished hot water. Each person sips the mate through the same metal straw.

11. Freire, *Pedagogy of the Oppressed*; Centro Ecuménico de Educación Popular, *Técnicas participativas para la educación popular*; Gustavo Romero et al., *La Participación en el diseño urbano y arquitectónico en la producción social del hábitat* (Mexico City: UNAM, 2004); María Teresa Sirvent, *Estrategias participativas en educación de adultos: Sus alcances y limitaciones* (San José, Costa Rica: Centro Interamericano para la Educación, la Ciencia y la Cultura, 1984).

12. In Spanish, staff refer to many of these game mechanics as "técnicas lúdicas" (playful techniques).

13. Salen and Zimmerman, *Rules of Play: Game Design Fundamentals*, 316–17.

14. Csikszentmihalyi, *Flow: The Psychology of Optimal Experience*; Salen and Zimmerman, *Rules of Play: Game Design Fundamentals*, 315; Laurel, *Computers as Theater*, 161.

15. Bachrach and Baratz, "The Two Faces of Power"; John Gaventa, *Power and Powerlessness: Quiescence and Rebellion in an Appalachian Valley* (Chicago: University of Chicago Press, 1980).

16. *Jugar y Jugarse: Las Técnicas y la dimensión lúdica de la educación popular*, 9.

17. *Rules of Play: Game Design Fundamentals*, 475.

18. Hughes, "Beyond the Rules of the Game: Why Are Rooie Rules Nice?" This occurs most commonly in casual sports and playground games, although digital games increasingly allow players to modify the parameters of gameplay as well.

19. *What Video Games Have to Teach Us about Learning and Literacy*, 110.

20. Robert Chaskin, "Democracy and Bureaucracy in a Community Planning Process," *Journal of Planning Education and Research* 24, no. 4 (2005): 408–19.

21. Huizinga, *Homo Ludens: A Study of the Play Element in Culture*, 10.

22. *Pobres ciudadanos. Las Clases populares en la era democrática* (Buenos Aires, Argentina: Editorial Gorla, 2005).

23. Patsy Healey, *Collaborative Planning: Shaping Places in Fragmented Societies* (Vancouver: UBC Press, 1997); Judith Innes and David Booher, "Reframing Public

Participation: Strategies for the 21st Century," *Planning Theory and Practice* 5, no. 4 (December 2004): 419–36.

24. Fung, "Varieties of Participation in Complex Governance."

25. Salen and Zimmerman, *Rules of Play: Game Design Fundamentals*, 80.

26. Paulo M. Filho-D'Avila, Vladimyr Jorge-Lombardo, and Ana Fernanda Coelho, "Acesso ao poder. Clientelismo e democracia participativa desconstruindo uma dicotomia," *Civitas—Revista de Ciências Sociais* 4, no. 2 (2004): 4211–33; Auyero, *Poor People's Politics: Peronist Survival Networks and the Legacy of Evita*.

27. Fullerton, *Game Design Workshop*, 2nd ed., 32.

28. This process is similar to the cultural politics of Alvarez, Dagnino, and Escobar, *Cultures of Politics, Politics of Cultures: Re-visioning Latin American Social Movements* (Boulder: Westview Press, 1998).

29. Borries, Walz, and Böttger, *Space Time Play: Computer Games, Architecture and Urbanism*; Steffen P. Walz, *Toward a Ludic Architecture: The Space of Play and Games* (Pittsburgh: ETC Press, 2010); Al-Kodmany, "Visualization Tools and Methods for Participatory Planning and Design"; Arias, "Bottom-up Neighbourhood Revitalisation: A Language Approach for Participatory Decision Support."

30. William Baker, H. Lon Addams, and Brian Davis, "Critical Factors for Enhancing Municipal Public Hearings," *Public Administration Review* 65, no. 4 (August 2005): 490–99; Fung, "Varieties of Participation in Complex Governance"; Innes and Booher, "Reframing Public Participation: Strategies for the 21st Century."

Chapter 6

1. Cora Giordana, "Rosario sigue siendo una gran receptora de inmigrantes," *Clarín* (Rosario, Argentina, November 3, 2007), sec. Suplemento Rosario; City of Toronto, "Toronto Facts, Toronto's Racial Diversity," 2011, http://www.toronto.ca/toronto _facts/diversity.htm.

2. *Rob Ford's Compassion for the Homeless*, 2002, http://www.youtube.com/ watch?v=8YZQ4oQjxgc.

3. Abers, *Inventing Local Democracy: Grassroots Politics in Brazil*; Baiocchi, *Militants and Citizens: The Politics of Participatory Democracy in Porto Alegre*.

4. Santos, "Participatory Budgeting in Porto Alegre: Toward a Redistributive Democracy"; Baiocchi, *Militants and Citizens: The Politics of Participatory Democracy in Porto Alegre*.

5. Baiocchi and Ganuza, "The Power of Ambiguity: How Participatory Budgeting Travels the Globe."

Notes to Pages 152–159

6. *Participatory Budgeting* (Washington, DC: The World Bank, 2007); UN-Habitat, "Participatory Budgeting," *2010 Best Practices Database*, 2010, http://www .unhabitat.org/bestpractices/2010/mainview04.asp?BPID=2548.

7. Josh Lerner and Jez Hall, "Participatory Budgeting: A New Tool for Democratic Decision Making," *Transformation* 5 (Spring 2007): 10–15; Nick Mahony, "Making Democracy Spectacular," *Representation* 46, no. 3 (2010): 339.

8. Elizabeth Pinnington, Josh Lerner, and Daniel Schugurensky, "Participatory Budgeting in North America: The Case of Guelph, Canada," *Journal of Public Budgeting, Accounting and Financial Management* 2/3, no. 21 (2009).

9. Josh Lerner and Megan Wade Antieau, "Chicago's $1.3 Million Experiment in Democracy: Participatory Budgeting in the 49th Ward," *YES! Magazine*, April 20, 2010, http://www.yesmagazine.org/people-power/chicagos-1.3-million-experiment -in-democracy.

10. City of Toronto, "Toronto Facts, Toronto's Racial Diversity."

11. City of Toronto, "Toronto Facts, Business and Economic Development," 2011, http://www.toronto.ca/toronto_facts/business_econdev.htm.

12. Toronto Public Health, *The Unequal City: Income and Health Inequalities in Toronto* (Toronto, October 2008).

13. United Way Toronto, *Losing Ground: The Persistent Growth of Family Poverty in Canada's Largest City* (Toronto, 2007), http://www.unitedwaytoronto.com/ whatWeDo/reports/losingGround.php.

14. Unless otherwise noted, all statistics are from Toronto Community Housing, "Frequently Asked Questions," 2010, http://www.torontohousing.ca/media_centre/ faq.

15. Rita Daly, "A Tenant Revolution, but Is Anyone Listening?" *The Toronto Star*, September 15, 2007, http://www.thestar.com/news/gta/2007/09/15/a_tenant _revolution_but_is_anyone_listening.html.

16. Toronto Community Housing, "Participatory Planning and Budgeting in Toronto Community Housing Corporation: Our Own Story" (presented at the Lifelong Citizenship Learning, Participatory Democracy and Social Change Conference, Toronto, October 18, 2003).

17. Ibid.

18. Joe Friesen, "Low on Maintenance Funds, Toronto Community Housing Holds a Competition," *The Globe and Mail* (Toronto, May 20, 2006).

19. Megan Oglivie, "Tenants Lobby Each Other in Ultimate Reality Show," *The Toronto Star*, April 6, 2008, http://www.thestar.com/news/gta/2008/04/06/ tenants_lobby_each_other_in_ultimate_reality_show.html.

240   Notes to Pages 160–203

20. Ibid.

21. All statistics are from the participatory evaluation that I led for TCH, which is discussed in chapter 7.

Chapter 7

1. Yoland Wadsworth, *What Is Participatory Action Research?* (Action Research International, 1998), http://www.aral.com.au/ari/p-ywadsworth98.html.

2. Marisol Estrella and John Gaventa, *Who Counts Reality? Participatory Monitoring and Evaluation: A Literature Review* (Brighton, UK: Institute of Development Studies, 1998), http://www.ntd.co.uk/idsbookshop/details.asp?id=421.

3. Alice McIntyre, *Participatory Action Research* (Thousand Oaks, CA: Sage, 2007); Wadsworth, *What Is Participatory Action Research?*; Estrella and Gaventa, *Who Counts Reality? Participatory Monitoring and Evaluation: A Literature Review*.

4. Boal, *Games for Actors and Non-Actors*, 85.

5. McGonigal, *Reality Is Broken*, 205.

6. Ibid., 85.

7. Gilda Haas, "3 Exercises for Decision-Making," *Dr. Pop*, February 13, 2010, http://drpop.org/2010/02/3-exercises-for-group-decision-making/.

8. The Toronto Star, "Crisis at the TCHC: A Timeline," *The Toronto Star*, March 17, 2011, http://www.thestar.com/news/gta/2011/03/17/crisis_at_the_tchc_a_timeline.html.

9. Lindsey Reed, "TCHC: Looking beyond the Spin," *The Toronto Star*, March 11, 2011, http://www.thestar.com/opinion/editorialopinion/2011/03/11/tchc_looking_beyond_the_spin.html.

10. Daniel Dale, "Council Ousts TCHC Board, Appoints Ootes as Temporary Leader," *The Toronto Star*, March 10, 2011, http://www.thestar.com/news/gta/2011/03/10/council_ousts_tchc_board_appoints_ootes_as_temporary_leader.html.

Chapter 8

1. Fung, "Varieties of Participation in Complex Governance"; David Easton, *The Political System: An Inquiry into the State of Political Science* (New York: Knopf, 1953); Verba, Schlozman, and Brady, *Voice and Equality*.

2. Fullerton, *Game Design Workshop*, 2nd ed., 249.

Notes to Pages 204–209

3. Boaventura de Sousa Santos and Leonardo Avritzer, "Introduction: Opening up the Canon of Democracy," in *Democratizing Democracy: Beyond the Liberal Democratic Canon* (New York: Verso, 2007).

4. Salen and Zimmerman, *Rules of Play: Game Design Fundamentals*, 269.

5. Malcolm Gladwell, "Twitter, Facebook, and Social Activism," *The New Yorker*, October 4, 2010, http://www.newyorker.com/reporting/2010/10/04/101004fa_fact _gladwell?.

6. Kay Lehman Schlozman, Sidney Verba, and Henry E. Brady, "Weapon of the Strong? Participatory Inequality and the Internet," *Perspectives on Politics* 8, no. 02 (2010): 487–509.

7. Baiocchi, *Radicals in Power: The Workers' Party and Experiments in Urban Democracy in Brazil*.

8. Álex Ayala, "Teatro del oprimido, una voz para la gente," *La Razón* (La Paz, Bolivia, March 18, 2005), http://www.bolivia.com/noticias/AutoNoticias/DetalleNoticia 25567.asp.

9. El Ciudadano, "De la Boleta a la bolita," *El Ciudadano* (Rosario, Argentina, May 26, 2010), http://www.elciudadanoweb.com/?p=63519.

10. Municipalidad de Rosario, "Presupuesto participativo," 2011, http://www .rosario.gov.ar/sitio/informacion_municipal/pp_anteriores.jsp#2011.

Bibliography

Abers, Rebecca. *Inventing Local Democracy: Grassroots Politics in Brazil.* Boulder, CO: Lynne Rienner Publishers, 2000.

Abramson, Paul R., John Herbert Aldrich, and David W. Rohde. *Change and Continuity in the 2004 and 2006 Elections.* Washington, DC: CQ Press, 2007.

Abt, Clark. *Serious Games.* New York: Viking Press, 1970.

Addonizio, E. M., D. P. Green, and J. M. Glaser. "Putting the Party Back into Politics: An Experiment Testing Whether Election Day Festivals Increase Voter Turnout." *PS: Political Science and Politics* 40, no.4 (2007): 721–27.

Agger, Michael. "How Video Games Can Make Us Heroes." *Slate*, January 24, 2011. http://www.slate.com/articles/arts/books/2011/01/how_video_games_can_make_us _heroes.html.

Aldrich, John. "Rational Choice and Turnout." *American Journal of Political Science* 37, no. 1 (1993): 246–78.

Algava, Mariano. "Cuando el Pueblo Se Juega (juego, subjetividad y Realidad)." In *Pedagogía de la resistencia: Cuadernos de educación popular*, ed. Claudia Korol. Buenos Aires: Asociación Madres de Plaza de Mayo, 2004, 237–46.

Algava, Mariano. *Jugar y jugarse: Las Técnicas y la dimensión lúdica de la educación popular.* Rosario, Argentina: Ediciones América Libre, 2006.

Alinsky, Saul. *Rules for Radicals.* New York: Vintage Books, 1972.

Al-Kodmany, Kheir. "Visualization Tools and Methods for Participatory Planning and Design." *Journal of Urban Technology* 8, no. 2 (August 2001): 1–37.

Allegretti, Giovanni, and Carsten Herzberg. *Participatory Budgets in Europe: Between Efficiency and Growing Local Democracy.* The Transnational Institute Briefing Series. Amsterdam: Transnational Institute, 2004.

Bibliography

Almansi, Florencia. "Regularizing Land Tenure within Upgrading Programmes in Argentina; the Cases of Promeba and Rosario Habitat." *Environment and Urbanization* 21, no. 2 (September 2009): 389–413.

Almansi, Florencia. "Rosario's Development; Interview with Miguel Lifschitz, Mayor of Rosario, Argentina." *Environment and Urbanization* 21, no. 1 (April 2009): 19–35.

Altschuler, Glenn, and Stuart Blumin. "Limits of Political Engagement in Antebellum America: A New Look at the Golden Age of Participatory Democracy." *Journal of American History* 84, no. 3 (1997): 855–85.

Alvarez, Sonia, Arturo Escobar, and Evelina Dagnino. *Cultures of Politics, Politics of Cultures: Re-visioning Latin American Social Movements.* Boulder, CO: Westview Press, 1998.

Amadea, Sonia. *Rationalizing Capitalist Democracy: The Cold War Origins of Rational Choice Liberalism.* Chicago: University of Chicago Press, 2003.

American Public Media. "Budget Hero," 2008. http://www.marketplace.org/topics/economy/budget-hero.

Anderson, Craig, Douglas Gentile, and Katherine Buckley. *Violent Video Game Effects on Children and Adolescents.* Oxford: Oxford University Press, 2006.

Andreoni, James. "Cooperation in Public-Goods Experiments: Kindness or Confusion?" *American Economic Review* 85, no. 4 (1995): 891–904.

Arias, Ernesto. "Bottom-up Neighbourhood Revitalisation: A Language Approach for Participatory Decision Support." *Urban Studies (Edinburgh, UK)* 33, no.10 (December 1996): 1831–48.

Arnold, Rick, and Bev Burke. *A Popular Education Handbook.* Toronto: OISE, 1982.

Arnold, Rick, Barndt Deborah, and Bev Burke. *A New Weave: Popular Education in Canada and Central America.* Toronto: OISE, 1985.

Arnstein, Sherry. "A Ladder of Citizen Participation." *Journal of the American Institute of Planners* 35 (4) (1969): 216–224.

AT&T. "AT&T Announces the Eighth Season of 'American Idol' Smashes All-Time Record for Fan Engagement through Text Messaging," May 22, 2009. http://www.att.com/gen/press-room?pid=4800&cdvn=news&newsarticleid=26832.

Auyero, Javier. *Poor People's Politics: Peronist Survival Networks and the Legacy of Evita.* Durham, NC: Duke University Press, 2000.

Avedon, Elliot, and Brian Sutton-Smith, eds. *The Study of Games.* New York: Wiley, 1971.

Bibliography

Ayala, Álex. "Teatro del Oprimido, Una Voz para la gente." *La Razón*. La Paz, Bolivia, March 18, 2005. http://www.bolivia.com/noticias/AutoNoticias/DetalleNoticia 25567.asp.

Bachrach, Peter, and Morton Baratz. "The Two Faces of Power." *American Political Science Review* 56 (4) (1962): 947–52.

Baiocchi, Gianpaolo. *Militants and Citizens: The Politics of Participatory Democracy in Porto Alegre*. Stanford: Stanford University Press, 2005.

Baiocchi, Gianpaolo. "Participation, Activism, and Politics: The Porto Alegre Experiment." In *Deepening Democracy: Institutional Innovations in Empowered Participatory Governance*, ed. Archon Fung and Erik Olin Wright. New York: Verso, 2003, 45–76.

Baiocchi, Gianpaolo, ed. *Radicals in Power: The Workers' Party and Experiments in Urban Democracy in Brazil*. London: Zed Books, 2003.

Baiocchi, Gianpaolo, and Ernesto Ganuza. "The Power of Ambiguity: How Participatory Budgeting Travels the Globe." *Journal of Public Deliberation* 8, no. 2 (2012). http://www.publicdeliberation.net/jpd/vol8/iss2/art8/.

Baker, William, H. Lon Addams, and Brian Davis. "Critical Factors for Enhancing Municipal Public Hearings." *Public Administration Review* 65, no. 4 (August 2005): 490–99.

Bakhtin, Mikhail. *Rabelais and His World*. Indianapolis: Indiana University Press, 1984.

Ballesteros, María Paula. *Los Chicos quieren saber de Qué Se Trata*. Universidad Nacional de Rosario, 2009.

Barber, Benjamin R. *Strong Democracy: Participatory Politics for a New Age*. Los Angeles: University of California Press, 2003.

Bartle, Richard. "Hearts, Clubs, Diamonds, Spades: Players Who Suit MUDs." *MUSE Ltd.*, 1996. http://www.mud.co.uk/richard/hcds.htm.

Beck, John C., and Mitchell Wade. *The Kids Are Alright: How the Gamer Generation Is Changing the Workplace*. Boston: Harvard Business Press, 2006.

Berelson, Bernard, Paul Lazarfeld, and William McPhee. *Voting*. Chicago: University of Chicago Press, 1954.

Billionaires For Bush. "Billionaires For Bush Website," 2009. http://www .billionairesforbush.com/.

Birdwell, Ken. "The Cabal: Valve's Design Process for Creating Half-Life." *Gamasutra*, December 10, 1999. http://www.gamasutra.com/view/feature/3408/the_cabal _valves_design_process_.php.

Björk, Staffan, and Jussi Holopainen. "Games and Design Patterns." In *The Game Design Reader*, ed. Katie Salen and Eric Zimmerman. Cambridge: MIT Press, 2006, 410–37.

Blunt, Richard. "Do Serious Games Work? Results from Three Studies." *eLearn Magazine*, December 1, 2009. http://elearnmag.acm.org/featured.cfm?aid=1661378.

Boal, Augusto. *Games for Actors and Non-Actors*, trans. Adrian Jackson. New York: Routledge, 2002.

Boal, Augusto. *Legislative Theatre: Using Performance to Make Politics*. New York: Routledge, 1998.

Boal, Augusto. *Theatre of the Oppressed*. New York: Theatre Communications Group, 1979.

Bobbio, Norberto. *The Future of Democracy*. Minneapolis: University of Minneapolis Press, 1984.

Bogad, L. M. *Electoral Guerrilla Theatre: Radical Ridicule and Social Movements*. New York: Routledge, 2005.

Bon, Gustave Le. *The Crowd: A Study of the Popular Mind*. New York: Macmillan, 1897.

von Borries, Friedrich, Steffen P. Walz, and Matthias Böttger. *Space Time Play: Computer Games, Architecture and Urbanism*. Boston: Springer, 2007.

Boyd, Andrew. "Irony, Meme Warfare, and the Extreme Costume Ball." In *From ACT UP to the WTO: Urban Protest and Community Building in the Era of Globalization*, ed. Benjamin Shepard and Ronald Hayduk. New York: Verso, 2002, 245–53.

Boyd, Andrew, and Stephen Duncombe. "The Manufacture of Dissent: What the Left Can Learn from Las Vegas." *Journal of Aesthetics and Protest* 1, no. 3 (2004): 34–47.

Branford, Sue, and Jan Rocha. *Cutting the Wire: The Story of the Landless Movement in Brazil*. London: Latin American Bureau, 2002.

Brienes, Wini. *Community and Organization in the New Left: 1962–1968*. South Hadley, MA: Praeger, 1982.

Brown, John Seely, and Douglas Thomas. "Breakthrough Ideas for 2008: The Gamer Disposition." *Harvard Business Review* (February 2008). http://blogs.hbr.org/cs/2008/02/the_gamer_disposition.html.

Brown, John Seely, and Douglas Thomas. "You Play World of Warcraft? You're Hired!" *WIRED*, April 2006. http://www.wired.com/wired/archive/14.04/learn.html.

Brown, Stuart, and Christopher Vaughan. *Play: How It Shapes the Brain, Opens the Imagination, and Invigorates the Soul*. New York: Penguin, 2010.

Bibliography

Burby, Raymond. "Making Plans That Matter: Citizen Involvement and Government Action." *Journal of the American Planning Association. American Planning Association* 69, no. 1 (2003): 33–49.

Button, Keith. "A 'Subtle' Approach: Soldiers Learn Nuances of Foreign Cultures through Video Gaming." *Training and Simulation Journal*, October 1, 2009.

Caillois, Roger. *Man, Play, and Games*, trans. Meyer Barash. Chicago: University of Illinois Press, 2001.

Canel, Eduardo. *Barrio Democracy in Latin America: Participatory Decentralization and Community Activism in Montevideo*. State College: Penn State Press, 2010.

La Capital. "Rosario Hábitat Beneficiará a 600 Familias En Molino Blanco." *La Capital*. Rosario, Argentina, December 16, 2003.

Cappella, Joseph N., and Kathleen Hall Jamieson. "News Frames, Political Cynicism, and Media Cynicism." *Annals of the American Academy of Political and Social Science* 546 (July 1996): 71–84.

Cappella, Joseph N., and Kathleen Hall Jamieson. *Spiral of Cynicism: The Press and the Public Good*. Oxford: Oxford University Press, 1997.

Fernández, Del Carmen María. "Con Los Niños, Para Todos." In Experiencia Rosario, ed. United Nations Development Program. Rosario, Argentina: United Nations Development Program, 2006, 173–222.

Castronova, Edward. "Virtual Worlds: A First-Hand Account of Market and Society on the Cyberian Frontier." CESifo Working Paper Series, SSRN (Social Science Research Network), no. 618 (December 2001).

Ecuménico de Educación Popular, Centro. *Técnicas participativas para la educación popular*. Buenos Aires: Editorial Lumen Humanitas, 1996.

Chaskin, Robert. "Democracy and Bureaucracy in a Community Planning Process." *Journal of Planning Education and Research* 24, no. 4 (2005): 408–19.

Chatfield, Tom. *Fun Inc.: Why Games Are the 21st Century's Most Serious Business*. London: Virgin Books, 2010.

Chavez, Daniel. *Polis and Demos: The Left in Municipal Governance in Montevideo and Porto Alegre*. Maastricht: Shaker Publishing, 2004.

Chavez, Daniel, and Benjamin Goldfrank. *The Left in the City: Participatory Local Governments in Latin America*. London: Latin American Bureau and Transnational Institute, 2004.

Chick, Tom. "Shoot Club: The DOOM 3 Review." In *The Game Design Reader*, ed. Katie Salen and Eric Zimmerman. Cambridge: MIT Press, 2006, 156–69.

Church, Doug. "Formal Abstract Design Tools." *Gamasutra*, July 16, 1999. http://www.gamasutra.com/view/feature/3357/formal_abstract_design_tools.php.

City of Toronto. "Toronto Facts, Business and Economic Development," 2011. http://www.toronto.ca/toronto_facts/business_econdev.htm.

City of Toronto. "Toronto Facts, Toronto's Racial Diversity," 2011. http://www.toronto.ca/toronto_facts/diversity.htm.

Ciudades, Educadoras América Latina. *Montevideo Ciudad Educadora: Identidad, cultura y participación a Través de la Música*. Rosario, Argentina: Ciudades Educadoras, 2002.

Clark, Susan, and Woden Teachout. *Slow Democracy: Rediscovering Community, Bringing Decision Making Back Home*. White River Junction, VT: Chelsea Green Publishing, 2012.

Colman, Andrew. *Game Theory and Its Applications in the Social and Biological Sciences*. New York: Routledge, 1995.

Converse, Phillip. "Change in the American Electorate." In *The Human Meaning of Social Change*, ed. Angus Campbell and Phillip Converse. New York: Russel Sage, 1972, 263–337.

Cook, D. "What Are Game Mechanics?" *Lost Garden*, October 23, 2006. http://www.lostgarden.com/2006/10/what-are-game-mechanics.html.

Coppedge, Michael. "The Dynamic Diversity of Latin American Party Systems." *Party Politics* 4, no. 4 (October 1, 1998): 547–68.

Córdova, Juana. *"El Año viejo. Un Medio de expresión popular."* *Revista Artesanías de América*. CIDAP, 2001.

Cornwall, Andrea, and Vera Schatten Coelho. *Spaces for Change?: The Politics of Citizen Participation in New Democratic Arenas*. London: Zed Books, 2007.

Costikyan, Greg. "I Have No Words & I Must Design." *Interactive Fantasy*, no. 2 (1994).

Costikyan, Greg. "Where Stories End and Games Begin." *Game Developer* (September 2000): 44–53.

Cox, Gary. "Centripetal and Centrifugal Incentives in Electoral Systems." *American Journal of Political Science* 34, no. 4 (1990): 903–35.

Cox, Gary. *Making Votes Count*. Cambridge, UK: Cambridge University Press, 1997.

Cox, Gary. "Electoral Rules and the Calculus of Mobilization." *Legislative Studies Quarterly* 24, no. 3 (1999): 387–420.

Crawford, Chris. *The Art of Computer Game Design*. New York: McGraw-Hill, 1984.

Csikszentmihalyi, Mihaly. *Flow: The Psychology of Optimal Experience*. New York: Harper Collins, 1991.

Dagnino, Evelina, Alberto Olvera Rivera, and Aldo Panfichi. *La Disputa por la construcción democrática en América Latina*. México City: Centro de Investigaciones y Estudios Superiores en Antropología Social, 2006.

Dahl, Robert. "The Concept of Political Power." *Behavioral Science* 2, no. 3 (1957): 201–15.

Dale, Daniel. "Council Ousts TCHC Board, Appoints Ootes as Temporary Leader." *The Toronto Star*, March 10, 2011. http://www.thestar.com/news/gta/2011/03/10/council_ousts_tchc_board_appoints_ootes_as_temporary_leader.html.

Dalton, Russell J. *Democratic Challenges, Democratic Choices: The Erosion of Political Support In Advanced Industrial Democracies*. Oxford: Oxford University Press, 2004.

Daly, Rita. "A Tenant Revolution, but Is Anyone Listening?" *The Toronto Star*, September 15, 2007. http://www.thestar.com/news/gta/2007/09/15/a_tenant_revolution_but_is_anyone_listening.html.

Davies, Russell. "Playful." *Russell Davies*, November 9, 2009. http://russelldavies.typepad.com/planning/2009/11/playful.html.

Debord, Guy. *Society of the Spectacle*. London: Rebel Press, 1983.

DeKoven, Bernard. "Changing the Game." In *The Game Design Reader*, ed. Katie Salen and Eric Zimmerman. Cambridge: MIT Press, 2006, 518–37.

Demming, Michael. *The Cultural Front: The Laboring of American Culture in the Twentieth Century*. New York: Verso, 1996.

Deterding, Sebastian. "Pawned. Gamification and Its Discontents," September 24, 2010. http://www.slideshare.net/dings/pawned-gamification-and-its-discontents.

Dewey, John. *The Public and Its Problems*. New York: Holt, 1927.

Dobuzinskis, Alex. "Global Movie Box Office Nears $30 Billion in 2009." *Reuters*, March 10, 2010. http://www.reuters.com/article/2010/03/10/us-boxoffice-idUSTRE62955520100310.

Downs, Anthony. *An Economic Theory of Democracy*. New York: Harper, 1957.

Duncombe, Stephen. *Dream: Re-imagining Progressive Politics in an Age of Fantasy*. New York: New Press, 2007.

Easton, David. *The Political System: An Inquiry into the State of Political Science*. New York: Knopf, 1953.

Ciudadano, El. "De La Boleta a La Bolita." *El Ciudadano*. Rosario, Argentina, May 26, 2010. http://www.elciudadanoweb.com/?p=63519.

Erikson, Erik. *Childhood and Society*. New York: Van Nostrand Reinhold Company, 1985.

Eskelinen, Markku. "The Gaming Situation." *Game Studies* 1, no. 1 (2001). http://www.gamestudies.org/0101/eskelinen/.

Estrella, Marisol, and John Gaventa. *Who Counts Reality? Participatory Monitoring and Evaluation: A Literature Review*. Institute of Development Studies, 1998. http://www.ntd.co.uk/idsbookshop/details.asp?id=421.

Fehr, Ernst, and Bettina Rockenbach. "Detrimental Effects of Sanctions on Human Altruism." *Nature*, 422, no. 6928 (2003): 137–40.

Ferguson, Christopher. "Video Games and Youth Violence: A Prospective Analysis in Adolescents." *Journal of Youth and Adolescence* 40, no. 4 (2010): 377–91.

Filho-D'Avila, Paulo M., Vladimyr Jorge-Lombardo, and Ana Fernanda Coelho. "Acesso ao poder. Clientelismo e democracia participativa desconstruindo uma dicotomia." *Civitas—Revista De Ciências Sociais* 4, no. 2 (2004): 4211–33.

Fiorina, Morris. "Extreme Voices: A Dark Side of Civic Engagement." In *Civic Engagement in American Democracy*, ed. Morris Fiorina and Theda Skocpol. Washington, DC: Brookings Institution Press, 1999.

Ford, Alberto, and Martín Carné. "Desafíos de la participación en la implementación de políticas públicas." In *Construyendo confianza. Hacia un nuevo vínculo entre estado y sociedad civil*, vol. 2, ed. Alejandro Belmonte. Buenos Aires: Fundación CIPPEC / Subsecretaría para la Reforma Institucional y Fortalecimiento de la Democracia de la Nación de Argentina, 2009, 49–80.

Forment, Carlos. *Democracy in Latin America: 1760–1900*, vol. 1. Chicago: University of Chicago Press, 2003.

Forment, Carlos. "The Democratic Dribbler: Football Clubs, Neoliberal Globalization, and Buenos Aires' Municipal Election of 2003." *Public Culture* 19, no. 1 (2007): 85.

Freeman, Jo. (aka Joreen). "The Tyranny of Stucturelessness." In *Radical Feminism*, ed. Anne Koedt, Ellen Levine, and Anita Rapone. New York: Quadrangle, 1973. http://www.jofreeman.com/joreen/tyranny.htm.

Freire, Paulo. *Pedagogy of the Oppressed*. New York: Continuum, 1970.

Friesen, Joe. "Low on Maintenance Funds, Toronto Community Housing Holds a Competition." *The Globe and Mail*, Toronto, May 20, 2006.

Fullerton, Tracy. *Game Design Workshop: A Playcentric Approach to Creating Innovative Games*, 2nd ed. New York: Morgan Kaufmann, 2008.

Bibliography

Fung, Archon. *Empowered Participation: Reinventing Urban Democracy*. Princeton: Princeton University Press, 2006.

Fung, Archon. "Varieties of Participation in Complex Governance." *Public Administration Review* 66, Special Issue (December 2006): 66–75.

Fung, Archon, and Erik Olin Wright, eds. *Deepening Democracy: Institutional Innovations in Empowered Participatory Governance*. New York: Verso, 2003.

Gagandeep. "PSP to Instill 'Team Play' In Hilton Garden Inn." *Gaming Blog*, September 29, 2008. http://www.gamingblog.org/psp-to-instill-team-play-in-hilton-garden-inn.html.

Games for Change. "Games for Change Website," 2009. http://www.gamesforchange.org/.

Gaudiosi, John. "New Reports Forecast Global Video Game Industry Will Reach \$82 Billion by 2017." *Forbes Tech*, July 18, 2012. http://www.forbes.com/sites/johngaudiosi/2012/07/18/new-reports-forecasts-global-video-game-industry-will-reach-82-billion-by-2017/.

Gautney, Heather, Omar Dahbour, Ashley Dawson, and Neil Smith. *Democracy, States, and the Struggle for Global Justice—Google Books*. New York: Routledge, 2009.

Gaventa, John. *Power and Powerlessness: Quiescence and Rebellion in an Appalachian Valley*. Chicago: University of Chicago Press, 1980.

Gawande, Atul. *The Checklist Manifesto*. New York: Metropolitan Books, 2009.

Gee, James Paul. *Good Video Games + Good Learning*. New York: Peter Lang Publishing, 2007.

Gee, James Paul. *What Video Games Have to Teach Us About Learning and Literacy*, 2nd ed., Palgrave Macmillan, 2007.

Gentile, Douglas, and Craig Anderson. "Violent Video Games: Effects on Youth and Public Policy Implications." In *Handbook of Children, Culture, and Violence*, ed. N. Dowd, D. G. Singer, and R. F. Wilson. Thousand Oaks, CA: Sage, 2006, 225–46.

Gibson, Edward L., ed. *Federalism and Democracy in Latin America*. Baltimore: Johns Hopkins University Press, 2004.

Gintis, Herbert, Samuel Bowles, Robert Boyd, and Ernst Fehr. *Moral Sentiments and Material Interests: The Foundations of Cooperation in Economic Life*. Cambridge: MIT Press, 2005.

Giordana, Cora. "Rosario sigue siendo una gran receptora de inmigrantes." *Clarín*. Rosario, Argentina, November 3, 2007, sec. Suplemento Rosario.

Gladwell, Malcolm. "Twitter, Facebook, and Social Activism." *The New Yorker*, October 4, 2010. http://www.newyorker.com/reporting/2010/10/04/101004fa_fact_gladwell?

Goldfrank, Benjamin. "The Fragile Flower of Local Democracy: A Case Study of Decentralization/participation in Montevideo." *Politics and Society* 30, no. 1 (2002): 51.

González, Chiqui. "Políticas de infancia: El Paisaje de La Ciudadanía." In *Experiencia Rosario*, ed. Municipalidad de Rosario. Rosario, Argentina: United Nations Development Program, 2006.

Goodwin, Jeff, James Jasper, and Francesca Polletta, eds. *Passionate Politics: Emotions and Social Movements*. Chicago: University of Chicago Press, 2001.

Greco, JoAnn. "Can Do in San Juan's Cano." *Planning*, April 2009.

Green, Donald, and Ian Shapiro. *Pathologies of Rational Choice Theory: A Critique of Applications in Political Science*. New Haven: Yale University Press, 1994.

Guilloud, Stephanie, and William Cordery. "Fundraising Is Not a Dirty Word: Community-Based Economic Strategies for the Long Haul." In *The Revolution Will Not Be Funded: Beyond the Non-profit Industrial Complex*, ed. INCITE! Women of Color against Violence. Cambridge, MA: South End Press, 2007.

Guinier, Lani, and Gerald Torres. *The Miner's Canary: Enlisting Race, Resisting Power, Transforming Democracy*. Cambridge: Harvard University Press, 2003.

Haas, Gilda. "3 Exercises for Decision-Making." *Dr. Pop*, February 13, 2010. http://drpop.org/2010/02/3-exercises-for-group-decision-making/.

Haas, Gilda. "Gilda's Gaming Adventure." *Dr. Pop*, April 13, 2010. http://drpop.org/2010/04/gildas-gaming-adventure/.

Hagel, John, and John Seely Brown. "How World of Warcraft Promotes Innovation." *Bloomberg Businessweek*, January 14, 2009. http://www.businessweek.com/stories/2009-01-14/how-world-of-warcraft-promotes-innovationbusinessweek-business-news-stock-market-and-financial-advice.

Hajnal, Zoltan. *America's Uneven Democracy: Race, Turnout, and Representation in City Politics*. Cambridge, UK: Cambridge University Press, 2010.

Hand, Martin, and Karenza Moore. "Community, Identity and Digital Games." In *Understanding Digital Games*, ed. Jason Rutter and Jo Bryce. London: Sage Publications, 2006, 166–83.

Hanisch, Carol. "A Critique of the Miss America Protest." In *Notes from the Second Year: Women's Liberation*, ed. Shulamith Firestone and Anne Koedt. New York: New York Radical Women, 1968 , 86–88.

Hay, Colin. *Why We Hate Politics*. Oxford: Polity, 2007.

Bibliography

253

Healey, Patsy. *Collaborative Planning: Shaping Places in Fragmented Societies*. Vancouver: University of British Columbia Press, 1997.

Helgason, David. "2010 Trends." *Unity Technologies Blog*, January 14, 2010. http://blogs.unity3d.com/2010/01/14/2010-trends/.

Hindess, Barry. *Choice, Rationality, and Social Theory*. London: Unwin Hyman, 1988.

Hoffman, Abbie. "Museum of the Streets," 1980. http://theanarchistlibrary.org/library/Abbie_Hoffman__Museum_of_the_Streets.html.

Horkheimer, Max, and Theodor W. Adorno. *Dialectic of Enlightenment: Philosophical Fragments*. Stanford: Stanford University Press, 2002.

Howe, Nicholas. "Metaphor in Contemporary American Political Discourse." *Metaphor and Symbol* 3, no. 2 (1988): 87–104.

Hubers, J. C., M. C. van Veen, C. Kievid, and R. Siemerink, eds. *Game Set and Match*. Delft: Faculty of Architecture, DUT, 2004.

Hughes, Linda. "Beyond the Rules of the Game: Why Are Rooie Rules Nice?" In *The Game Design Reader*, ed. Katie Salen and Eric Zimmerman. Cambridge: MIT Press, 2006, 504–16.

Huizinga, Johan. *Homo Ludens: A Study of the Play Element in Culture*. Boston: Beacon Press, 1955.

Innes, Judith, and David Booher. "Reframing Public Participation: Strategies for the 21st Century." *Planning Theory and Practice* 5, no. 4 (December 2004): 419–36.

International Theatre of the Oppressed Organization. Augusto. "Theatre of the Oppressed Website," 2010. http://www.theatreoftheoppressed.org.

Involve. *Not Another Consultation! Making Community Engagement Informal and Fun*. London: Local Government Improvement and Development, November 2010. http://www.local.gov.uk/web/guest/health/-/journal_content/56/10171/3510888/ARTICLE-TEMPLATE.

Isaac, T. M., and Patrick Heller. "Democracy and Development: Decentralized Planning in Kerala." In *Deepening Democracy: Institutional Innovations in Empowered Participatory Governance*, ed. Archon Fung and Erik Olin Wright. New York: Verso, 2003, 77–110.

Isbister, Katherine. *Better Game Characters by Design: A Psychological Approach*. San Francisco: Morgan Kaufmann, 2006.

Iyengar, Shanto, Helmut Norpoth, and Kyu S. Hahn. "Consumer Demand for Election News: The Horserace Sells." *Journal of Politics* 66, no. 1 (February 2004): 157–75.

Jackson, Janna. "Game-Based Teaching: What Educators Can Learn from Videogames." *Teaching Education* 20, no. 3 (2009): 291.

Jackson, Robert. "Rationality and Political Participation." *American Journal of Political Science* 37, no. 1 (1993): 279–90.

Jacobson, Arthur. "Origins of the Game Theory of Law and the Limits of Harmony in Plato's Laws." *Cardozo Law Review* 20 (May–July 1999): 1335–55.

Järvinen, Aki. *Games without Frontiers: Theories and Methods for Game Studies and Design.* Tampere: Tampere University Press, 2008.

Jasper, James. *The Art of Moral Protest: Culture, Biography, and Creativity in Social Movements.* Chicago: University of Chicago Press, 1997.

Jenkins, Henry. "'Complete Freedom of Movement': Video Games as Gendered Play Space." In *The Game Design Reader*, ed. Katie Salen and Eric Zimmerman. Cambridge: MIT Press, 2006, 330–63.

Jenkins, Henry. "Game Design as Narrative Architecture." In *First Person: New Media as Story, Performance, and Game*, ed. Noah Windrip-Fruin and Pat Harrigan. Cambridge: MIT Press, 2004, 118–30.

Johns, Michael. "The Urbanisation of a Secondary City: The Case of Rosario, Argentina, 1870–1920." *Journal of Latin American Studies* 23, no. 3 (1991): 489–513.

Juul, Jesper. *Half-Real: Video Games between Real Rules and Fictional Worlds.* Cambridge: MIT Press, 2005.

Kadlec, Alison. "Play and Public Life." *National Civic Review* 98, no. 4 (2010): 3–11.

Kahne, Joseph, Ellen Middaugh, and Chris Evans. "The Civic Potential of Video Games." Chicago: The John D. and Catherine T. MacArthur Foundation, September 7, 2008.

Kalning, Kristin. "Does Game Violence Make Teens Aggressive?" *Msnbc.com*, December 8, 2006. http://www.nbcnews.com/id/16099971/ns/technology_and_science-games/.

King, Cheryl, Kathryn Feltey, and Bridget O'Neill Susel. "The Question of Participation: Toward Authentic Public Participation in Public Administration." *Public Administration Review* 58, no. 4 (1998): 317–26.

King, Martin Luther. "Religion's Answer to the Problem of Evil." In *The Papers of Martin Luther King, Jr.* Vol. I: Called to Serve, January 1929–June 1951. Berkeley: University of California Press, 1992.

Klopfer, Eric. *Augmented Learning: Research and Design of Mobile Educational Games.* Cambridge: MIT Press, 2008.

Bibliography

Klopfer, Eric, Scot Osterweil, and Katie Salen. *Moving Learning Games Forward*. The Educational Arcade, 2009. http://education.mit.edu/papers/MovingLearning GamesForward_EdArcade.pdf.

Koo, Gene. "Video Games and Democratic Participation." *Valuable Games*, April 21, 2009. http://blogs.law.harvard.edu/games/2009/04/21/video-games-and-democratic -participation/.

De Kosnik, Abigail. "Participatory Democracy and Hillary Clinton's Marginalized Fandom." *Transformative Works and Cultures* 1 (2008). http://journal.transformativeworks .org/index.php/twc/article/viewArticle/47.

Koster, Raph. *A Theory of Fun for Game Design*. Scottsdale, AZ: Paraglyph Press, 2005.

Kumar, Mathew. "GDC: Will Wright's Perspectives on Play." *Edge Magazine*, March 16, 2010. http://www.edge-online.com/features/gdc-will-wrights-perspectives-play/.

Laurel, Brenda. *Computers as Theatre*. Reading, MA: Addison-Wesley, 1991.

LeBlanc, Marc. "8KindsOfFun.com," 2010. http://algorithmancy.8kindsoffun.com/.

LeBlanc, Marc. "Tools for Creating Dramatic Game Dynamics." In *The Game Design Reader*, ed. Katie Salen and Eric Zimmerman. Cambridge: MIT Press, 2006, 438–59.

Leighninger, Matt. *The Next Form of Democracy: How Expert Rule Is Giving Way to Shared Governance . . . and Why Politics Will Never Be the Same*. Nashville: Vanderbilt University Press, 2006.

Lenhart, Amanda, Joseph Kahne, Ellen Middaugh, Alexandra Rankin Macgill, Chris Evans, and Jessica Vitak. *Teens, Video Games, and Civics*. Washington, DC: Pew Internet and American Life Project, September 16, 2008.

Lerner, Josh. "Communal Councils in Venezuela: Can 200 Families Revolutionize Democracy?" *Z Magazine* 20, no. 3 (2007): 45–49.

Lerner, Josh. "Let the People Decide: Transformative Community Development through Participatory Budgeting in Canada." *Shelterforce*, 146, 2006: 12–15.

Lerner, Josh, and Jez Hall. "Participatory Budgeting: A New Tool for Democratic Decision Making." *Transformation* 5 (Spring 2007): 10–15.

Lerner, Josh, and Daniel Schugurensky. "Who Learns What in Participatory Democracy? Participatory Budgeting in Rosario, Argentina." In *Democratic Practices as Learning Opportunities*, ed. van der Veen, Ruud, Danny Wildemeersch, Janet Youngblood and Victoria Marsick. Rotterdam: Sense Publishers, 2007: 85–100.

Lerner, Josh, and Donata Secondo. "By the People, For the People: Participatory Budgeting from the Bottom Up in North America." *Journal of Public Deliberation* 8, no. 2 (2012). http://www.publicdeliberation.net/jpd/vol8/iss2/art2/.

Lerner, Josh, and Megan Wade Antieau. "Chicago's $1.3 Million Experiment in Democracy: Participatory Budgeting in the 49th Ward." *YES! Magazine*, April 20, 2010. http://www.yesmagazine.org/people-power/chicagos-1.3-million-experiment -in-democracy.

Lewis, John Lowell. *Ring of Liberation: Deceptive Discourse in Brazilian Capoeira*. Chicago: University of Chicago Press, 1992.

Lichbach, Mark. *The Rebel's Dilemma*. Ann Arbor: University of Michigan Press, 1998.

Lijphart, Arend. "Unequal Participation: Democracy's Unresolved Dilemma." *American Political Science Review* 91, no. 1 (1997): 1–14.

Lippmann, Walter. *Public Opinion*. New York: Harcourt, Brace and Company, 1922.

Lowi, Theodore. "The State in Political Science: How We Become What We Study." *American Political Science Review* 86, no. 1 (1992): 1–7.

Lowndes, Vivien, Gerry Stoker, Lawrence Pratchett, David Wilson, Steve Leach, and Melvin Wingfield. *Enhancing Public Participation in Local Government*. London: UK Department of the Environment, Transport and the Regions, 1998.

Lukensmeyer, Carolyn. *Bringing Citizen Voices to the Table: A Guide for Public Managers*. San Francisco: Jossey-Bass, 2013.

Lukes, Stephen. *Power: A Radical View*. London: Macmillan, 1974.

Lundgren, Sus, and Staffan Björk. "Game Mechanics: Describing Computer-Augmented Games in Terms of Interaction." In *Terms of Interaction, Proceedings of TIDSE 2003* (2003): 45–56. http://citeseerx.ist.psu.edu/viewdoc/summary?doi=10.1.1.13.5147.

Mahony, Nick. "Making Democracy Spectacular." *Representation* 46, no. 3 (2010): 339.

Mangan, Katherine. "Future Business Leaders Cut Loose at MIT." *The Chronicle of Higher Education*, April 3, 2011, sec. Graduate Students. http://chronicle.com/article/ At-MIT-Future-Business/126981/.

Mansbridge, Jane. *Beyond Adversary Democracy*. Chicago: University of Chicago Press, 1983.

Mansbridge, Jane, ed. *Beyond Self-Interest*. Chicago: University of Chicago Press, 1990.

Mansbridge, Jane. "Does Participation Make Better Citizens?" *The Good Society* 5, no. 2 (1995): 1–7.

Mateas, Michael, and Andrew Stern. Interaction and Narrative. In *The Game Design Reader*, ed. Katie Salen and Eric Zimmerman. Cambridge: MIT Press, 2006, 642–69.

Bibliography

Maxera, Lylia, ed. *Innovación y espacio local: En la Gestión municipal de La Ciudad de Rosario (1995–1999)*. Rosario, Argentina: Universidad Nacional de Rosario, 1999.

McGerr, Michael. *The Decline of Popular Politics: The American North, 1865–1928*. New York: Oxford University Press, 1986.

McGonigal, Jane. *Reality Is Broken: Why Games Make Us Better and How They Can Change the World*. New York: Penguin, 2011.

McIntyre, Alice. *Participatory Action Research*. Thousand Oaks, CA: Sage, 2007.

Medina, Abal, and Juan Manuel. *Participación y control ciudadano*. Buenos Aires, Argentina: Editorial Prometeo, 2009.

Merklen, Denis. *Pobres ciudadanos. Las Clases populares en la era democrática*. Buenos Aires: Editorial Gorla, 2005.

Monroe, Kristen, Michael Barton, and Ute Klingemann. "Altruism and the Theory of Rational Action: Rescuers of Jews in Nazi Europe." *Ethics* 101, no. 1 (1990): 103–22.

Moreno, Inés. *El Juego y los juegos*. Buenos Aires: Lumen Hvmanitas, 2005.

de Rosario, Municipalidad. *Experiencia Rosario: Políticas para la gobernabilidad*. Rosario, Argentina: United Nations Development Program, 2006.

de Rosario, Municipalidad. "Indicadores demográficos," 2011. http://www.rosario .gov.ar/sitio/caracteristicas/indicadores.jsp?nivel=Ciudad&ult=Ci_3.

de Rosario, Municipalidad. "Origen de Rosario," 2011. http://www.rosario.gov.ar/ sitio/caracteristicas/historia/historia1.jsp.

de Rosario, Municipalidad. "Presupuesto participativo," 2011. http://www.rosario .gov.ar/sitio/informacion_municipal/pp_anteriores.jsp#2011.

de Rosario, Municipalidad. "Presupuesto participativo joven," 2011. http://www .rosario.gov.ar/sitio/desarrollo_social/juventud/pp_joven_anteriores.jsp.

Nabatchi, Tina, John Gastil, Michael Weiksner, and Matt Leighninger, eds. *Democracy in Motion: Evaluating the Practice and Impact of Deliberative Civic Engagement*. Oxford: Oxford University Press, 2012.

Neblo, Michael A., Kevin M. Esterling, Ryan P. Kennedy, David M. J. Lazer, and Anand E. Sokhey. "Who Wants to Deliberate—And Why?" *American Political Science Review* 104, no. 3 (2010): 566–83.

Newman, Andy. "Raucous Meeting on Atlantic Yards Plan Hints at Hardening Stances." *New York Times*, August 24, 2006. http://www.nytimes.com/2006/08/24/ nyregion/24yards.html.

Norris, Pippa. *Critical Citizens: Global Support for Democratic Government*. Oxford: Oxford University Press, 1999.

Norris, Pippa. *Democratic Phoenix: Reinventing Political Activism*. Cambridge, UK: Cambridge University Press, 2002.

Obama, Barack. "Obama's Speech in Tampa, Florida." *RealClearPolitics*, October 20, 2008. http://www.realclearpolitics.com/articles/2008/10/obamas_speech_in_tampa _florida.html.

Oder, Norman. "AY Supporters Out in Force at Epic Hearing, but Opponents Go the Distance." *Atlantic Yards Report*, August 24, 2006. http://atlanticyardsreport.blogspot .com/2006/08/ay-supporters-out-in-force-at-epic.html.

OECD. *Focus on Citizens: Public Engagement for Better Policy and Services*. OECD Studies on Public Engagement. OECD, 2009.

Oglivie, Megan. "Tenants Lobby Each Other in Ultimate Reality Show." *The Toronto Star*, April 6, 2008. http://www.thestar.com/news/gta/2008/04/06/tenants_lobby _each_other_in_ultimate_reality_show.html.

Olsen, Stefanie. "Educational Video Games with a Mix of Cool and Purpose." *The New York Times*, November 1, 2009. http://www.nytimes.com/2009/11/02/ technology/02games.html.

Oosterhuis, Kas, and Lukas Feireiss, eds. *Game Set and Match II: On Computer Games, Advanced Geometries, and Digital Technologies*. Rotterdam: Episode Publishers, 2006.

Opp, Karl-Dieter. "Postmaterialism, Collective Action, and Political Protest." *American Journal of Political Science* 34, no. 1 (1990): 212–35.

Osborne, Martin J. *An Introduction to Game Theory*. Oxford: Oxford University Press, 2004.

Osborne, Martin J., and Ariel Rubinstein. *A Course in Game Theory*. Cambridge: MIT Press, 1994.

Palfrey, Thomas, and Jeffrey Prisbrey. "Anomalous Behavior in Public Goods Experiments: How Much and Why?" *American Economic Review* 87, no. 5 (1997): 829–46.

Pateman, Carole. *Participation and Democratic Theory*. New York: Cambridge University Press, 1970.

Patterson, Thomas, and Philip Seib. "Informing the Public." In *The Press*, ed. Geneva Overholser and Kathleen Hall Jamieson. Oxford: Oxford University Press, 2006, 189–202.

Pavlus, John. "Sixty-two Reasons Why 'Gamification' Is Played Out." *CoDesign* 8 (November 2010). http://www.fastcodesign.com/1662656/sixty-two-reasons -why-gamification-is-played-out.

Pearce, Celia, Tracy Fullerton, Janine Fron, and Jackie Morie. "Sustainable Play: Toward a New Games Movement for the Digital Age." *Games and Culture* 2, no.3 (2007): 261–78.

Pew Research Center. *Distrust, Discontent, Anger and Partisan Rancor.* Washington, DC: Pew Research Center, April 18, 2010. http://www.people-press.org/2010/04/18/distrust-discontent-anger-and-partisan-rancor/.

Pinnington, Elizabeth, Josh Lerner, and Daniel Schugurensky. "Participatory Budgeting in North America: The Case of Guelph, Canada." *Journal of Public Budgeting, Accounting and Financial Management* 21, no. 2/3 (2009): 455–84.

Plato. *The Dialogues of Plato.* Trans. J. Hayward. Chicago: University of Chicago Press, 1952.

Plunkett, Luke. "The McDonalds Nintendo DSi." *Kotaku*, April 19, 2010. http://kotaku.com/5520108/the-mcdonalds-nintendo-dsi.

Polletta, Francesca. *Freedom Is an Endless Meeting: Democracy in American Social Movements.* Chicago: University of Chicago Press, 2002.

Poundstone, William. *Prisoner's Dilemma.* New York: Doubleday, 1992.

Prensky, Marc. *Digital Game-Based Learning.* New York: McGraw-Hill, 2001.

PricewaterhouseCoopers. "Back on Track—Think Global, Win Local to Succeed in the Global Sports Market," May 26, 2010.

Przeworski, Adam. *Democracy and the Market.* Cambridge, UK: Cambridge University Press, 1991.

Przeworski, Adam, Ian Shapiro, and Casiano Hacker-Cordón. "Minimalist Conception of Democracy: A Defense." In *Democracy's Value*, ed. Ian Shapiro and Casiano Hacker- Cordon. Cambridge: Cambridge University Press, 1999, 23–55.

Putnam, Robert D. *Bowling Alone: The Collapse and Revival of American Community.* New York: Simon and Schuster, 2001.

Reed, Lindsey. "TCHC: Looking Beyond the Spin." *The Toronto Star*, March 11, 2011. http://www.thestar.com/opinion/editorialopinion/2011/03/11/tchc_looking_beyond_the_spin.html.

Reed, T. V. *The Art of Protest: Culture and Activism from the Civil Rights Movement to the Streets of Seattle.* Minneapolis: University of Minnesota Press, 2005.

Reeves, Byron, and J. Leighton Read. *Total Engagement: Using Games and Virtual Worlds to Change the Way People Work and Businesses Compete.* Boston: Harvard Business School Press, 2009.

Reynolds, Paul. "Survey Reveals Global Dissatisfaction." *BBC*, September 15, 2005, sec. Europe. http://news.bbc.co.uk/2/hi/europe/4245282.stm.

Rideout, Victoria, Ulla Foehr, and Donald Roberts. *Generation M2: Media in the Lives of 8- to 18-Year-Olds.* Menlo Park: Kaiser Family Foundation, 2010.

Rodriguez, Ana Maria, and Adriana Salomón. "The Rosario Habitat Experience: Project Management Applied to Government." *PM World Today* 11, no. 11 (November 2009): 1–9.

Rollings, Andrew, and Ernest Adams. *On Game Design*. Indianapolis: New Riders, 2003.

Romero, Gustavo, Rosendo Mesías, Mariana Enet, Rosa Oliveras, Lourdes García, Manuel Coipel, and Daniela Osorio. *La Participación en el diseño urbano y arquitectónico en la producción social del hábitat*. Mexico City: UNAM, 2004.

Rosanvallon, Pierre. *Counter-democracy: Politics in an Age of Distrust*. Cambridge, UK: Cambridge University Press, 2008.

Rouse, I. I. I. *Richard. Game Design Theory and Practice*. Plano, TX: Wordware Publishing, 2005.

Rusk, Jerrold. "The Effect of the Australian Ballot Reform on Voting: 1876–1908." *American Political Science Review* 64, no. 4 (1970): 1220–38.

Ryan, Mary. *Civic Wars: Democracy and Public Life in the American City During the Nineteenth Century*. Berkeley: University of California Press, 1997.

Salen, Katie, and Eric Zimmerman. *Rules of Play: Game Design Fundamentals*. Cambridge: MIT Press, 2004.

Salen, Katie, and Eric Zimmerman, eds. *The Game Design Reader: A Rules of Play Anthology*. Cambridge: MIT Press, 2006.

Santos, Boaventura de Sousa, ed. *Democratizing Democracy: Beyond the Liberal Democratic Canon*. New York: Verso, 2007.

"Santos, Boaventura de Sousa. "Participatory Budgeting in Porto Alegre: Toward a Redistributive Democracy." *Politics & Society* 26, no.4 (1998): 461–510.

Santos, Boaventura de Sousa, and Leonardo Avritzer. "Introduction: Opening Up the Canon of Democracy." In *Democratizing Democracy: Beyond the Liberal Democratic Canon*. New York: Verso, 2007, xxiv–lxxiv.

Schaffer, Amanda. "Why Video Games Really Are Linked to Violence." *Slate*, April 27, 2007. http://www.slate.com/articles/health_and_science/medical_examiner/2007/04/dont_shoot.html.

Schell, Jesse. "'Design outside the Box' Presentation." Presented at the DICE 2010, February 18, 2010. http://www.g4tv.com/videos/44277/DICE-2010-Design-Outside-the-Box-Presentation/.

Schlozman, Kay Lehman, Sidney Verba, and Henry E. Brady. "Weapon of the Strong? Participatory Inequality and the Internet." *Perspectives on Politics* 8, no. 2 (2010): 487–509.

Bibliography 261

Schumpeter, Joseph Alois. *Capitalism, Socialism and Democracy.* New York: Harper, 1975.

Schweizer, Bobby. "The Difference between Newsgames and Gamification." *Newsgames*, December 3, 2010. http://newsgames.gatech.edu/blog/2010/12/the-difference-between-newsgames-and-gamification.html.

Scott, James C. *Domination and the Arts of Resistance: Hidden Transcripts.* New Haven: Yale University Press, 1992.

Scott, James C. *Weapons of the Weak: Everyday Forms of Peasant Resistance.* New Haven: Yale University Press, 1987.

Scott, Joan. "The Evidence of Experience." *Critical Inquiry* 17, no. 4 (1991): 733–97.

Selee, Andrew, and Enrique Peruzzotti, eds. *Participatory Innovation and Representative Democracy in Latin America.* Baltimore: Johns Hopkins University Press, 2009.

Sethi, Rajiv, and E. Somanathan. "Norm Compliance and Strong Reciprocity." In *Moral Sentiments and Material Interests: On the Foundations of Cooperation in Economic Life,* ed. Herbert Gintis, Samuel Bowles, Robert Boyd, and Ernst Fehr. Cambridge: MIT Press, 2003, 229–50.

Shepard, Benjamin. "If I Can't Dance: Play, Creativity, and Social Movements." City University of New York, Graduate Faculty in Social Welfare, 2006.

Shepard, Benjamin. *Play, Creativity, and Social Movements.* New York: Routledge, 2009.

Shepard, Benjamin, and Ronald Hayduk. *From ACT UP to the WTO: Urban Protest and Community Building in the Era of Globalization.* New York: Verso, 2002.

Sicart, Miguel. "Defining Game Mechanics." *Game Studies* 8, no. 2 (2008). http://gamestudies.org/0802/articles/sicart.

Simon, Herbert. "Human Nature in Politics: The Dialogue of Psychology with Political Science." *American Political Science Review* 79, no. 2 (1985): 293–304.

Singer, P. W. "Meet the Sims . . . and Shoot Them: The Rise of Militainment." *Foreign Policy,* April 2010. http://www.foreignpolicy.com/articles/2010/02/22/meet_the_sims_and_shoot_them.

Sirvent, María Teresa. *Estrategias participativas en educación de adultos: Sus Alcances y limitaciones.* San José, Costa Rica: Centro Interamericano para la Educación, la Ciencia y la Cultura, 1984.

Skocpol, Theda. *Diminished Democracy: From Membership to Management in American Civic Life.* Norman: University of Oklahoma Press, 2004.

Skocpol, Theda, and Morris P. Fiorina. *Civic Engagement in American Democracy.* Washington, DC: Brookings Institution Press, 1999.

Smith, Rogers M. "Putting the Substance Back in Political Science." *The Chronicle of Higher Education*, April 5, 2002, sec. The Chronicle Review. http://chronicle.com/article/Putting-the-Substance-Back-in/35557/.

Smith, Rogers M. *Stories of Peoplehood: The Politics and Morals of Political Membership*. Cambridge, UK: Cambridge University Press, 2003.

Sniderman, Stephen. "Unwritten Rules." *The Life of Games*, October 1999. http://www.gamepuzzles.com/tlog/tlog2.htm.

Solnit, David, ed. *Globalize Liberation*. San Francisco: City Lights Books, 2004.

Squire, Kurt. "From Content to Context: Video Games as Designed Experiences." *Educational Researcher* 35, no. 8 (2006): 19–29.

Squire, Kurt, and Henry Jenkins. "Harnessing the Power of Games in Education." *Insight (American Society of Ophthalmic Registered Nurses)* (2004): 7–33.

Steinkuehler, Constance. "The Mangle of Play." *Games and Culture* 1, no. 3 (2006): 199.

Steinmetz, George. "Positivism and Its Others in the Social Sciences." In *The Politics of Method in the Human Sciences: Positivism and Its Epistemological Others*, ed. George Steinmetz. Durham, NC: Duke University Press, 2005, 1–56.

Stepanek, Marcia. "Game Theory." *Stanford Social Innovation Review*, July 12, 2010. http://www.ssireview.org/blog/entry/game_theory/.

Stockburger, Axel. "Listen to the Bulk of the Iceberg." In *Space Time Play: Computer Games, Architecture and Urbanism: The Next Level*. Boston: Springer, 2007, 110–13.

World, Street Football. "Streetfootballworld Website," 2010. http://www.streetfootballworld.org/.

Suits, Bernard. *Grasshopper: Games, Life, and Utopia*. Orchard Park, NY: Broadview Press, 2005.

Sutton-Smith, Brian. *The Ambiguity of Play*. Cambridge: Harvard University Press, 1997.

Swain, Chris. "Pre-launch Trip to Washington." *Buzz About the ReDistricting Game*, May 23, 2007. http://redistrictinggame.blogspot.com/2007/05/jonathan-aronson-and-i-went-to.html.

Swain, Chris. "The ReDistricting Game," 2009. http://www.redistrictinggame.org/.

Swain, Chris. "The Redistricting Game Being Used in PA Lobbying Effort." *Buzz About the Redistricting Game*, March 30, 2008. http://redistrictinggame.blogspot.com/2008/03/redistricting-game-being-used-in-pa.html.

Bibliography

Teppa, Carla. *Proyecto La Ciudad de Las Niñas y Los Niños.* Rosario, Argentina: Municipalidad de Rosario, 2009.

Thaler, Richard H., and Cass R. Sunstein. *Nudge: Improving Decisions About Health, Wealth, and Happiness.* New Haven: Yale University Press, 2008.

The Entertainment Software Association. "Industry Facts," 2011. http://www.theesa.com/facts/index.asp.

The Toronto Star. "Crisis at the TCHC: A Timeline." *The Toronto Star,* March 17, 2011. http://www.thestar.com/news/gta/2011/03/17/crisis_at_the_tchc_a_timeline.html.

The Trust for Public Land. "NYC Playgrounds Program," 2009. http://www.tpl.org/what-we-do/where-we-work/new-york/ny-city-playgrounds.html.

Thompson, Clive. "Halo 3: How Microsoft Labs Invented a New Science of Play." *Wired,* September 2007: 140–92. http://www.wired.com/gaming/virtualworlds/magazine/15-09/ff_halo?currentPage=all.

de Tocqueville, Alexis. *Democracy in America.* New York: Harper Perennial, 1966.

Tonucci, Francesco. *La Ciudad de Los Niños: Un Modo nuevo de pensar La Ciudad,* Buenos Aires: Editorial Losada, 1996.

Housing, Toronto Community. "Frequently Asked Questions," 2010. http://www.torontohousing.ca/media_centre/faq.

Housing, Toronto Community. "Participatory Planning and Budgeting in Toronto Community Housing Corporation: Our Own Story." Presented at the Lifelong Citizenship Learning, Participatory Democracy and Social Change Conference, Toronto, October 18, 2003.

Toronto Public Health. *The Unequal City: Income and Health Inequalities in Toronto.* Toronto: City of Toronto, October 2008.

UN-Habitat. "Participatory Budgeting." *2010 Best Practices Database,* 2010. http://www.unhabitat.org/bestpractices/2010/mainview04.asp?BPID=2548.

United Way Toronto. "Losing Ground: The Persistent Growth of Family Poverty in Canada's Largest City." Toronto, 2007. http://www.unitedwaytoronto.com/whatWeDo/reports/losingGround.php.

Urie, Heather. "Trying to Entice Public to Meetings, Boulder Offers Prizes." *Boulder Daily Camera,* October 17, 2010. http://www.dailycamera.com/ci_16339442.

Valderrama, Ana. "Sueños de plaza." *Matéricos Periféricos* no. 10 (2009): 48–61.

Verba, Sidney, Kay Lehman Schlozman, and Henry Brady. *Voice and Equality: Civic Voluntarism in American Politics.* Cambridge: Harvard University Press, 1995.

Volkswagen. "The Fun Theory," 2010. http://www.thefuntheory.com/.

Vygotsky, Lev Semenovich. *Mind in Society: The Development of Higher Psychological Processes*. Cambridge: Harvard University Press, 1978.

Wadsworth, Yoland. *What Is Participatory Action Research?* Action Research International, 1998. http://www.aral.com.au/ari/p-ywadsworth98.html.

Wainwright, Hilary. *Reclaim the State: Adventures in Popular Democracy*. London: Verso, 2003.

Walters, Lawrence, James Aydelotte, and Jessica Miller. "Putting More Public in Policy Analysis." *Public Administration Review* 60, no.4 (2000): 349–59.

Walz, Steffen P. *Toward a Ludic Architecture: The Space of Play and Games*. Pittsburgh: ETC Press, 2010.

Wark, McKenzie. *Gamer Theory*. Cambridge: Harvard University Press, 2007.

Warman, Peter. *Newzoo Games Market Report: Consumer Spending on Key Platforms and Business Models*. Amsterdam: Newzoo, May 2010.

Welp, Yanina, and Serdült Uwe, eds. *Armas de doble filo: La Participación ciudadana en la encrucijada*. Buenos Aires: Prometeo Libros, 2009.

Whiteley, Paul. "Rational Choice and Political Participation—Evaluating the Debate." *Political Research Quarterly* 48, no. 1 (1995): 211–33.

Winnicott, D. W. *Playing & Reality*. London: Tavistock Publications, 1971.

Wolfinger, Raymond, and Steven Rosenstone. *Who Votes?* New Haven: Yale University Press, 1980.

Wood, Elisabeth. *Insurgent Collective Action and Civil War in El Salvador*. Cambridge, UK: Cambridge University Press, 2003.

World Bank, *Participatory Budgeting*. 2007. Washington, DC: World Bank.

Wu, Jia. *Global Video Game Market Forecast*. Strategy Analytics, February 5, 2010. http://strategyanalytics.com/default.aspx?mod=ReportAbstractViewer&a0=5282.

Young, Iris Marion. *Inclusion and Democracy*. Oxford: Oxford University Press, 2002.

Yuen, Eddie. "Introduction." In *Confronting Capitalism: Dispatches from a Global Movement*, ed. Eddie Yuen, Daniel Burton-Rose, and George Katsiaficas. Brooklyn: Soft Skull Press, 2004: vii–xxix.

Zysman, Guillermo. "Eramos Tan Pobres." *Rosario 12*. Rosario, Argentina, May 22, 2008. http://www.pagina12.com.ar/diario/suplementos/rosario/9-13644-2008-05-22 .html.

"Columbia Institute," 2013. http://www.columbiainstitute.ca/.

Bibliography

"Epic Win—Level-Up Your Life," January 30, 2010. http://www.rexbox.co.uk/epicwin/.

"Erradican a 200 familias en villa La Lata y Abren Calles." *La Capital*, August 13, 2003. http://archivo.lacapital.com.ar/2003/08/13/ciudad/noticia_27064.shtml.

"Future Search Network," 2013. http://www.futuresearch.net/.

"Games For Learning Institute," 2010. http://g4li.org/.

"Games Learning Society Website," 2010. http://www.gameslearningsociety.org/.

"Gamification Blog," 2011. http://www.gamification.co/.

"Healthy Democracy," 2013. http://healthydemocracy.org/.

How to Rig a Public Hearing—Coverage of the Scam Atlantic Yards D.E.I.S. Proceedings, 2006. http://www.themusicdrop.com/fbr/deis_hearing_show_web_1.mov.

"Institute of Play," 2010. http://www.instituteofplay.com/.

"MoveOn.Org," 2013. http://front.moveon.org/.

"National League of Cities: Democratic Governance and Civic Engagement," 2013. http://www.nlc.org/find-city-solutions/center-for-research-and-innovation/governance-and-civic-engagement/democratic-governance-and-civic-engagement.

"Occupy Wall Street," 2013. http://occupywallst.org/.

"Quest to Learn Website," 2010. http://q2l.org/.

"Red FAL: Forum of Local Authorities for Social Inclusion and Participatory Democracy," 2013. http://www.redfal.org/.

"Right to the City," 2013. http://www.righttothecity.org/.

Rob Ford's Compassion for the Homeless, 2002. http://www.youtube.com/watch?v=8YZQ4oQjxgc.

"The Center for Deliberative Democracy," 2013. http://cdd.stanford.edu/polls/.

"The Education Arcade," 2010. http://www.educationarcade.org/.

"The World Café," 2013. http://www.theworldcafe.com/.

Index

Numbers in italics refer to pages with illustrations.

Abt, Clark, *29*
Activation phenomenon, 104
Activist play, 40–42
ACT UP, 40–41, 42
Addams, Jane, 40
Age, voting, 13
Alinsky, Saul, 30–31
Allocation Days, TCH, 161–70
American Idol, 19, 27
America's Army, 19, 27, 81, *82*
Analysis games, 191, 201
Animation games, 190
Architects, 84–85
Argentina. *See* Rosario, Argentina; Rosario Hábitat
Army 360, 20
Arnstein, Sherry, 32
Aronson, Jonathan, *38*
Artificial conflict. *See* Conflict
Assassin's Creed, 72
Atlantic Yards, 1–2, 3
Attitudes toward political authority, 12–13
Australia, 30, *31*
Avendon, Elliot, *29*
Avritzer, Leonardo, 204
Ayiti: The Cost of Life, 36

Balancing feedback loops, 59–60, 192–93

Ballantyne, Derek, 161–62, 187
Barber, Benjamin, 11
Bartle, Richard, 52
Baseball, 66
Beck, John, 83
Billionaires for Bush, 41, *41*, 42
BINGO, 56
Binner, Hermes, 91, 92
Björk, Staffan, 53
Blackjack, 67
Blunt, Richard, 18
Boal, Augusto, 43–44, 47, 98
Boero, Estevez, 91
Bowling, 74, *74*
Bowling Alone, 7–8
Boyd, Andrew, 16
Brazil, 39, 43–44, 87, 89
Bread and Puppet, 40
Brecht, Bertolt, 16
Broad Front, 89
Brown, John Seely, 83, 84
Budget Hero, 20

Caillois, Roger, *29*, 219n4
Cambiemos, 35
Canada. *See* Toronto Community Housing (TCH)
Capacity-building games, 190–91, 201
Cardoso, Henrique, 89
Castronova, Edward, 49

Catalyst Centre, 43
Celebrity (game), 72
Center for Community Change, 45
Chance, 69–70, 194
Characters, 78–79, *79*, 195
Chatfield, Tom, 19
Children's Councils (Rosario, Argentina). *See* City of the Children
Chile, 87
China, 87
Choice points, 75, *76*, 195
Church, Doug, 52–53
Citizens' Initiative Review, 12
City of the Children, 5, 87–88, 91, 92–94, 190, 197, 198
  games as political change and, 116–17
  legislation and, 97–106
  manipulation and, 198–99
  Monumento a las Ideas and, 94–97
  separating work from play, 107–12
Civilization, 75, 77–78
Civil rights movement, 40
Clear goals and objectives, 67, 194
Collaboration and conflict, 192–93
Collaborative competition, 135–41, *136*, *138*, 184, 201–202
Colman, Andrew, 27
Columbia Institute, 12
Community organizing, 4–5, 30–31. *See also* Rosario Hábitat
Competition, collaborative, 135–41, *136*, *138*, 184, 201–202
Conflict, 16, 29, 54–56
  balancing feedback loop, 59–60
  collaboration and, 192–93
  collaborative competition and, 135–41
  in democratic processes, 192–93
  magic circle, 57–59, 137, 140, 192
  reinforcing feedback loops, 60
  type, 56–57, *58*, 137, 140, 160, 192
Core mechanics, enjoyable, *74*, 74–75, 195

Costikyan, Greg, *29*, 75
Crawford, Chris, *29*
Critical citizens, 12–13
Criticism of games, 19–22
Csikszentmihalyi, Mihaly, 60
Cuenca, Ecuador, 39, *39*

Dangers, lurking, 196–99
Davies, Russell, 22
Decision-making, 17, 32–33
  games, 191, 201
  game theory and, 33–35
  participatory, 131–35, *132*
Dekoven, Bernard, 65
Deliberative Polling, 12
Democracy
  causes of broken, 12–16
  demand for, 13, 15
  design in, 3, 17
  disempowerment and, 10–12, 13
  disengagement from, 7–9, 12
  distrust of, 9–10, 12–13
  as fun, 2–3, 21–22, 189–90
  game mechanics in, 192–96
  games in processes of, 190–91
  new frontiers for games and, 46–47
  our love-hate relationship with, 6–12
  public hearings and, 1–2
  rethinking games and, 204–207
  similarities of games to, 16–17
  supply side of, 13
  winning strategies for using games with, 199–204
Democrazy, 65, 65–66
Demographic changes and democracy, 13
Deterding, Sebastian, 21, 22
Dewey, John, 9
Disempowerment, 10–12, 13
Disengagement, 7–9
  technological changes and, 12
Dissident play, 38, 39–40

Index

Distrust, 9–10, 12–13
Downs, Anthony, 33
Duncombe, Stephen, 16

Ecuador, 39, *39*
Education Arcade, The, 83
Electoral festivities, 38–39
Electronic Arts, 51
Engagement
  characters and, 78–79, *79*, 195
  choice points and, 75, *76*
  enjoyable core mechanics and, *74*,
    74–75, 195
  hidden information and, 76–78, *78*,
    161, 195
  metagaming and, 81, 196
  narrative and, 79–81, 134, 195–96
  resources and, 195
  by Rosario Hábitat, 126–31, 195–96
  of the senses, 126–31, 200
  sound effects and, 195
  by Toronto Community Housing,
    160–70, 195–96
  vibrant visuals and, 195
Enjoyable core mechanics, *74*, 74–75,
  195
Epic Win, 21
Eskelinen, Markku, 80
Evaluation, participatory, 173, 174–75
  game mechanics and, 183–87
  games used in, 175–82
  learning by playing and, 187–88
Evans, Chris, 36
EverQuest, 49

Facebook, 81
Farmville, 74
Feedback loops
  balancing, 59–60, 192–93
  reinforcing, 60, 192–93
FIERCE, 45
Fiorina, Morris, 8, 12

Flow state, 60
Football, 66
Formal abstract design tools, 53
Forum of Local Authorities for Social
  Inclusion, 12
Foster, Ralph, 15
Freeman, Jo, 61
Freire, Paulo, 43
Frente Amplio, 89
Fullerton, Tracy, 17, 52, 53, 62
Future Search, 12

Game design, 3, 17, 47. *See also* Game
  rules
  architects, 84–85
  artificial conflict in, 16, 29, 54–60
  for community participation, 145–47
  engagement in, 72–81
  establishing legitimate rules, 201
  game design theory and, 50–52
  game mechanics and, 52–54, 205–206
  influence of, 81–85
  intentions, 20–21
  iterative, 52, 203–204
  for participants, 203–204
  participatory evaluation and, 175–82
Game Developers Conference, 15
Game mechanics, 52–54, *55*, 120, 183–
  87, 205–206
  in democratic processes, 192–96
  linking participation to measurable
    outcomes, 202
Game rules, 16, 18, 29, 53, 61–62
  balanced feedback loops, 59–60,
    192–93
  in democratic processes, 193–94
  establishing legitimate, 200–201
  just-in-time information, 62–63, *64*,
    134, 193
  magic circle, 57–59, 137, 140, 159–60,
    192
  modeling, 63–64, 134, 193

Game rules (continued)
multimodal presentation, 62, *63*, 133–34, 159, 193
player generated, 65–66, 193
reinforcing feedback loops, 60, 192–93
rulings, 66
sanctions, 66, 193–94
Games. *See also* Conflict; Engagement; Outcomes
about politics, 35–38
analysis, 191, 201
animation, 190
attracting and enabling massive participation, 17
capacity-building, 190–91, 201
changing landscape of, 208–209
criticism of, 19–22
decision-making, 17, 32–33, 191, 201
defined, 16–17
in democratic processes, 190–91
dynamics, 53–54
formal abstract design tools, 53
formal elements, 53
growing influence of, 18
informal engagement events, 44–45
lack of fun in, 197
lurking dangers of, 196–99
making democracy fun, 5–6, 21–22, 189–90
manipulating participation, 20
manipulation through, 198
measurable outcomes of, 16, 29
as metaphors for politics, 30–33
new frontiers for democracy and, 46–47
nondigital, 25, 35–36, 207
play and, 28–30, 219n4, 219n7
players rarely losing faith in, 18
as political action, 42–46
as political change, 116–17
procedures, 53
as research method, 33–35
rethinking democracy and, 204–207

role-playing, 78–79, *79*
rules, 16, 18, 29, 53, 57–59, 61–66
scholars, 15, 34, 62
similarities to democracy, 16–17
social issue, 35–36
team-building, 190
trivialization and, 197–98
trust in, 18
unfair outcomes of, 21
used in participatory evaluation, 175–82
used in politics, 4–5, 27–28
video (*see* Video games)
violence in, 19, 196–97
virtual worlds in, 49–50
winning strategies for democracy and, 199–204
Games for Change, 27, 35
Games for Learning Institute, The, 83
Game theory, 4, 33–35
game design theory and, 51
Gamification, 20–21, 22
Gans, Joshua, 21
Garzia, María Isabel, 123
Gee, James, 62–64, 82, 120, 133
Gershenfeld, Alan, 27
Goals and objectives, 67, 194
González, María de los Ángeles (Chiqui), 92–93, 207
Good Day, 175–76, 182, 190
Grand Theft Auto, 19, 78–79, *79*
Greenpeace, 8
Green Yellow Red Cards, 182
Group vs. group conflict, 56–57, 160, 192
Group vs. system conflict, 57, *58*, 137, 140, 160
Grupo de Teatro del Oprimido (GTO) Rosario, 98–105, 115–16

Haas, Gilda, 180
Hagel, John, 84
Halo, 72

Halo 3, 52
Hay, Collin, 10, 13
Hibbing, John, 8
Hidden information, 76–78, *78*, 161, 195
Highlander Center, 43
Hoffman, Abbie, 40
Holopainen, Jussi, 53
Howard, John, 30, *31*
Hughes, Linda, 62, 65
Huizinga, Johann, *29*, 57, 219n4

Individual vs. group conflict, 56, 192
Individual vs. individual conflict, 56, 192
Individual vs. system conflict, 56
Influence of games, growing, 18
Informal engagement events, 44–45
Inherently participatory nature of games and democracy, 17
Institute of Play, 83
Intentions, game design, 20–21
Iterative design, 52, 203–204

Jenkins, Henry, 72
Jeopardy, 60, 176–77, 182, 191, 193
Just-in-time information, 62–63, *64*, 134, 193

Kahne, Joseph, 36
Kids Are Alright: How the Gamer Generation Is Changing the Workplace, The, 83
King, Martin Luther, Jr., 30–31
Kriegspiel, 35

Lacalle, Luis Alberto, 89
Lack of fun in games, 197
Lack of time for democratic participation, 14
La Ley del Patronato, 98–99
Landless Workers Movement, 12
Learning by playing, 187–88

LeBlanc, Marc, 15, 53
Legislative theater, 43–44
Levels, 71–72, 160, 194
LGBT activism, 40–41, 45
Life, 79–80, *81*
Link between participation and outcomes, 141–44, *143*, 202–203
Living Theater, The, 40
Lord of the Rings, 57, *58*
Lowering of the voting age, 13
Lusory attitude, 57

Magic circle, 57–59, 137, 140, 159–60, 192
Manipulation through games, 198
Massively multiplayer online role-playing games (MMORPGs), 49
Matching Puzzle, *178*, 178–79, 182, 191
Measurable outcomes, 16, 29, 68, *68*, 142, 194
    linking participation to, 202–203
Mechanics, game, 52–54, *55*, 120
Meier, Sid, 75, 77
Menem, Carlos, 89
Metagaming, 81, *82*, 196
Metaphors for politics, games as, 30–33
Mexico, 39
Microsoft Games User Research, 52
Middaugh, Ellen, 36
Modeling, 63–64, 134, 193
Monopoly, 56, 62, *63*, 133–34
Monumento a las Ideas, 94–97
Mortal Kombat, 71, *71*
MoveOn, 8, 12, 45
Multimodal presentation, 62, *63*, 133–34, 159, 193
Myst, 73

Narrative and engagement, 79–81, 134, 195–96
National League of Cities, 12
Neblo, Michael, 15
New Games Movement, 35

New Left, 40
Newspaper Game, 94–95, 190
Nintendo, 51
Nondigital games, 25, 35–36, 207
Nonprofit organizations and games, 45
Norris, Pippa, 12

Obama, Barack, 27
Objectives and goals, 67, 194
Occupy movement, 7, 12
Occupy Wall Street, 7
Osborne, Martin, 33
Outcomes
  chance, 69–70, 194
  clear goals and objectives, 67, 194
  in democratic processes, 194
  levels, 71–72, 194
  linking participation to, 141–44, *143,*
    202–203
  measurable, 16, 29, 68, *68,* 142, 194,
    202–203
  points, 70, *70,* 144, 161, 194
  status indicators, 71, *71,* 194
  uncertain, 69, 142, 144, 194
  unfair, 21, 197
  vivid presentation of, 142–44, *143*

Pac-Man, 50
Paraguay, 87
Participation, 6–7
  changing attitudes toward political au-
    thority and, 12–13
  declining civic participation and social
    capital effect on, 12
  defined, 6
  demographic changes effect on, 13
  disempowerment and, 10–12, 13
  disengagement from, 7–9, 12
  distrust and, 9–10, 12–13
  effect of lowering voting age on, 13
  encouraged through games, 44–46
  as fun, 2–3
  game design for community, 145–47

games manipulating, 20
lack of citizen interest in, 13–14
linked to outcomes, 141–44, *143,*
  202–203
participatory democracy in Rosario
  and, 88–91
play and, 42
technological changes effect on, 12
as tedious and uncomfortable, 1–2
Participatory budgeting, 45, 66
  engagement and, 160–70
  game mechanics and, 183–87
  participatory evaluation of, 173,
    174–75
  by Toronto Community Housing
    (TCH), 151–71
Participatory Democracy, 12
Participatory evaluation, 173, 174–75
  game mechanics and, 183–87
  games used in, 175–82
  learning by playing and, 187–88
Participatory redevelopment, 88
Participatory rule-making, 131–35, *132*
Partido dos Trabalhadores, 88, 151
Partido Socialista, 91
Plato, 30
Play
  activist, 40–42
  dissident, 38, 39–40
  games and, 28–30, 219n4, 219n7
  increasing impact of participation, 42
  learning through, 187–88
  populist, 38
  social movements and, 40–42, 43
Player generated rules, 65–66, 193
Playful democracy, 88
Playtesters, 52, 179
Plaza Dreams, 107–12, *109,* 117, 198
Points, 70, *70,* 144, 161, 194
Politics. *See also* Democracy
  games about, 35–38
  games as metaphors for, 30–33
  games as political action and, 42–46

increasing use of games in, 4–5, 27–28
informal engagement events, 44–45
play as political action and, 38–42
Popular education, 43
Popular Front, 40
Populist play, 38
Poundstone, William, 33
Project South, 43
Protección Integral de las niñas, niños y adolescentes, 97–98
Proyectistas, 107, 110
Proyecto ENLACE, 45
Public hearings, 1–3
Puerto Rico, 45
Putnam, Robert, 7–8, 12

Queers for Economic Justice, 45
Quest, 83

Rational choice, 35
Reclaim the Streets, 42
ReDistricting Game, 37, 37–38
Reinforcing feedback loops, 60, 192–93
Research method, games as, 33–35
Resources and engagement, 75–76, *77,* 161, 195
Right to the City Alliance, 12
Risk, 19
Robinson, Ken, 20
Role-playing games, 78–79, *79*
Rosario, Argentina, 4–5, 87
  City of the Children in, 92–117
  demographics, 89–90
  elections, 91
  games as political change in, 116–17
  legislation and, 97–106
  participatory democracy in, 88–91
  Plaza Dreams, 107–12
  Theater of the Oppressed in, 5, *101,* 101–106, 112–16, *114*
Rosario Hábitat, 5, 88, 91, 190, 207
  changing landscape of games and, 208–209

collaborative competition and, 135–41, *136, 138,* 192
community meetings, 119–20
engagement by, 126–31, 195–96
game design for community participation in, 145–47
linking participation to measurable outcomes, 203
linking participation to outcomes, 141–44, *143*
manipulation and, 199
objectives of, 121–23
outcomes, 194
problems experienced by, 123–26
rules, 131–35, 193, 201
violence and, 196–97
Rouse, Richard, 53
Rubeinstein, Ariel, 33
Rules, game, 16, 18, 29, 53, 61–62
  balanced feedback loops, 59–60, 192–93
  in democratic processes, 193–94
  establishing legitimate, 200–201
  just-in-time information, 62–63, *64,* 134, 193
  magic circle, 57–59, 137, 140, 159–60, 192
  modeling, 63–64, 134, 193
  multimodal presentation, 62, *63,* 133–34, 159, 193
  player generated, 65–66, 193
  reinforcing feedback loops, 60, 192–93
  Rosario Hábitat and, 131–35
  rulings, 66
  sanctions, 66, 193–94
Rules of Play, 29
Rulings, 66, 193–94

Salen, Katie, 29, 30, 133
  on game design, 50, 51, 54, 65
  on goals, 67
Sanctions, 66, 193
San Francisco Mime Troupe, 40

Santos, Boaventura de Sousa, 204
School Bus, 176–77, 182
Scores, 144
Scrabble, 70, *70*
Senses, stimulating and engaging the, 126–31, 200
Serious Games Initiative, 35
Settlement House Movement, 40
SimCity, 63, *64*
Sims, The, 80
Skocpol, Theda, 8, 12
Slot machines, 72, *73*
Slow Democracy, 12
Smith, Rogers M., 81
Social capital, 12
Social issue games, 35–36
Social movements and play, 40–42, 43
Social networking, 20
Solitaire, 56
Sound effects, 73, 161, 195
Space Invaders, 59, 59–60
Spaces of possibility, 51
Speed Dating, 180–81, 182
Spitzer, Elliot, 42
Star Wars, 80
Status indicators, 71, 160–61, 194
Stealth Democracy, 8
Stonewall Inn, 40
Stop, 190
Sueños de Plaza, 107–12, *109,* 117, 198
Suits, Bernard, 57
Super Mario Brothers, 75–76, *77*
Supply side of democracy, 13
Sutton-Smith, Brian, *29*
Swain, Chris, 37

Team-building games, 190
Tea Party, 7
Technological changes and disengagement, 12
Teenage Mutant Ninja Turtles, 64

Tetris, 56, 75, *76*
Texas Chainsaw Massacre, The, 19
Theater of the Oppressed, 43–44, *44,* 88, 197
   manipulation and, 199
   participatory evaluation and, 175–76
   potential failures of, 112–16
   in Rosario, Argentina, 5, *101,* 101–106, 112–16, *114*
Theiss-Morse, Elizabeth, 8
Theory of Fun for Game Design, A, 15
Thomas, Douglas, 83
Tonucci, Francesco, 91, 92
Toronto Community Housing (TCH), 5, 149–50, 170–71, 173, 190, 207
   Allocation Days, 161–70
   conflict and collaboration in, 192
   conflicts types, 160
   engagement by, 160–61, 195–96
   learning by playing and, 187–88
   linking participation to measurable outcomes, 202–203
   map, *154*
   1.8 Day, 155–61, *156, 157,* 197
   outcomes, 194
   participatory budgeting at, 151–71
   participatory evaluation, 173, 174–75
   rules, 193, 201
   size of, 153
   skeptics of games and game mechanics, 150–51
   staff manipulation and, 198–99
   tenant delegates, 156–60, 185–86
   unfair outcomes and, 197
Trivialization, 197–98
Trivial Pursuit, 68, *68*
Trust
   in games, 18
   in government, 9–10, 12–13
21st Century Town Meetings, 12
"Tyranny of Structurelessness, The," 61

Index

Uncertain outcomes, 69, 142, 144, 194
Unfair outcomes of games, 21, 197
United Nations, 7
  Development Programme, 91
Uruguay, 35, 39, 87, 89

Vázquez, Tabaré, 89
Venezuela, 2–3
Vibrant visuals and engagement, 72, *73*, 161, 195
Video games, 4, 17, 35
  criticism of, 19–20
  design, 50–52
  engagement, 72–81
  violence, 19
  virtual worlds, 49–50
Villa Corrientes, *124*, 145
Violence, game, 19, 196–97
Virtual worlds, 49–50
Visuals, vibrant, 72, *73*, 161, 195
Vivid presentation of outcomes, 142–44, *143*
Volkswagen, 16
Voting age, 13

Wade, Mitchell, 83
Wadsworth, Yoland, 174
What Changed?, 179–80, 182, 191, 192
What Video Games Have to Teach Us about Learning and Literacy, 82
Wheel of Fortune, 69–70
Who Wants to Be a Millionaire, 69
Wilde, Oscar, 2
Winnicott, D. W., 18
Worker's Party (Argentina), 88, 89, 151
World Bank, 7
World Café, 12
World of Warcraft, 19

Yippies, 40
Young, Iris Marion, 2, 14

Youth participation, 88
YouTube, 81

Zimmerman, Eric, 29, 30, 133
  on game design, 50, 51, 54, 65
  on goals, 67

Printed in the United States
by Baker & Taylor Publisher Services